DATE DUE			
FEB 1 1 2002			
AUG - 6 2002			
MAY 2 0 2003			
MAY 0 9 2017			

201-9500   PRINTED IN U.S.A.

WALKING
THE
ALPINE PARKS
OF FRANCE & NORTHWEST ITALY

MARCIA R. LIEBERMAN

PHOTOGRAPHS BY PHILIP LIEBERMAN

THE
MOUNTAINEERS

Published by
The Mountaineers
1011 SW Klickitat Way
Seattle, Washington 98134

87 6 5 4
5 4 3 2 1

Published simultaneously in Canada by Douglas & McIntyre, Ltd., 1615 Venables Street, Vancouver, B.C. V5L 2H1

Published simultaneously in Great Britain by Cordee, 3a DeMontfort Street, Leicester, England, LE1 7HD

Manufactured in the United States of America

Edited by Christine Clifton-Thornton and Dana Lee Fos
Maps by Word Graphics
All photographs by Philip Lieberman
Cover design by Bookends
Typesetting by The Mountaineers Books
Layout by Word Graphics

Cover photograph: Lac Negre, Parc National du Mercantour
Frontispiece: On the way to the Refuge du Clot

Library of Congress Cataloging-in-Publication Data
Lieberman, Marcia 1936–
        Hiking the Alpine parks of France and northwest Italy / Marcia Lieberman.
        p.   cm.
    Includes index.
    ISBN 0-89886-398-8
    1. Hiking--France--Alps, French--Guidebooks. 2. Hiking--Italy--Alps, Italian--Guidebooks. 3. National parks and reserves--France--Alps, French--Guidebooks. 4. National parks and reserves--Italy--Alps, Italian--Guidebooks. 5. Alps, French (France)--Guidebooks. 6. Alps, Italian (Italy)--Guidebooks. I. Title.
GV199.44.F82A4445 1994
796.5'1'09449--dc20   94-25059
                                                    CIP

CONTENTS

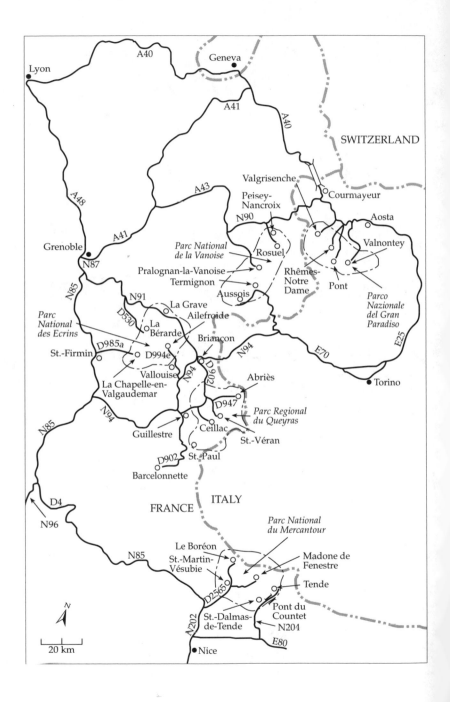

Parc Naturel Régional du Queyras 69

Parc National des Ecrins 112

THE ALPINE PARKS OF NORTHWEST ITALY

Parco Nazionale del Gran Paradiso 186

Key to Map Symbols

━ ‥ ━ ‥ ━ ‥ ━	Country border	ⓘ	Junction
━ ‧ ━ ‧ ━ ‧ ━	Park boundary	▲	Peak
++++++++++++	Ski lift, cablecar, or télépherique	) (	Col, pass
━━━━━━━	Road	‖	Bridge (foot or auto)
------------	Trail	■	Ruin
∿∿∿	River	⇑	Accommodations: hut or refuge
⬤	Lake	⩜	Campground
○	City	⸙	Church
●	Town, village, or hamlet	†	Cross
ⓟ	Parking	⫲	Buildings

Dedication

To our dear friends Marianne Spalding and Arthur S. O'Grady, who shared our love of walking.

Acknowledgments

I am very grateful to a number of people who provided very valuable assistance in the preparation of this book. Marion Fourestier of the French Government Tourist Office in New York was a helpful source of information and assisted with French translations; Dr. Martin St. André of Butler Hospital in Providence, and David Ascher at Brown University also assisted with these translations. Umberto Lombardo of the Italian Government Tourist Office in New York provided useful information about Italy. Dr. Lynn Gunzberg of Brown University graciously assisted with Italian translations.

The following persons generously shared their knowledge of hiking routes in their respective regions.

Mercantour

Jean Grinda, Bureau des Guides, St.-Martin-Vésubie; Claude Baringo, Refuge Des Merveilles.

Queyras and Ubaye

Yves Fouque, Accompagnateur en Montagne, Ceillac; Jean-Marc Plichon, St.-Véran; Luc Lemoël, Ristolas; Jean-Marc Bourillon, Fouillouse.

Ecrins

Christiane Amevet, La Bérarde; Emmanuelle Mourey, Hôtesse at La Bérarde; Paul Rousset, La Grave; Vincent Tonnelier, La Grave.

Vanoise

Marie-Odile Guth, Director of the Parc National de la Vanoise, Chambéry; Martine Pouyé, Hôtesse at the Office du Tourisme, Peisey-Nancroix; Brigitte Grand-Touvier, Office du Parc National de la Vanoise, Bourg St. Maurice; Paul Burlet, Accompagnateur en Montagne, Pralognan; Marielle Gaçon, Hôtesse at the Office du Tourisme, Pralognan; Henri and Lise-Marie Favre, Pralognan; Beatrice and Alain Ghiachino, Rosuel; Marion Caullireau, Office du Tourisme, Aussois.

Gran Paradiso

Stefano Carletto and Maria Caterina Viani, Office du Tourisme, Communauté de Montagne Grand Paradis, Villeneuve; Signor Gex, Planaval, Valgrisenche; Signor Luigi Gerbelle, Bonne, Valgrisenche; Angelo Cavagnet, Rifugio Vittorio Sella, Valsavarenche; Adriana Chabod, Pont, Valsavaranche; Luciano Herren, Valnontey.

I also wish to express my warm thanks to my editor, Christine Clifton-Thornton, whose excellent judgment and meticulous care were of the greatest value in the preparation of this book.

INTRODUCTION

The Alps of France and northwestern Italy comprise a beautiful and varied region of impressively high peaks and steep glaciers, mountain tarns and alpine meadows, and lonely valleys. What sets these western Alps apart from the better-known mountains of Switzerland and Austria is the wildness of the country. There are, for example, only two cablecars in all the regions described in this book, whereas in any single Swiss or Austrian mountain resort there is usually at least one lift and often several. The little mountain villages are mostly simple and unaffected, which is the source of their charm. And it is impossible to write honestly about the pleasures of hiking in the French and Italian Alps without mentioning the wonderful food.

There are many reasons to go to the Alps—they are easily accessible and are located in politically stable and peaceful countries, the water and food are safe, and you don't need to travel with a small pharmacy in your luggage—but surely the primary reason is their beauty. All mountains are endowed with grandeur, but from what I have seen, no other mountain chain can compare with the Alps for sheer loveliness. Because of their northern latitude—they are 1,500 miles north of the Himalayas—the Alps have a low snowline and the grass grows near the snow. The sight of green meadows, ablaze with the brilliance of myriad wildflowers, shining against a white backdrop of snowclad peaks is enough to make one's heart sing. Glaciers are abundant; in the Alps, you will see many hundreds of them, whereas in other mountain regions they are often higher and more hidden.

Few North Americans are found on the French or Italian alpine trails because few of us know anything about these regions. Mention the French Alps and most North Americans think of Chamonix and Mont Blanc, although urbanized Chamonix is not characteristic of a French alpine village, and the Mont Blanc massif is only the northernmost of several extensive and important alpine regions in France. This highest of all alpine peaks is called Monte Bianco on its Italian side, but while it is generally known that Italy is a mountainous country and home of many of the world's greatest climbers, how many people can name even one all-Italian alpine peak?

The grand mountain range known as the Alps was formed millions of years ago after what is now Italy collided with the landmass of Europe. As a result, the Alps wrap around the bulge at the northern end of present-day Italy. A glance at a map shows that the western edge of the Alps be-

Opposite: *St.-Martin-Vésubie*

gins near the Mediterranean and rises northward along the French–Italian border, then swings eastward along the Swiss–Italian and Austrian–Italian borders into Slovenia, while additional bands of mountains extend across Austria and southern Germany. The highest mountains belong to the western Alps, that portion of the range belonging to France, northwestern Italy, and Switzerland; and along much of the border country between France and Italy there are glorious areas of mountains and glaciers.

The French have established a series of parks to protect the four major alpine regions south of Mont Blanc. The Parc National du Mercantour is located in the Maritime Alps, the southernmost part of the entire mountain range. Directly to the north, in the Cottian Alps, is the Parc Naturel Régional du Queyras. West of the Queyras are the great Dauphiné Alps, now part of the Parc National des Ecrins. And north of the Queyras and Ecrins is the Parc National de la Vanoise, containing the western section of the Graian Alps, a range that extends across the border in Italy and is the setting for the magnificent and historic Parco Nazionale del Gran Paradiso. The Mont Blanc massif was not incorporated into either a national or regional park. It is the only area of the French Alps that is well known outside of France. The Tour du Mont Blanc, the hiking route that encircles the Mont Blanc massif, is very popular, and there are guidebooks in English for this route. Consequently, the Mont Blanc massif is not included in this book. The highly developed Chamonix–Mont Blanc area is, moreover, not typical of the wildness of these mountains.

Ibex

In France, the Mercantour is close to the Mediterranean, easily accessible from the coasts of France and Italy, and its mountain villages have a Provençal character. It is a country of high lakes and rugged mountains, although the region is low in comparison to other alpine regions. The Mercantour is also the site of one of the most interesting groups of outdoor prehistoric rock engravings found in Europe. The distinctive landscape of the Queyras is that of an upland pleated by long, craggy ridges; some of its villagers still perform pilgrimages that celebrate ancient myths and legends. The Ecrins contains the most dramatic scenery to be found in France apart from the Mont Blanc massif; its deep, narrow valleys are enfolded between high, snowclad peaks and massive glaciers. A somewhat different effect is seen in the Vanoise, whose landscape, although studded with mountains and glaciers, is a high plateau, more spacious than that of the Ecrins and offering long vistas.

Just across the border from the Vanoise, the Gran Paradiso in Italy is a region of dramatic alpine scenery, of great mountains encircled by glaciers, overlooking wild valleys that are home to superb wildlife. The national park established here, one of the earliest in Europe, was instrumental in saving the ibex from extinction. Today no other alpine region offers an opportunity equal to that afforded in this park to view these handsome animals in the wild. The Gran Paradiso is also enriched by an intercultural setting, mixing elements of Italian and French cultures.

Those already acquainted with the Alps of Switzerland and Austria naturally will find some differences as well as many similarities when hiking in the French and Italian Alps. As in Switzerland and Austria, hikers for the most part do not camp out in the mountains but stay in mountain huts or villages. A major difference between the Swiss and Austrian Alps and the French and northwestern Italian Alps derives from the nature of these communities. At the base of most of the great mountains in Switzerland and Austria are all-season alpine resorts that serve as hiking centers in the summer and ski resorts in the winter. Most were originally simple villages based on the alpine pastoral economy—in which farmers drove their animals up to higher pastures for the summer—and in these resorts traditional houses and old churches are often still found.

With certain notable exceptions, the Alps of France and northwestern Italy are more wild and less developed. The few farming communities that still survive are small and simple. Moreover, such great mountains as the Barre des Ecrins have neither a resort nor even a village very near them. (This is not to say, however, that there are no accommodations available in the vicinity: the location of accommodations will be explained for each region throughout this book.) Excluding the Mont Blanc area, which is served by Chamonix and Courmayeur, in the Alps of France and northwestern Italy the famous ski resorts and the primary hiking/climbing centers are generally completely different places. Nearly all the best-known French ski resorts are, in fact, totally artificial places, built from scratch on sites where no previous village existed, for the sole purpose of creating ski centers near some skiable mountains. Most of these French ski resorts consist of contemporary, multi-story apartment houses and condominiums, often made of concrete (reflecting French fondness for *la modernité*), like little portions of a Parisian suburb dropped at the base of

Vegetable garden at Venanson

some mountain. No remnant of a village is seen because no village was ever there, and there is no pretense of village quaintness. These ski resorts are generally quite dead in the summer.

The hiker, fortunately, does not have to pass through or even see these sterile places. The hiking and climbing centers are, in contrast, mostly very quiet, unassuming little towns and villages that remain pleasingly undeveloped because there is no alpine ski industry with its lure of gigantic profits. The rare hiker who desires five-star standards of hotel luxury on his or her alpine vacation will find almost nothing that meets such requirements in the areas covered in this book.

Because large areas of the Alps of France and northwestern Italy have not been developed for downhill skiing, mechanical lifts in these regions are almost nonexistent. This is in great contrast with Switzerland and Austria (and with the Mont Blanc massif and the Dolomites), where numerous cablecars, *télépheriques* (generally a larger, single car), and funiculars that were built for downhill skiers give summer hikers a boost to higher altitude. There are no cablecars in the parks of the Mercantour, the Queyras, or the Gran Paradiso, and only one cablecar close to the central Vanoise and one *télépherique* in the region of the Ecrins. A few tow-lifts, however, are found here and there for such small-scale downhill skiing as has been developed. This means that hikers are by and large on their own and must gain their altitude on foot.

These western Alps are beautiful and wild, with wonderful hiking, but it would be sheer hypocrisy to deny their additional attractions. There is great charm in the different cultures of these regions. To begin with, there is food—a subject dear to the hearts and stomachs of all hikers and mountaineers. Hiking in France and Italy does not always look different from hiking in other countries, but it certainly tastes different! At the huts of the Club Alpin Français (CAF), for example, a four-course dinner is mandated by club rules; it usually includes a cheese course and such astonishing dishes (for hut food, that is) as *Daube de Boeuf* cooked in wine and veal stew with polenta. In a hut in the Mercantour where I stopped one warm afternoon for a soft drink, the hut keeper—a sprightly, gray-haired man with an apron tied around his waist and sleeves rolled up to the elbow— left off chopping onions for a stew he was simmering in order to serve sodas; two open-lattice blueberry tarts sat cooling on the table. While hut food is certainly not up to the standards of a Michelin one-star restaurant, it can be remarkable as hut food, and of course down in the villages, in hotels and simple inns, the fare is very good as well.

Part of the charm of walking in the western Alps comes from the villages themselves. They are often simple and sweet, less prettified than, say, a certain type of English village in the Cotswolds, without that kind of tearoom-quaintness. Along the lanes and back streets are plain, ungentrified old houses, sometimes with cow sheds attached, set next to barns, kitchen gardens, and small hayfields. The inhabitants are not gentleman farmers or retired stockbrokers tending their rosebushes, but real farmers and dairymen whose ancestors not so long ago would have been called peasants.

In such a place, a visitor can sometimes get a taste of village life.

Auguste Mathon, le cordonnier, *or old cobbler, at La Grave*

In La Grave, a small French climbing center, I asked our hotel keeper (she spoke excellent English) if there was a cobbler in town because I wanted to get a new pair of boots stretched out a little. Alas, she said, the last of the *cordonniers* was a very old man, now retired, but he had kept his shoemaker's tools and was, moreover, her neighbor. "Let's go see him," she said. "Perhaps he can help." So she led me next door to the house of 86-year-old Guste (short for Auguste) Mathon, who not only widened my boot (and would take no money) but also invited me down to his field the next day to watch him mow. During the haying season, old Guste marches down every day to his ancestral plot along the river, a scythe on his back, to cut grass for the large colony of rabbits he keeps in his front yard.

In *la France profonde,* which means something like the old American phrase "the deep South," people often go out of their way to be helpful and friendly. The same thing is true in rural Italy. They are interested in our countries and our cultures. Of course if you can speak French you have greater opportunities for conversation (northwestern Italy is historically a French-speaking region and French is understood everywhere). People in both France and northwestern Italy appreciate even high-school French but will try to speak whatever English they can if you speak no French or Italian.

While public transportation does exist, and it is possible to get to many alpine villages by bus, it is certainly much easier and more convenient to do so by car. Because the countryside is very beautiful, driving is pleasant.

Hiking trails are numerous in the western Alps. France has a great network of long-distance trails known as the Grandes Randonnées, or GR (pronounced *zhay air*), some of which are very long-distance indeed, crossing whole sections of the country (they are found throughout France, not only in the alpine regions). Each GR is numbered. The GR 5, for example, extends from northern France to the Mediterranean (crossing the Alps in the process), while the GR 54 makes a great loop around the Parc National des Ecrins. There are also numerous trails in the northwestern Italian Alps, including the long-distance *alte vie*. Hiking is very popular in both France and Italy. The holiday season in France extends from about July 15 to August 15 or 20, while many Italians take their holiday in August. Huts are crowded during this period, and accommodations can be tight. You can, however, phone virtually all huts for reservations; call two to seven days in advance. At many huts someone will speak English. Hiking is good, however, from June to early October; during the off season there generally are few people around and reservations are not necessary.

Although this book is organized into sections based on alpine parks, not all the walks described here are inside a park, nor are all parts of each walk necessarily within a park. This is not a guide to every walk in these parks but, rather, a varied selection that includes the highlights of each region.

How to Use This Book

This book is organized into three sections. The Introduction presents a wide range of basic information. It gives practical advice and information on conditions and customs in the western Alps—the mountains along and near the border of eastern France and northwestern Italy—and in the five parks established in these regions. Travel Basics provides information about hotel accommodations, alpine club huts, and *gîtes d'étape*, transportation, languages, weather, and other general topics. Advice about how to condition yourself for alpine hiking, what pace to take, and what to pack is also included, as well as tips on buying food and supplies. The final part in the Introduction, The Alpine Environment, briefly explains regional environmental problems and goals and points out what you need to know about the laws and customs of the parks covered in this book.

Valleys provide the approaches into the mountains. Visits to these five parks in the western Alps are organized according to the valleys that serve as entry points for the various sections of each park. Within each valley, the village, hamlet, or parking area that provides the closest point from which to get into the mountains is described. Several multi-day tours, as well as individual hikes, are included; as you thumb through this book, you'll see that tours are set off from individual hikes by horizontal bars:

Part I describes the four parks in the French Alps, Parc National du Mercantour, Parc Naturel Régional du Queyras and the Ubaye, Parc National des Ecrins, and Parc National de la Vanoise, and details a selection of hikes in each park.

Part II describes the Parco Nazionale del Gran Paradiso in northwestern Italy and details a selection of hikes in that park.

The appendices provide some useful addresses, glossaries, a list by hike number of corresponding topographic maps, sample correspondence in French and Italian showing how to write for reservations at hotels, inns, and huts, and a metric conversion table.

Walk Information

For each walk in this book there is a brief list of basic information printed above the walk description. Throughout this information, "m" means meters, and "km" means kilometers.

Ratings. Just below the walk's name (which is usually based on the walk's high point or destination), each walk is rated. Routes are graded in terms of how physically demanding and how technically difficult they are. Although none of the routes described here are considered technical climbs, some necessitate a level of skill that will safely see you through descents on loose scree, traverses on snow, and walks on narrow paths with significant exposure.

Easy. A well-graded route with about 500 meters of ascent.

Moderate. A route of moderate length and about 700 to 800 meters of ascent.

Strenuous. Long, with a considerable ascent, steep sections, and a possibility of exposed sections of narrow trail, scree, snow traverses, et cetera. These are typically 6- to 8-hour walks involving an ascent of 1,000 meters or more.

Very strenuous. A very long route that may have some difficulties that approach a technical climb.

These grades are based on normal conditions for the route, but please note that in bad conditions such as fog, snow, or ice, routes must be upgraded. Many walks that can be safely taken in good weather on a dry trail should not be attempted in mist or snow. In inclement weather, a "strenuous" route might well become "very strenuous" or should be avoided altogether.

When considering whether a route's grade is suitable for you and/or your party, also review the information on Pace in the following section, Travel Basics.

Distance and type of walk. The next listing characterizes the type of hike for the route and gives the distance in kilometers. Three types of hikes are described. A trip "one way" starts in one place and ends in another. A "round trip" starts and ends at the same place, so that you return from the destination by retracing your route. The total distance out and back for such walks is given. A "loop trip" goes to its destination by one route and returns by a different route. Again, the total distance is given. A few loop trips involve the use of a car or bus to complete the trip.

High point and altitude. The "high point" gives the altitude in meters of the highest point reached on the route. "Total climb" gives the total amount of ascent or descent required, in meters. Alpine walks do not necessarily continually rise in one direction and descend in the other but may jog up and down along the way. Therefore, the ascent or descent may be greater than the distance between the high point and the starting point. (When a hike incorporates the use of a lift, the "total climb" figure includes the ascent of the lift.) For round trip walks the ascent and descent must be the same, so the term "total climb" indicates the vertical distance that you must ascend and descend.

Time. The times given here, which exclude lunch stops, are not necessarily those on the signposts found on the trails, which sometimes are too fast. The descents for this book were not calculated by formula but, rather, according to actual time for a careful descent, because descent on a rough trail can take longer than descent on an easy one.

Also, keep in mind the guidelines provided under the section Ratings, earlier in this chapter, and those under Pace, in Travel Basics.

Other Important Facts

LEFT BANK, RIGHT BANK

The orientation for trail directions is given facing downstream: that is, if you stand alongside a stream bank and face downstream with the stream to your left, the left bank is the one to your far left, the right bank is the one on which you are standing.

MAPS

Each walk in this book is shown on a sketch map. Hike numbers correspond to numbers on the sketch maps.

Lac Ste.-Anne, Parc Naturel Régional du Queyras

The sketch maps in this book are based on both 1:25,000 and 1:50,000 hiking maps published in France and Italy for these regions. Along with trail information, these sketch maps indicate locations of overnight accommodations as well as some prominent features such as glaciers, lakes, rivers, and major peaks. Sometimes names will appear on maps indicating meadows or "places." This practice of naming areas that are not set off by significant geographic features is common, and you will find such names on all topographic maps of these regions as well.

I strongly recommend that you also purchase the maps cited in Appendix 5 for each walk. The walk descriptions in this book are keyed to the suggested topographic maps, which show mountains and other features that are not shown on the sketch maps, as well as land contours. Although many of the major geographic features in each region are indicated on the sketch maps provided in this book, the limited scale of these sketch maps cannot include everything you will see on the route (or its topographic map), and possession of the topographic map will enhance the interest of each walk. Moreover, should a hiker lose the route, a topographic map with its fine detail will be extremely useful, perhaps essential. Many of the maps recommended here can be obtained only in the region they describe. You can buy them at bookstores, sport shops, grocery or general stores, or local tourist offices. Topographic maps are absolutely essential to the hiker.

TRAIL SIGNS AND BLAZES

A single logo has been adopted for all the French national parks, and you may see it on signposts, brochures, park buildings, et cetera. It looks like a fuzzy-edged spiral nebula, but on closer view (or when it is enlarged) you can see that the spiral is a montage made of all sorts of animals, birds, insects, trees, and flowers. The logo symbolizes the richness, complexity, and biological diversity of life. The general emblem is black, but each park displays the same logo in a different color (for example, dark blue for the Vanoise, purple for the Ecrins, green for the Mercantour).

In France, blazes on the Grande Randonnée, or GR, network are fairly standardized, consisting of a white bar above a red one, painted on a tree, rock, wall, or wood post. Sometimes the GR's number appears as well. The mark repeated twice plus an arrow indicates a turn, and an x indicates that you are going in the wrong direction. On non-GR trails the blazes may be of various, and even changing, colors, even on the same trail. Any flash of color indicates that you are on the trail, and junctions are usually marked.

Contrary to the general alpine custom of red and white trail blazes— usually a white bar over a red one, or two bars of one color sandwiching a third bar of another color, or even just a red mark—in the Gran Paradiso area trails are blazed with yellow marks, while red and white marks there usually indicate a property boundary.

Actual trail signs are less frequent along the routes in France and Italy than in Switzerland and Austria, but signs are always posted at a trailhead. Unlike Swiss signs, which normally give hiking times, French and Italian signs only occasionally give hiking times. It is not customary in the Alps to give distances on trail signs. French signs post hiking times that may sometimes be a little fast, and many Italian signs assume an ascent rate of 400 meters per hour, which is much faster than the 300-meter-per-hour ascent commonly regarded throughout the Alps as the standard, moderate rate of ascent.

ROADS

In France, road types are designated with letters. An A road is an *autoroute,* a toll road with limited access; the speed limit is 130 kilometers per hour. Some A roads are part of a trans-European network and are also designated "E." An N road is a *route nationale,* a major through-route; they are usually two-lane roads. A D road is a *route departementale,* a local road; some D roads are as good as the N roads.

In Italy, an A road is an *autostrada,* a limited-access toll road similar to the French *autoroutes.* Regional and local roads are not given special designations.

Often there is only one road through these small villages, and many main roads and side streets are unnamed. Where road names have been left out of the text, generally the villages are so small that you cannot miss the landmarks mentioned in the description.

There are references in the trail descriptions to "jeep roads" or "farm roads," by which is meant dirt or gravel roads that may be used by jeeps or farm vehicles. Their use is usually restricted to local inhabitants and farmers. Despite references to jeep roads, you need not infer that these roads are full of vehicles; as a rule you'll see very few, if any.

Note: In France, people refer to jeeps and other four-wheel-drive vehicles as *quatre-quatres* (sometimes written as "4x4s"), and jeep roads are often called *une route pour voiture 4x4.* Whichever way it is written, it is pronounced "quatre quatre"—phonetically, this sounds like "cat cat."

STREAM AND BROOK CROSSINGS

In the region of Italy covered here, many streams and brooks are unbridged. (In France, most streams are bridged, with few exceptions.) I have indicated in most cases whether the crossings are easy or difficult, although that judgment is subjective and can also be affected by the time of day (glacier-fed streams are fuller in the late afternoon) and by the season. A reference to stepping stones implies a fairly shallow stream, where you don't have to leap from rock to rock. Trekking poles are a great help in all such cases. I generally call a smaller flow a brook, a larger one a stream.

Travel Basics

Accommodations

HOTELS

Local tourist offices (*office du tourisme* or *syndicat d'initiative* in France; *azienda di soggiorno é turismo* or *ufficio informazioni turistiche* in Italy) sometimes offer printed lists of hotels (*liste des hotels* in France; *annuario alberghi* in Italy). These can be obtained upon arrival, or you can write to any town or village before you leave home and request such information. Guidebooks to French and Italian hotels are available in North America. Books such as the *Michelin Red* guides (updated annually) describe selected hotels and restaurants in categories ranging from simple to elegant. The Michelin guides are published by Michelin, Services de Tourisme Du Pneu Michelin, 46 avénue de Breteuil, F-75324 Paris cedex 07, France; tel. 33(1) 45 66 1234. They can be purchased in the United States at many bookstores or from Michelin, P.O. Box 19001, Greenville, SC 29602-9001. The annually updated *Guides des Hotels-Restaurants Logis de France* guidebook lists members of an association of simple, inexpensive, and generally very agreeable hotels, and I have found them the best for our purpose. A *Logis de France* hotel is more likely to be found in an obscure mountain village than a Michelin-listed hotel and is usually less expensive as well. The *Logis de France* guidebook can be purchased in bookshops in France, or you can request a copy of the book from the organization that publishes it, Fédération nationale des Logis de France (see Appendix 1 for the address).

All of France once went on holiday in the month of August, but years of government campaigns to persuade people to stagger their vacations have succeeded somewhat, and the summer season now runs from about July 15 to August 15. The Italians still seem to take their vacations in August. Reservations are certainly advisable for this period. Hotels and inns in mountain villages are generally open from early or mid-June until the end of September or mid-October, although some are open year-round or nearly so.

GÎTES D'ÉTAPE

Scattered along and near French hiking trails, especially near the Grande Randonnée (GR) trails, are very simple inns or hostels known as *gîtes d'étape*: literally, "stopping places along a road." (*Gîte* means a lodging or resting place; an *étape* is a halting place or day's march.) You may see the phrase *gîte chambre d'hôte*, sometimes defined as a simple bed-and-breakfast, usually with dinner also available. The *gîte* is roughly the equivalent of the Swiss *Berghotel* or mountain inn, with several differences. Some of the French *gîtes* are located in villages and towns through

Dining at the gîte d'étape *at Fouillouse*

which hikers pass, whereas Swiss *Berghotels* are always up in the mountains. Moreover, unlike *Berghotels*, some *gîtes* are also their owners' home. While some *gîtes* have a few private rooms, most consist of dormitories similar to those in alpine club huts (see later). *Gîtes d'étape* usually have indoor toilets and may have simple shower rooms, but they do not provide towels or soap. Some also have a *coin cuisine* (which literally means a kitchen corner), where guests can cook their own meals. *Gîtes* generally serve an evening meal, however, and these can be very good. For example, at one *gîte* in the Mercantour, dinner began with a tasty soup, followed by a large casserole of gratinéed yellow squash and rice, *Daube de Boeuf* with salad, and apple tart for dessert. *Gîtes* also serve the typical continental breakfast of bread with butter and jam and coffee or tea.

You can purchase guidebooks to the *gîtes* in bookstores in France. One book that includes both French alpine club huts and *gîtes* is the *Guide des Refuges et Gîtes des Alpes*, edited by the Association de la Grande Traversée des Alpes Cimes, and published by Editions Glénat, BP 177, 38008 Grenoble cedex, France. Another such book is *Gîtes Refuges, France et Frontières*, by Annick and Serge Mouraret, published by Editions La Cadole, 74 rue Albert Perdreaux, 78140 Vélizy, France.

VACATION APARTMENTS

It is possible to rent a furnished vacation apartment or house in some parts of the French Alps. These apartments are called *locations de vacances.* Kitchen equipment and blankets are provided, but you generally must bring towels and bedsheets; inquire about this when you make reservations.

You can obtain a list of vacation apartments in a region by writing to Maison des Gîtes de France (see Appendix 1). If you rent directly through a vacation apartment owner, write and state your name, address, and telephone number, the dates required, and the number of persons in your party (adults and children) and enclose two international postal reply coupons. Request that the owner send you two copies of the rental contract. You can also write to Maison des Gîtes de France directly and ask them to book for you; they will charge a fee for this service. The booking service is open weekdays from 9:00 A.M. to 12:00 P.M. and 2:00 P.M. to 4:30 P.M. Weekly rental usually extends from 4:00 P.M. on a Saturday to 10:00 A.M. the following Saturday, although other arrangements can be made.

ALPINE CLUB HUTS

The Club Alpin Français (CAF) and Club Alpino Italiano (CAI) run mountain huts like those in Switzerland and Austria. A hut in France is a *refuge de montagne* (whereas in French-speaking Switzerland it is a *cabane*); in Italy it is a *rifugio*. Club members receive a discount, with reciprocal discounts for members of the clubs of other alpine countries. Membership in the French and Italian clubs is open to all. For information contact the Club Alpin Français, 24 avénue de la Laumière, 75019 Paris, France; tel. (1) 42 02 68 44. Or contact the Club Alpino Italiano, Fons. Pimentel 7, 20100 Milano, Italy; tel. 0039 2 2614 1378.

The dormitories or bunk rooms found at alpine club huts and *gîtes d'étape* are very simple. They usually consist of sleeping shelves or platforms on which people sleep side by side. There may also be bunkbeds. CAI huts in the Gran Paradiso region often have small rooms with bunkbeds for four persons, in addition to dormitories. You are provided with a thin mattress, pillow, and blankets, which are generally plentiful, but not with sheets or pillowcases. Some guests bring sheet sacks or thin sleeping bags but many do not.

Many French alpine club huts now sell a disposable, biodegradable paper sheet sack, or *sac de couchage*, that is popularly called, oddly, a *sac à viande*—literally, "meat sack." Some alpine club huts sell a disposable, fitted bottom sheet called a *drap housse* or *drap couchette*, a dust sheet that covers only the mattress.

Some *gîtes* may have partitions within the dormitory separating pairs of guests. The code of behavior is decorous. Although both sexes share the dormitories and nobody brings a bathrobe, people are quiet and discreet. In the morning you are expected to fold up the blankets and place them neatly at the foot of your mattress. Note: Unlike Italian huts, many French huts do not provide toilet paper. You should also bring your own handtowel and soap.

Alpine club huts serve hikers as well as climbers. Some, like the Refuge des Merveilles, are frequented almost solely by hikers, while others, near great mountains or glaciers, are mainly used by climbers or persons undertaking a glacier tour.

In alpine-style climbing, a team of climbers erects a series of base camps and takes several weeks to accomplish a climb. At a hut in the Alps, climbers rise well before dawn, sometimes as early as 2:00 A.M. They start the climb with headlamps, reach the summit before midmorning and descend by noon, before the afternoon sun softens the snow and raises the risk of avalanches and falling rocks. Alpine club huts are built as high as is practicable near major mountains in order to facilitate these swift ascents. You do not have to rise in the dark, however, if you stay at a hut frequented by climbers; hikers get up at about 7:00 A.M. Climbers go to bed early, and most everyone else turns in by 9:00 P.M. or 10:00 P.M. at the latest.

At the beginning of the season, about the middle of June, the French and Italian huts are provisioned by helicopter. After that, new supplies are brought up by the hut keeper (in French, *gardien;* in Italian, *custode*) or by his or her family or friends. (In France I found many huts kept by *gardiennes.*) Each hut is run by a particular section of the country's alpine club.

The huts are very simple: dining room, kitchen (closed to the public), and dormitories. The toilet may be indoors or out. Solar-generated hot showers operated by a coin or token are increasingly to be found, but there is usually no hot water at the sinks. Meals are simple but filling. They have to be. The caloric expenditure of climbers is prodigious, and they require mountainous portions. (For that matter, your own caloric output will be pretty high. A hiking vacation in the Alps may be the surest method of dieting ever devised.) In French refuges and in most Italian ones, the hut keeper makes one menu for everyone—always a four-course meal in France and a three- or four-course meal in Italy—and serves everyone together (there may be two consecutive services if the hut is crowded). Such a dinner begins with a soup in France or pasta in Italy, followed perhaps by a stew or a platter of meat or chicken with rice or pasta and vegetables, a cheese course, and then a dessert of canned fruit, *mousse au chocolat*, flan, or sometimes a tart. Soft drinks are always available, and wine and beer are usually available. Many climbers and hikers bring their own food with them; at some huts they are allowed to cook simple meals in a special room and eat *hors sac* (out of the rucksack). A very few huts do not serve meals but have a stove, pots, and fuel available for hikers to cook food they have brought with them. Only two such huts are mentioned in this book and they are identified as such. Note that breakfast is comparatively small and typically European: bread, jam, and butter, and tea or coffee, which the French like to drink out of bowls.

In the Vanoise, many of the huts are privately owned and sell take-out picnic lunches. *Un casse croûte* or *un pique-nique* (now sometimes spelled "picnic") may consist of a sandwich, boiled egg, fruit, tomato, and cookie—a great help to hikers who have to carry their own provisions on multi-day tours.

Boots must be parked in the hut entryway on special shelves. Ice axes and trekking poles should also be left there. Huts provide rubber overshoes or slippers to wear indoors, although some guests bring their own slippers or sneakers.

On summer weekends during spells of fine weather the huts may be crowded, especially ones that are easily accessible and that serve popular climbs. You can telephone most huts (they have radio telephones) and reserve a place. Otherwise, people get accommodations in the order in which they arrive. Huts that are easily accessible may post cards at the trailhead announcing that they are full (*complet* in French, *completo* in Italian); this usually occurs only on a weekend.

The huts are popular with hikers because they almost invariably occupy locations that range from splendid to breathtaking. An evening at a hut has a special appeal. After the climb it took to get there, you will eat with relish whatever they serve, and the camaraderie is often incomparable.

Some of the privately owned refuges in the Vanoise permit camping between July 1 and August 31, but hikers may camp for one night only, between 7:00 P.M. and 7:00 A.M., in small tents (ones in which a person cannot stand upright), for a small per-person fee.

Demi-pension (in French) or *mezza pensione* (in Italian) means the price of a night's stay plus evening meal and breakfast. Prices are the same for all alpine club huts of the same category in France and are also uniform in Italy, but prices at privately owned huts vary.

Logistics

TRANSPORTATION

Although it is possible to get to many places in these regions using local buses, renting a car certainly makes things easier. Buses run daily although not frequently, and the traveler who uses them has less flexibility. It is easier and less expensive to arrange car rentals if you do so before you arrive. Shop around for the best buy, which you may find through an organization such as the American Automobile Association (AAA), or through other well-known agencies.

Note: If you rent a car in France and your itinerary includes driving into Switzerland, you will have to buy an autoroute sticker for your car at the Swiss border. If you neglect to do so, you may be pulled over and fined.

WEATHER

During any part of the summer in the Alps you may encounter spells of warm or cool temperatures, with rainy or dry weather; therefore, you should bring clothing for all contingencies. Even during what counts in the mountains as a "heat wave," when temperatures may reach 25 to 27 degrees Celsius (80 to 85 degrees Fahrenheit), evenings are always cool. Such a period of warm weather can last for a week or two, or there may be an extended period of cool or wet weather.

In planning your vacation, note that there may be a good deal of snow left until mid- to late June that may restrict your hiking. Good weather occurs about equally in July or in August. Some hikers prefer to go hiking at the end of August or in September because there are far fewer tourists then, much less snow on the passes, and some say better and more settled weather. On the other hand, the alpine flowers are more abundant earlier in the summer. The hiking season ends by late September or early October.

LANGUAGES

Hikers who can brush up their high school French will be pleased to learn that it will be of use in both France and northwestern Italy. The area covered in this book forms not only a geographic but also a linguistic unit, and you can use French throughout. The northwest corner of Italy was part of the ancient state of Savoy, which was French-speaking. Savoy was split apart during the upheavals of the nineteenth century; its western region was absorbed by France in 1860, and its eastern region was joined to the new nation of Italy in 1861. The natives of this part of Italy still speak French and also a *patois* (a dialect resembling Provençal French), as well as the Italian they learn in school as a second language. In this book, words from these languages are given first in French and then in Italian. For the Italian region represented here, place names are generally given in Italian, although frequently the Italian and the French names are used interchangeably on maps and trail signs. Because of this, an alphabetical listing of these names is included in the glossary. A glance at any map of the region shows numerous French place names, sometimes slightly Italianized on official maps. There are towns and villages with such names as Villeneuve and Rhêmes-Notre Dame and mountains called La Grande Traversière and L'Herbetet. Indeed, because of its linguistic heritage, this is one of only a few regions in Italy that enjoy a measure of autonomy.

It is undeniable that the more you can speak of a country's language, the more interaction you can enjoy and the easier it will be to make arrangements. But I do not think that unfamiliarity with the language is a reason to stay away. Although many French and Italian people speak no English, a surprising number do, and if you make an effort to speak a little French or Italian you can often meet people half way; the good will this generates helps make friendships. Almost everywhere I went, there was someone who spoke English. At one hotel I found a Welsh waitress working there for the summer. A hotel owner, with an uncle in Chicago, spoke colloquial English. At another hotel, a young employee had lived in Canada for a while and also spoke good English, as did the guide at the historic bakery in the village of Villar-d'Arène, where they used to make bread only once a year. At hotels or alpine club huts you may run into other guests who speak English. During dinner at one hotel I sat next to a friendly Belgian man who had worked for years in Washington, D.C. On another night, at an alpine club hut, I sat with a German woman who had married an Englishman; her sister had married a Frenchman and they had come to the Alps to share a little time together. The hut keeper's assistant at this same hut was multilingual, speaking French, Italian, English, and Greek! And the next night at dinner, our table partners were several charming young Italian hikers eager to speak English.

HIKING GUIDES

Accompagnateurs en Montagne, a special class of licensed, nonalpinist guides, offer guided private-party and group hiking tours through some of the local tourist offices. These *accompagnateurs* take special classes and must pass a state exam before they can escort clients. Along with guiding they explain regional geology and identify fauna and flora; in addition, they often know where chamois and ibex are found and can lead clients to see them. They are not authorized to take clients rock climbing or onto glaciers. Notices for regular, scheduled group tours led by *accompagnateurs* often are posted at local tourist offices.

TELEPHONES

The French have developed a pay phone system that accepts special cards called *télécartes* as payment instead of coins. You can buy these cards, valid for various numbers of message units, at any post office. Insert the card into the machine at any telephone booth set up for the cards (a picture diagram on the machine shows you which way to insert the card). According to where you phone or how long you speak, a certain number of message units will be used up on the card. Not all French phone booths are set up for cards, so you may still need to carry change.

A similar system is being introduced into Italy. Some Italian pay phones take tokens, called *gettoni.* You can buy these at cafés, bars, and tobacco shops.

CURRENCY

Travelers' checks are universally accepted by banks. The foreign exchange rates are always posted in the bank. Most hotels, stores, and restaurants will accept major American credit cards; however, alpine club huts and *gîtes* will not. Also, in the Val d'Aosta area of Italy, small hotels usually do not accept credit cards. Hotels give a poor exchange rate on travelers' checks. You can often exchange currency at railway stations outside of banking hours. If you change money in France at a bank called a *Société Générale,* there is no tax on the transaction.

BUSINESS HOURS

Many people use the European timetable, in which the hours of 1:00 P.M. to midnight are numbered 13:00 to 24:00. Shop hours are generally 8:00 to 12:00 (8:00 A.M. to 12:00 P.M.) and 13:30 or 14:30 to 18:30 hours (1:30 P.M. or 2:30 P.M. to 6:30 P.M.). Banking hours are generally 8:30 to 12:00 and 13:30 to 16:00 or 16:30 hours. Post offices are closed from 12:00 to 13:45 and then reopen from about 14:00 to 18:00 or 18:30 hours, but there may be local variations. Italian banks and post offices may be closed in the afternoon; travelers should check the posted schedules. In alpine villages frequented by hikers, food shops and even other shops may be open on Sunday, but you should inquire or look for a card on the door: open and closed are, respectively, *ouvert* and *fermé* in French and *aperto* and *chiuso* in Italian. In Italy, grocery stores may be closed on Sundays or may not get fresh bread that day; stock up on Saturdays with picnic supplies.

Walking Tips

CONDITIONING

It is important to be in good condition before you start an alpine vacation. Various forms of aerobic exercise, including walking, can provide this kind of conditioning.

Sometimes the obvious needs to be said. For your first day in the Alps, select a route with only a moderate ascent. Information on the ascent in meters is noted for every route I list. If there are any hills near your home, walk in them a few days before you leave, if possible. Climbing up and down stairs, ramps, or steep streets can also help. If you live in a flat region, expect that it will take a few days in the mountains to get your thigh and calf muscles into condition. The soles of your feet also get less sore and tender after a couple of days of climbing.

PACE

Setting the proper pace is crucial in the mountains. It can mean the difference between arriving at your destination comfortably or in a state of exhaustion. Even small mountains seem tall. This makes people think that if they don't move quickly, they won't get to the top. Consequently, the pace that some inexperienced hikers take would wear out anyone but an Olympic long-distance runner. After several minutes of rapid ascent they fall to the side of the trail, panting, then as soon as they recover their breath they start up again as fast as possible. All-out rushes alternate with short and ever–less satisfactory periods of rest, and they arrive at the top ready to collapse.

A nineteenth-century English traveler described his disappointment at watching the Swiss in motion. Instead of gracefully bounding up mountains like chamois, he complained, they plodded like peasants. But what he saw was the right pace—and the only way to handle these mountains or any others. On one of my first trips to the Alps, I was resting by the side of a steep trail when two figures approached: young men with full

Roman road on the way to Col de Mary, the Ubaye

packs topped with ropes, ice axes, and crampons, obviously making for an alpine club hut and some serious climbs. They moved upward so slowly that they appeared almost to be taking baby steps. I watched in fascination as they slowly but steadily mounted the steep trail. Although my pack was light compared to theirs, they passed me and I never caught up with them.

This is the way licensed alpine guides teach novices to ascend a trail. When walking uphill, move slowly, steadily, and regularly. Although your objective looks high, the vertical distances are less than you might think. Plodding methodically uphill can give you an ascent rate of 300 meters an hour, which is considered the standard ascent rate. On a moderate slope, this might translate into about fifty-five or sixty fairly short steps a minute; on a steep slope, about forty-five steps a minute. It's counterinstinctive. When the trail starts to rise, slow down. With the proper pace even elderly people (in good health) can hike in the mountains, and in the Alps they do.

This said, it also needs to be observed that hiking styles differ across the Alps. French and Italian hikers often try to speed at the start of a hike; I would urge you not to be tempted to join the race. Keep to the proper pace, and before the hike is over you'll probably pass most of them.

ALTITUDE ACCLIMATIZATION

Unless you already live at high altitude, you will need to acclimatize to it. High altitude produces various effects on the human body, chiefly because of the reduced amount of oxygen in the air. Yet the body begins to adapt, generally within two to three days, to these new conditions. Respiration increases in volume and depth, and blood vessels open up, allowing oxygen to be more efficiently absorbed. Other biochemical adaptations occur as well, enabling larger amounts of oxygen to be carried to body tissues. This adjustment process occurs faster for some people than for others. There is an upper limit of 18,000 to 20,000 feet in altitude to which anyone can acclimatize, but this is considerably higher than what one encounters anywhere in the Alps: even the highest alpine summits are lower than this.

You acclimatize to higher altitudes mainly by going up and staying there. This adjustment is a silent process, but you need to give it a few days to take effect. During the first day, physical activity should be fairly light. It is advisable not to drink alcohol until you are acclimatized. Mild to acute altitude sickness can occur if you try to rush the process. The symptoms of mild altitude sickness include shortness of breath and mild insomnia. In the Alps, acute symptoms are likely only among people who attempt a major climb (4,000 meters or higher) within a few days after their arrival. They may also occur occasionally in persons who sleep in the few alpine club huts that are over 3,500 meters high; none of these huts are listed in this book. Acute symptoms include severe headache, confusion, problems with motor coordination, weakness, chills, nausea, and vomiting. Alpine hiking is done at much lower altitudes than where these acute symptoms can ordinarily be expected to occur.

For some reason not yet fully understood, teenagers run a greater risk of altitude sickness than older people, although it cannot be predicted who will be affected. At the first sign of nausea, dizziness, or breathing problems during a climb, descend at once.

Just as you condition your leg muscles for mountain walking, you must also condition yourself for altitude. When you first arrive in the Alps, even if you think your leg muscles are ready for anything, do not attempt any climbs that take you up a considerable distance (1,000 meters or more) before you are at least conditioned to the altitude of the town you are starting from. Your first hike should be only a moderate climb of less than 500 meters. On your second hike, go a little higher depending on how you feel.

Although there is always a temptation to rush to get to the top once you see the summit, go slowly!

What To Bring

CLOTHING AND EQUIPMENT

Boots and socks. If you don't have boots, it's better to buy them at home than to wait until you get to the Alps so you have a chance to break them in. Wear them at home on as many walks as possible, even if you are just clumping along the sidewalk.

In selecting boots, look for ones with lugged rubber outsoles; they are sturdy and have the best grip. Technical climbing boots are too stiff for hiking. I recommend a medium-weight leather boot with a three-quarter-inch steel shank or one of the new plastic-laminated insoles. The problem with lightweight boots is that they don't give enough support on rubble and scree, and the soles are too flexible for rock. They also tend to disintegrate after one season of hard use; moreover, the lightweight boots of leather and laminated cloth are not waterproof and may not keep your feet dry in snow, which you may encounter because the alpine summer is unpredictable. If you are thinking of trying some of the mountain pass routes where you may encounter snow, a medium-weight leather boot will serve you best.

Whether you are being fitted for boots in a store or measuring your own foot for a catalog order, wear a couple of pairs of socks. The most comfortable arrangement for hiking is a thin inner liner sock and a heavier outer sock, preferably a wool or thick "wick-dry" sock. A variety of socks is available from mail-order houses.

It's a good idea to apply a seal treatment to leather boots; you can have relatively waterproof boots this way. If conditions are wet or snowy, you'll have to repeat this treatment as often as once a week.

If you have a little extra room in your boot, various insole pads now on the market provide wonderful cushioning. If you are buying new boots, allow room for an insole.

A special note for beginners: If your feet hurt on the trail, consider relacing your boots. You may not be aware that you have put a little too much pressure over your toes and arches, yet this can cause pain. Lace your boots fairly loosely near the toes and instep, and only tighten at the ankle, where your foot flexes. When going downhill, however, tighten the lacing slightly along your instep and toes if your foot is sliding forward and your toes are hitting the front of your boot. If you tie the top too tightly, you may feel a sort of burn later around your leg above the ankle.

Packs. The most useful pack is a medium-capacity rucksack, with a volume between thirty-five and fifty liters. American internal-frame packs are often large and have elaborate suspension systems, but these packs are heavy and expensive, and unnecessary unless you intend to carry fifty-pound loads. Get the smallest one that feels comfortable on your back and that will hold your necessities as well as your camera in case of rain. I recommend a simple top-loading pack that weighs between two and three and a half pounds. It will be more comfortable if it has an internal frame consisting of light aluminum stays or a fiberglass-reinforced panel that conforms to the shape of your back. A load-bearing waist belt is a useful feature since it allows you to shift weight between your hips and shoulders from time to time during a long hike.

Also note that packs are sized to different back lengths. Look for one that is long enough for your back, because a pack whose lower edge hits the small of your back can be painful during a long trip. Short men, many women, and children will be more comfortable with a pack whose shoulder straps are set closer together than is the case for many packs designed for tall men. Several excellent packs are now available in North America, but if you can't find one you can easily buy one in larger European alpine towns and some resorts.

No pack is entirely waterproof. Since they all leak in a downpour, you should pack items you really want to keep dry in a large waterproof stuff sack or a plastic bag.

Trekking poles. These devices began to be seen in the Swiss and Austrian Alps toward the end of the 1980s. At first many people thought they were merely a new fad, but nearly everyone who tried them was immediately converted, and they are now standard equipment for hikers in Switzerland and Austria. Climbers even carry them for nontechnical portions of a route and for moderate-angle snow climbs. Trekking poles are three-sectioned, collapsible ski poles that when collapsed fit neatly alongside your pack, strapped onto it; this makes them much easier to transport than a walking stick. The points of high-quality poles are made of carbide steel and will not wear down. Baskets may be attached around the points, according to your preference; with baskets, they can be used for ski mountaineering.

I cannot say enough in favor of trekking poles, and I no longer hike anywhere without them. Using a pair is even better than using one. They are wonderful in many situations: on muddy or slippery trails, for example, or on scree, or when there is a little snow. They help provide stability and balance. I love using them when rock-hopping across an unbridged stream, or for security on a narrow, exposed trail. They also help protect your knees when going down a steep slope. They do not, however, replace an ice ax when one is needed. Trekking poles have not yet swept the French or Italian Alps but are bound to do so soon. They can be bought in North America and in larger European alpine towns and many resorts.

Clothing. In the past, many European mountain hikers traditionally wore knickers in the Alps. The advantage of knickers was that you could roll down your knee socks if it became hot, but you were snug and warm when it was cold. Proponents also claimed they gave you freer knee movement. The fashion has now changed, and many alpine hikers have switched to "trekking pants," long pants with extra pockets rather like what Americans call trail or cargo pants. Obviously, you can do well in any comfortable pants, as long as they are not too tight. Jeans are not a good idea, as they take too long to dry if they get wet. A synthetic–cotton blend is best for warm weather, and an all-synthetic or synthetic–wool blend is best for cold, wet weather (for the most part, these heavier pants are not needed in summer). A pair of shorts will greatly enhance your comfort should the weather turn warm, which it often does; French and Italian hikers wear shorts most of the time. At higher altitudes there is a lot of radiant energy, and it can occasionally get very warm.

Bring both long- and short-sleeved shirts. A tanktop is nice in hot weather; the only disadvantage is the added risk of sunburn. And bring at least one warm garment. I recommend a wool sweater (a Shetland type is both lightweight and warm) or pile jacket. A cotton sweater won't provide much warmth.

You also need full rain protection. Climbers used to carry both wind and rain suits, but a good two-piece rain suit can serve both functions. The new "breathable" coated and laminated jackets are preferable to the older impermeable ones since they provide this dual protection. I advise against ponchos because they blow around in strong wind. If you have old rain clothes, check them before you leave home and seal the seams if necessary.

A sun hat with a good brim is a must. A bandana can be used to shade your neck. I also recommend that you bring a warm cap and a pair of gloves or mittens.

Gaiters—waterproof leggings that fit over boots and seal the tops—are useful for keeping snow, scree, and water out of your boots. You can buy knee-high ones or short ones that extend just above the ankle. The latter weigh much less and work very well with shorts. Long gaiters protect long pants from mud and snow.

Other equipment, preparations, and gear. Sunglasses are essential. The best kind screen ultraviolet rays. Don't go out onto a glacier or take an extended snow walk without good sunglasses; otherwise, you could get temporary snowblindness. Consider bringing glacier goggles if you are certain you will do some snow trips. If you wear eyeglasses, you can buy lightweight glacier goggles that fit over glasses. You can even wear them over your sunglasses for extra protection.

Since skin burns faster at high altitudes, wear a sunblock or a good sunscreen, and apply sunblock lip protection on your lips as well. For glacier travel use glacier cream on all exposed skin and a total sunblock on your lips. You can buy these items in Europe although sunblock is almost twice as expensive there as in North America.

You can make up your own first-aid kit in a self-sealing plastic bag. Include aspirin, a small bottle of disinfectant, a variety of small adhesive bandages, a few large sterile wound dressings, a roll of stretch-type adhesive tape for bandages and sprained ankles, tweezers for removing splinters, plus any sort of medication you need. You can get the equivalent of practically any standard over-the-counter U.S. medication in Europe but remember to bring prescriptions for any special medication that you regularly use. Carry a small supply of moleskin for blisters and irritations.

A compass is essential should you have to find a route or should you become lost. An altimeter is also useful but not essential, and they are expensive. European maps, particularly the 1:25,000 scale series, have detailed, generally accurate (the Italian maps can contain small errors) altitude data for points along the trail, and an accurate altimeter enables you to quickly find your location. Note: If you have an altimeter, you should not necessarily reset it every time you see a park sign; the altitudes on signs are often off by 30 meters or more. Pack a whistle in case you need to call for aid.

Most people will need a water bottle that holds at least 0.75 liter. Screwtop plastic bottles are light and odor-resistant. In Europe you can get ceramic-coated metal bottles that are easier to drink from but are slightly heavier than plastic bottles.

The longest blade of the traditional multi-blade pocket knife is a little short for slicing bread. I find a three-inch folding "lockblade" a useful size and not too heavy.

An ice ax is usually unnecessary, but it is a useful safety measure on certain walks where steep snow-covered slopes are traversed. If you prefer not to carry an ice ax, you can avoid routes where snow may be found on a slope by inquiring at local tourist offices. If the season is unusually snowy, you may want to take an ice ax on certain other walks such as mountain pass routes. For hiking, an ice ax of sixty-five to seventy centimeters in length is useful.

Photographic equipment should be simple, rugged, and light. Do not take equipment that you will want to get rid of after ascending the first 500 meters. My husband usually carries photographic equipment in a small bag that can be put into his pack in heavy rain. Kodachrome, Fuji, and Ilford film can be easily purchased in Europe at about the standard U.S. price, but you will not find discount rates.

In our experience, telephoto lenses are rarely necessary if your subject material is alpine scenery. The thirty-five-millimeter focal length is perhaps the most useful lens, and the fifty millimeter is the second most useful. Items like motor drive units are not necessary, and neither are many filters. Ultraviolet filters for lens protection are all one needs for color photography; medium-orange filters are occasionally useful for black and white photography. Keep in mind the weight of film on a cross-country trip. A roll of thirty-five millimeter film, without its cardboard box, weighs one ounce. Pack some lead-lined film protection bags in your suitcase. Hand-inspection of film is not possible; all carry-on and some checked luggage will be x-rayed by airport security.

What to Bring on a Day Trip

You will probably see some people out on alpine trails carrying next to nothing. This is extremely inadvisable, as mountain weather is changeable and you should therefore bring at least rain gear on every hike. Although you set off on a sunny morning, you may come back in rain. You also need something to keep you warm. The air becomes about 2 degrees Celsius cooler for each 300 meters you climb (about 4 degrees Fahrenheit for every 1,000 feet). If you climb 1,000 meters, you will not only be in much cooler air, but also possibly in stronger winds.

A basic list of what you should always carry starts, therefore, with a rain suit and a sweater or pile jacket—unless there has been a sustained spell of warm weather; however, always carry a warm garment if you are going fairly high or on a long route. You can use your rain jacket for additional warmth. Also bring a warm cap and mittens if you are going to climb fairly high. For a long hike or a hike where you may encounter snow, bring gaiters. When I start a hike in shorts on a warm morning, I always pack my long pants in case the weather changes or if I'm planning to climb fairly high. But weather is unpredictable regardless of the length or altitude of your hike. If it turns cold, adding rain pants over your shorts may give you sufficient protection. When I start a hike in a T-shirt, I pack a long-sleeved shirt for the same reason.

You should always bring sun protection: a sun hat with a good brim, sunglasses and sunscreen or sunblock, and a small container of sunblock for your lips. Carry a basic first-aid kit, including a square of moleskin in case of foot irritations. You also need a water bottle, compass, whistle, and food. If you are taking a long route, bring a flashlight or headlamp; it's also a good idea to carry a small reserve supply of high-energy food.

What to Bring on an Overnight Trip

If you are planning a multi-day trip, you must carry everything you need, but the primary consideration when packing is weight. If you plan to walk over passes, you will be hauling your wardrobe up a few thousand feet on your back. Experienced alpine walkers consider the weight of every toilet article and every item of clothing. For example, the weight difference between your comfortable old cotton canvas shorts and a nylon or polyester pair can be considerable—as much as half a pound.

Boots are not allowed inside alpine club huts. The huts provide indoor footwear resembling old-fashioned rubbers or else clogs, but some hikers bring a pair of lightweight slippers or running shoes for use inside the huts.

Sleepwear is optional. Europeans as a rule do not haul pajamas or nightgowns up to huts. Although both sexes share the dormitories, people look the other way or dress under the blankets.

A small, lightweight flashlight or headlamp is essential at alpine club huts because the toilet may be outside. Pack some toilet paper as well. At huts you'll also need a small handtowel, although some people manage with a washcloth. Bring half or a quarter of a bar of soap and, for a longer trip, a tiny supply of biodegradable soapflakes or detergent in a self-sealing plastic bag if you think you'll want to wash your clothes.

If you want to shave, consider a plastic, disposable razor and a small amount of brushless shaving cream in an empty plastic thirty-five millimeter film can. You can also carry skin conditioner and face cream in one of these tiny cans.

A brief note about what you don't need: Because camping is for the most part prohibited, you don't need a tent, and because all huts and *gîtes d'étape* provide blankets, you don't need a sleeping bag.

FOOD

For nearly every hike in this book you will need only lunch and snacks. Virtually every hut provides breakfast, lunch, and dinner (the few exceptions are noted in the text). This section offers general information and the French and Italian names of basic foods for picnic lunches and snacks. For information on hut meals, see the section on alpine club huts.

The long and narrow loaf that we know as French bread actually comes in different lengths. The standard *baguette* is usually an adequate lunch bread for two hikers. The *flute* is longer and the *ficelle* shorter. *Pain de campagne* (country bread) and *pain complet,* also called *pain noir,* are darker, whole-grain breads. *Pain de seigle* is made with rye flour, although it is not quite the same as what we call rye bread. These darker breads are a mixture of white and whole-grain flour and are quite pale compared to our whole-wheat breads. Five-grain bread—*pain aux cinq céréales*—although difficult to find, is delicious. These large, dark breads are good to take along if you are heading up to a hut or remote hamlet for a few days, but since they have no preservatives, they quickly turn hard. I found that storing a *pain de campagne* in a self-sealing bag kept it soft enough to eat. A roll is a *petit pain* in French or *panino* in Italian. Bread made with whole-wheat flour is *pane integrale* in Italian.

Peanuts, raisins, and other dried fruits are widely available. Wonderful selections of cheese as well as sliced cold meats and even pâté are available at grocery stores, supermarkets, or shops that specialize in prepared foods. Persons on a low-fat diet who don't eat cheese might consider canned fish: in France, several varieties of canned *salade niçoise*—tuna fish with piquant vegetables—are available, as are other canned salads. Sliced fresh tomatoes and green peppers with a little mustard (available *en tube* for the convenience of picnickers) make a tasty low-fat trail sandwich.

You can generally get herb tea at hotels, cafés, *gîtes d'étape,* and even huts. The ones most often available seem to be verbena (*verveine* in French, *verbena* in Italian), linden (*tilleul* in French, *tiglio* in Italian), mint (*menthe* in French, *menta* in Italian), or some mixture of these; you may be offered *verveine-menthe,* for example. The general word for such a tea is *une tisane* (in French) or *una tisana* (in Italian), but you should specify the herb you prefer.

A cheese course is served after almost every French meal, even at huts. You may be offered a choice of *fromage sec, blanc* or *frais. Fromage sec* is cheese such as we know it (e. g., camembert, blue cheese, et cetera); *fromage blanc* has the consistency of custard, although it isn't sweet; *fromage frais* is similar to cottage cheese.

WATER

Is stream water safe? This is not guaranteed, as there may be animals grazing above you. You should always fill your water bottle from a safe source before you start on the trail in the morning. You can carry a small bottle of iodine tablets for emergency use. Tap water in villages and water at huts are generally as safe as water supplies in the United States and Canada.

Safety

GENERAL CONSIDERATIONS

Hiking in the mountains entails unavoidable risks that every hiker assumes and must be aware of and respect. The fact that a route or area is described in this book is not a representation that it will be safe for you or your party. In the route descriptions a grading code is used to indicate the degree of difficulty of each route, but this code can only provide a rough guide: within each category, trails may vary greatly in difficulty and in the degree of physical conditioning and agility one needs to enjoy them safely.

Trail conditions and even routes may have changed or deteriorated since these descriptions were written. Winter storms and avalanches may produce rock slides over a section of trail and spring torrents can wash out small bridges. Also, trail conditions can change from day to day due to weather and other factors. A trail that is safe on a dry day may be unsafe in rain, snow, or fog; a trail that is safe for a well-conditioned, properly equipped hiker may be unsafe for someone else. This book does not and cannot list every hazard that may confront you, because of changing terrain and weather and the varying capabilities of different hikers.

Thousands of people have safe and enjoyable hikes every year; however, while the Alps in general are not a wilderness area, risks can be present that do not confront people at home. When you hike you assume those risks. Exercising your good judgment and common sense will help. You can minimize many risks by being well prepared, alert, and knowledgeable. Be aware of your own limitations and of conditions when and where you are hiking. If conditions are dangerous or if you or anyone in your party is unwell or exhausted, wait a day or turn back if you have already started on the trail.

The areas described in this book have long been safe and peaceful, but political conditions may add to the risks of travel in Europe in ways that this book cannot predict. When you travel, you assume this risk, and should keep informed of political developments that may make safe travel difficult or impossible.

SPECIFIC RISKS AND HAZARDS

Climbers distinguish two sorts of dangers: objective and subjective. Objective dangers stem from external factors, such as the greater likelihood of rock falls and avalanches in the afternoon; subjective ones arise from one's own bad judgment, inexperience, poor condition, or lack of equipment. There are several objective factors to which hikers are exposed. Check your local library or an outdoor supplies store for books that will prepare you for any of the following dangers.

Inclement weather. Do not start a long route if the morning looks ominous or the forecast is threatening. If you are out on a trail and the sky becomes heavy and dark, turn around. You should always carry both warm and waterproof clothes in your pack and extra food for energy. Because lightning is most likely to strike high, exposed points and ridge lines, you should descend from a peak or exposed ridge at once if the sky looks threatening. Most thunderstorms occur in the afternoon, so you should plan your hike so that you will be down from exposed places by then. (See the Weather section under Travel Basics.)

Rockfall. Occasionally, signs are posted warning of falling stones (*chute de pierres* in French, *caduta di sassi* in Italian). If you are passing under or close to a slope, you should both watch and listen. Animals grazing above you can knock down loose stones with their hoofs, and so can climbers or hikers above. If you knock down a stone yourself, shout a warning in case anyone is below you. Likewise, watch out if you hear a shout: "watch out" is *attention* in French, *attento* (masculine) or *attenta* (feminine) or *occhio* in Italian. Never sit down for lunch directly under a cliff or a steep slope littered with scree. Snow avalanches are not a hazard on hiking trails in the summer hiking season; they are a danger only on certain technical climbing routes in the summer. Avalanches can occur at lower altitudes in the spring skiing season, so anyone intending to snowshoe or ski on hiking routes in the spring should consult a local guides' office.

Loose scree. Some of the more difficult trails may involve a descent or traverse on loose scree. You can best descend these slopes by coming down first with the heel of your boot. Since there may be great exposure as well, you should avoid these routes if you are doubtful of your ability. (In the vocabulary of alpinism, "exposure" means simply a great vertical drop below you.) Remember that rain can make a route on solid rock difficult and snow can turn a walking trail into a technical climb.

Snow. Traversing a snow slope can be dangerous. You should always be careful on steep snow. If you have to make a traverse across a steep slope and you are not equipped with an ice ax, pick up a long, pointy stone and hold it ready to jam into the snow should you fall (this is called a "self-arrest"). Should you decide to carry an ice ax, make sure you get instruction in its use, and practice self-arrest techniques in a safe location. An ice ax can cause serious injury if used improperly. Note that snow stays longer on northern slopes.

Glaciers are always dangerous. When a glacier is covered with snow, crevasses are invisible. Even an uncovered glacier, however, can be dangerous. Stay off them unless you are roped and led by a guide or other trained professional. There are only a handful of glacier crossings that are considered safe for unequipped hikers; the local guides or tourist bureau can always advise you.

Wet grassy slopes. Wet grass is slippery, and people have slid off meadows with steep slopes. The alpine fatality lists include such cases among the climbing statistics. Avoid crossing steep meadows after rainfall.

Lakes. On a hot afternoon, a clear alpine lake may look inviting, but the glacier-fed water is icy-cold and can shock a person's heart. Whatever others are doing, play it safe.

Animals and plants. Poisonous snakes exist in the Alps but are rare; in over twenty years I have seen only one snake. There are no bears left in the Alps. Also, although you will probably walk past many cows, farmers do not send bulls out to graze in open pastures.

Rabies is now found in parts of Europe. Beware of wild animals that appear ill or unnaturally friendly. Do not attempt to touch any wild animal. Seek medical help immediately if you have been bitten by a wild animal.

Neither poison ivy, poison oak, nor poison sumac exist in Europe. One plant, however, is a nuisance—stinging nettle. Its touch causes a stinging pain, and the affected area may turn red. Fortunately the effects do not last long, and if you are near a stream, a splash of cold water helps a great deal. Look out for these tall plants (about 1.5 to 2 feet tall), with notched, pointy leaves. Stinging nettle has little sprays of dusty gray-green or purple tiny flowers, especially near the top of the plant and growing on its tip, above the leaves. The stalk is reddish green. Note: Monkshood (*Aconitum napellus*), wolfbane (*Aconitum vulparia*), and false hellebore (*Veratrum album*), all found in these regions, are poisonous.

IN CASE OF EMERGENCY

The alpine S.O.S. signal is a series of six signals evenly spaced within one minute, and then a repetition of six more after a minute's pause. The signals may be six whistle blasts, six light flashes, et cetera. Standing upright with both arms stretched above one's head signals a request for a helicopter rescue; holding only one arm up, with the other arm held down at your side, indicates that helicopter rescue is not needed.

The helicopter is the ambulance of the Alps. Should one fall ill at a hut, one can be evacuated by helicopter directly to a hospital within minutes after a call for help is transmitted. Virtually all alpine club huts have radio telephones for emergency use. Evacuation after a climbing injury or illness on a trail is also rapid, once a call for help is received.

Important. Consult your doctor before undertaking an alpine walking holiday if you are middle-aged or older, sedentary, out of condition, overweight, or a smoker, or have any cardiac or respiratory problem, high blood pressure, diabetes, or any other chronic health problem. Allow yourself to get acclimatized to the altitude before making any major exertions. And don't rush on the trail, especially when ascending. Listen to your body: if you are exhausted or unwell, take a day or two off.

The Alpine Environment

The creation of each of the parks described in this book represented an important advance of the environmental movement in France and Italy. Some aspects of that movement as it has evolved in these alpine countries may be familiar to North Americans, but other aspects may not be.

One common problem for all the parks was the result of excessive hunting and trapping. In these alpine regions, several species of wildlife, some of which were deemed pests such as lynx, wolf, bear, and certain vultures, have been killed off altogether. There was even an effort to kill off the golden eagle. On the other hand, the magnificent ibex, prized instead of despised, was nearly hunted to extinction. Its eleventh-hour salvation is bound up with the history of Italy's Parco Nazionale del Gran Paradiso and is related in more detail in the chapter on that park. The establishment of the Gran Paradiso and the other parks described in this book permitted the reintroduction of the ibex and other alpine species into these newly protected areas and has helped to save other wildlife as well.

A more recent and very grave threat to the alpine environment derives from the development and tremendous popularity of downhill skiing. Where it has been allowed to flourish, the effects of this sport on every aspect of the environment—the landscape, wildlife, and even the local population and culture—have been profound. Roads and transportation systems have had to be built to transport legions of skiers to formerly remote mountain areas. Hillsides and mountain slopes have been scraped, gouged, and cleared to create ski runs. The stanchions and towers for cablecar systems had to be driven into the ground or the ice. And in some instances quiet, traditional alpine villages have been transformed into fashionable resorts replete with fancy hotels and boutiques. Large numbers of people must be enticed to the mountains so that building investments can be turned into big profits. (Since many people love downhill skiing, this has not proved very difficult.) The creation of parks in the western Alps has limited the commercialization of the environment caused by development for downhill skiing.

A third area of concern reveals the extent to which the concept of the environment in these alpine regions differs from the North American concept. In North America we are concerned with preservation of wilderness areas in which nomadic peoples may once have wandered, but which generally were never settled or cultivated. We regard this wilderness as our great heritage. In contrast, alpine valleys are the site of an ancient human culture that survived by adapting to very difficult conditions. The mountain people drove the flocks and herds that were their chief means of sustenance up to very high meadows in summer, so that they could repeatedly mow the lower pastures and store hay for the animals' winter fodder. These high summer farms are often called *alpages* in France and in the Gran Paradiso region of Italy. Because fuel was precious, people conserved their forests. In Villar-d'Arène, just outside the Ecrins National Park in France, you can still visit the communal bakery where, until this century, the whole village annually baked their year's supply of bread— thus conserving the wood that fired the oven. Dependent for their existence upon a fragile natural environment, they were relatively cautious about making changes. When they left their mountain villages as part of the great demographic movement from farms to cities, the montagnard culture—like certain animal species—was threatened with extinction. Moreover, the alpine regions were left open to other kinds of exploitation.

In Europe, montagnard culture is regarded as part of a national patrimony, and its preservation is one of several important goals of the environmental movement.

To meet these various concerns, the French devised a system in which national parks contain two zones: central zones and peripheral zones. The central zones were created outside inhabited areas. New construction is prohibited, and wildlife and plants are strictly protected. The peripheral zones include villages, resorts, and ski developments. The French natural regional parks, however, such as the one in the Queyras, include inhabited zones. These natural regional parks, like the peripheral zones of the national parks, aim not only to protect the landscape and wildlife but also to safeguard and foster traditional montagnard culture. This can mean agricultural assistance to the remaining farmers and herders, preservation of old buildings such as churches, communal ovens, and mills, and efforts to record local folklore and traditions.

The impact of hikers on the environment is contained by the prevalent alpine custom of sleeping in alpine club huts or inns rather than camping. Overnight use is thus concentrated within a relatively small area. Neither camping nor campfires are allowed in the national parks, although bivouacs are allowed under certain conditions. No dogs are allowed, not even on leashes. Wild animals may not be disturbed. No gathering of flowers, fruit, shrubs, or minerals, no noise, no littering, no weapons, and no motorized vehicles are allowed. There are stiff fines for infractions of any of these rules.

One wild animal most commonly seen in the Alps is the marmot. This plump, furry rodent is about the size of a woodchuck. The holes of its burrows are seen everywhere on the slopes. The short, shrill whistle you often hear in the Alps is a marmot call. The largest alpine animals are chamois and ibex: one way to tell them apart is by the series of deep notches on the horns of an ibex. You may also see ermine, foxes, and eagles.

Hundreds of different wildflowers grace the alpine slopes and meadows; their profusion, variety, and color are dazzling. Several illustrated flower guides are available in local bookstores and can help you identify most of the ones ordinarily seen.

There are unwritten rules as well as specific environmental laws that hikers must observe.

Gates and fences. These are used to keep cattle, sheep, and goats from wandering into or out of certain areas. You should close any gate you open.

Fire. It is forbidden to make a fire within the central zone of the national parks; fires should be made only in picnic areas where they are permitted.

Garbage. Littering is forbidden within the parks. When hiking you should pack out all your personal trash.

Personal matters. The protocol for toileting between huts is to be discreet and leave nothing in sight. Bury any waste as deeply as possible and at least 200 feet from any water source. Pack out toilet paper.

Protected plants. All plants are protected within the national parks, and it is illegal to pick them. In peripheral zones, it may also be illegal to pick mushrooms or gather snails; signs are posted concerning this. In any case, even if you are not in a national park, you should not gather flowers.

THE ALPINE PARKS
OF FRANCE

PARC NATIONAL DU MERCANTOUR

The Mercantour region in southeastern France has more surprises than any other section of the Alps. It is part of the Maritime Alps, the southernmost tip of the alpine chain, the great crescent of mountains that curves around Italy as it bulges northward into Switzerland. The wild, often savage character of the landscape in these mountains belies its proximity to the French Riviera. Yet in little more than an hour's drive from Nice, with its palm trees and semitropical flowers, you can be in a high alpine valley surrounded by craggy mountains. The Maritime Alps share much of the typical fauna and flora characteristic of the entire alpine chain: animals, birds, and flowers such as chamois, marmot, ermine, golden eagle, ptarmigan, black grouse, spring gentian, houseleek, and rusty alpenrose are all found in these mountains. Among the characteristic alpine features, only glaciers are lacking. Plenty of snow falls in these mountains, however, and in June or even early July hikers may find snow near the high passes and ice floating on some of the beautiful blue and green tarns that are a distinguishing feature of the Maritime Alps. These little lakes are the destination of many of the trails in this region. There are hiking trails and

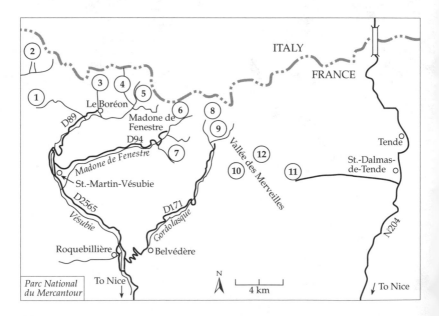

Medieval fresco in the chapel at Venanson

routes here as demanding as in any other part of the Alps as well as trails of moderate and easy grade—something for everyone. Moreover, there are so many trails that several weeks of daily hiking would not exhaust all the possibilities in the Mercantour.

The reason for the rapid contrasts of vegetation and climate found here—from olive and chestnut trees to fir and larch—is that the mountains rise so steeply and abruptly. From Nice on the Mediterranean coast it is 45 kilometers as the crow flies to St.-Martin–Vésubie, which is at 960 meters, while 7 or 8 kilometers from St.-Martin–Vésubie are high alpine valleys and lakes at about 2,500 meters.

Another feature of this region deserves special notice and makes hiking here an unusual treat. At the foot of these alpine valleys lie several typical, picturesque Provençal villages, far enough from the heavily touristed coast to have remained simple and unspoiled. Yellow-and-cream-colored houses capped by orange tile roofs are set close together above medieval streets, narrow, winding, and paved with cobblestones. As you walk down such a street, suddenly an even narrower passage darts off to one side, or an arch is flung up overhead, or the street becomes stepped—an outdoor stairway—to descend a grade. St.-Martin–Vésubie is a particularly charming and characteristic little town above the left bank of the Vésubie River. Venanson, a tiny, walled town perched high on a spur facing

St.-Martin–Vésubie from across the valley of the Vésubie, is quiet, forgotten, and enchanting.

The delights of the Provençal table and market cannot be overlooked, even—or especially—in a hiking guidebook, and will surely not be forgotten by anyone who comes here to walk; after all, we hikers are as hungry as any other traveler, if not more so. My husband and I have come down from a hike here, ravenous, and ducked into a village bakery even before taking off our boots for a square of *pissaladière,* a pizzalike crust topped with sauteed onions and slices of olive instead of cheese. Among our other favorites are *mescluns,* a salad made of tangy, wild greens, and *pistou,* a soup fragrant with basil.

The Parc National du Mercantour, founded in 1979, is the most recently created of the French alpine parks. Its central zone, in which no building is allowed and where all wildlife and plants are protected, covers 68,500 hectares. The visitor may occasionally see the slogan *"Non au Parc"*—"no to the park"—painted on a rock. These signs reflect the controversy that initially accompanied the creation of this park. Inhabitants of the region were planning to build a downhill ski area, which has now forever been blocked by the establishment of the park. Locals also objected to the park regulations that forbid hunting game and shooting birds and prohibit dogs, even when leashed, inside the park.

An outside visitor, however, is likely to see things differently. The beautiful, wild Mercantour remains unspoiled because it has not been developed for downhill skiing. There is no ski resort in any area described in this chapter—not even a small one. And it is not only the landscape, vegetation, and wildlife that have been spared. The absence of a downhill ski center has also preserved the quiet charm of the region's villages. Although the people of the Mercantour feel that they have been the losers, economically, by the establishment of a national park in their region, the land and all those who love untouched mountain country are the winners.

Note: The Mercantour is close to the Mediterranean, from which moist, warm air may rise toward the mountains. Rain or thunderstorms occasionally occur, generally in the afternoon; it is therefore advisable to start hikes early and be down from any high ridges by mid-afternoon.

The nearest large city, Nice, is accessible by train and plane. There is daily bus service between Nice and St.-Martin–Vésubie.

CENTRAL MERCANTOUR

The highest mountains of the Maritime Alps lie near and along the French–Italian border in the Haute Vésubie, the country of the upper Vésubie River. The region derives its name from the Cime (peak) du Mercantour (2,772 meters), long thought by local people to be the highest mountain in their region. It is easily visible from the valley of the Vésubie, from where its sharp profile dominates the skyline. The Cime du Gélas (3,143 meters), although less visible, is higher, as are several other peaks, while the Cima de l'Argentera (3,297 meters), on Italian territory and the highest point in the massif, is blocked from view.

The valley of the Haute Vésubie provides the main approach to the central part of the Mercantour and its national park. Three tributaries of the

Haute Vésubie climb into the mountains and are used by hikers to get to the trailheads. These three tributaries are the valley of Le Boreón, the valley of Madone de Fenestre, and the valley of the Gordolasque.

The charming little medieval town of St.-Martin–Vésubie can be reached from Nice by taking N202 and then D2565. The town is situated at the confluence of the streams of Le Boreón and Madone de Fenestre, where they form the Vésubie; St.-Martin–Vésubie is thus near the entrance to the valleys of Le Boreón and Madone de Fenestre and is also reasonably close to the valley of the Gordolasque (a half-hour's drive to its entrance). Vestiges of the town's fourteenth-century walls remain, along with one of its original four gateways. It makes an excellent base from which to explore the area. Roquebillière, 13 kilometers to the south on D2565, and closer to the entrance to the Gordolasque valley, is another pleasant small town whose two sections are divided by the Vésubie River. Portions of the town have been rebuilt, so it is less ancient than St.-Martin–Vésubie. Both St.-Martin–Vésubie and Roquebillière have several hotels and simple restaurants, and both are good places to shop for outdoor equipment. There are hotel accommodations and a small shop for provisions at Le Boreón, near the entrance to the valley of the same name, and a gîte d'étape nearby. Belvédère is a picturesquely situated village offering accommodations part way up the valley of the Gordolasque, and other simple hotels and gîtes d'étape are found farther along the valley.

Note: The large green hexagonal symbols painted on rocks are not trail blazes but, rather, mark the boundaries of the national park. Signposts in the park are also numbered and correspond to numbers on topographic regional hiking maps.

Vallée des Merveilles

Walks from Le Boreón

From St.-Martin–Vésubie, the road northward to Le Boreón (D2565, then D89) follows the stream of the same name, passing a fine waterfall, then two hotels, a restaurant, and a tiny shop selling basic provisions. This little cluster of buildings is Le Boreón. The valley of the same name is the starting point for some of the finest walks in the Mercantour. The walks are described here, from west to east.

Le Boreón, West

From Le Boreón, continue eastward on D89. Just beyond the artificial lake is a junction. Turn left (west) on D89 and cross the bridge here. This road leads to the Col de Salèsc (2,031 meters), a very low pass at the western edge of the valley of Le Boreón.

The starting point for two good walks is found at the end of this road to the Col de Salèse. Drive up D89 for about 3 kilometers (the last 0.6 kilometer may still be poorly paved) to the parking area. The road continues beyond here but is restricted to people holding special passes. At the end of the parking area are signposts for the Col de Salèse (which is on the GR 52), Les Adus, Lac Nègre, and several other destinations.

1. Lac des Adus

Rating: easy
Distance loop trip: 9 km
High point: 2,232 m

Total climb: 540 m
Time: 1 hour 50 minutes to high
    point, 1 hour 20 minutes down

This is a short but rewarding tour. Lac des Adus is a small lake of vivid color set among wild meadows and offering an excellent panoramic view of the skyline of the Mercantour range. The only drawback to this loop trip is that it begins up a very steep and narrow trail. By climbing up to the lake on the route described here for the descent, you can avoid this more difficult ascent, although you then use the same trail for both ascent and descent.

For the loop trip, start from the parking area at the end of the public road to the Col de Salèse. Immediately upon starting the trail, cross a signposted bridge to the left. Just across the bridge, sign No. 397 points right (southwest) to Lac des Adus. This path follows the right bank of the stream through woods marked with an occasional yellow blaze. Here the trail ascends steeply and becomes narrow in a few places, sometimes no more than 10 inches wide, with steep, grassy slopes to one side. After 1 hour 10 minutes (at 2,110 meters), sign No. 396 points straight ahead (west) to Lac des Adus and the Col de la Vallette des Adus. Cross a small talus slope and in 5 more minutes reach a log cabin. At a junction here, sign No. 395 points west to Lac des Adus and the Col de la Vallette des Adus. The trail to that col passes to the left of the lake, while the trail that passes to the right of the lake, heading west and later northwest, is the route for this walk.

Beyond the log cabin is a little bowl with a ridge line above on your left. Climb a few more minutes and the trail levels out; reach the lake in an-

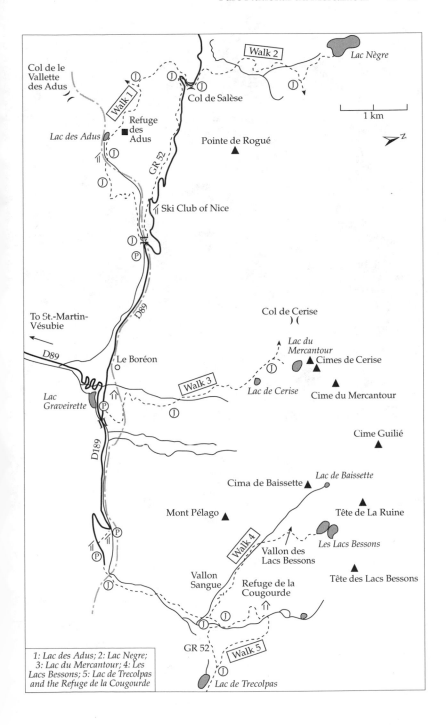

Col de le
Vallette
des Adus

Walk 1

Refuge
des
Adus

Lac des Adus

GR 52

Walk 2

Lac Nègre

Col de Salèse

1 km

Pointe de Rogué

Ski Club of Nice

To St.-Martin-
Vésubie

D89

D89

Le Boréon

Col de Cerise
) (

Lac du
Mercantour

Cimes de Cerise

Walk 3

Lac de Cerise

Cime du Mercantour

Cime Guilié

Lac
Graveirette

D189

Lac de Baissette

Cima de Baissette

Tête de La Ruine

Mont Pélago

Les Lacs Bessons

Walk 4

Vallon des
Lacs Bessons

Tête des Lacs Bessons

Vallon
Sangue

Refuge de la
Cougourde

GR 52

Walk 5

Lac de Trecolpas

1: Lac des Adus; 2: Lac Negre;
3: Lac du Mercantour; 4: Les
Lacs Bessons; 5: Lac de Trecolpas
and the Refuge de la Cougourde

Lac des Adus

other 10 minutes, at 2,145 meters. From this blue-green lake the profile of the Mercantour skyline is spread before you.

Continue northwest on the trail, climbing a little higher through the meadows. In 10 minutes reach the ruins of a stone cabin, the remains of the old Refuge des Adus. This spot, beside a meadow full of rusty alpenrose, offers an even finer panoramic view of the mountains of the Mercantour.

From here, begin the descent to the Col de Salèse. At the first junction, signed No. 437 at 2,220 meters, take the trail to the right (north and northwest) for the Col de Salèse; the trail to the left heads up to the Col de la Vallette des Adus. The trail to the Col de Salèse follows the top of a crest. Do not take a washed-out old section of trail that descends precipitously to the right (southeast), marked by a crossed-out green and yellow blaze. Instead, continue ahead along the crest on the trail blazed both red and white and also green and yellow, bearing northeast. This is a narrow path leading down on switchbacks to the road, which it reaches at sign No. 436, at the Col de Salèse jeep road (unpaved), 30 or 40 minutes after beginning the descent.

Turn right onto the road. In a few yards, a red and white blaze indicates the footpath, which enters the woods. This crosses the Col de Salèse road once again. Look for another red and white blaze on the right to resume the path as it cuts across the loops of the road and is thus more direct as well as more pleasant than following the road itself. Continue through the woods, reaching the parking area in about 1 hour 20 minutes after beginning the descent.

2. Lac Nègre

Rating: moderate
Distance round trip: 12.5 km
High point: 2,345 m
Total climb: 680 m
Time: 2 hours 40 minutes up, 2 hours 5 minutes down

Begin as for the previous walk to Lac des Adus (hike 1), at the parking area at the end of the public road to the Col de Salèse. A signpost points west to the Col de Salèse and Lac Nègre, along with other destinations. This stretch of trail, part of the GR 52, shows its characteristic red and white blazes. It leads through the woods, passing the hut of the Ski Club of Nice in 10 minutes. In another 10 minutes, cross to the right bank of the stream on a little bridge. Follow this pleasant, easy forest path. Twenty minutes later (at 1,940 meters), the trail crosses over the Col de Salèse jeep

Lac Nègre

road (unpaved), continuing to the left on the other side of the road and into the woods again. At 2,000 meters (sign No. 435) it returns to the jeep road, then climbs up to the col on switchbacks. Reach the Col de Salèse in about 1 hour after starting the hike. (At the col, you can turn left, heading west at first, for the better of the two trails up to Lac des Adus.)

Continue along the jeep road past the col. In 5 minutes the trail diverges to the right with a signpost for Lac Nègre and the Col de Frémamorte. As the trail climbs north and sometimes east, several mountains with pointed peaks of bare rock begin to appear. About 20 minutes past the col, cross the river on a bridge, continuing mainly northward toward the lake. Some of the blazes here are green and yellow. The trail jogs right to cross a shallow brook several times, on logs and then on stepping stones, and then turns left again, climbing up by gentle switchbacks. Reach a small pond and a junction about 2 hours 15 minutes after starting the hike.

At signpost No. 270 (2,270 meters) turn left (northwest) for Lac Nègre (the trail to the right climbs to the Col de Frémamorte), and reach the lake in another 30 minutes. The turquoise lake is surrounded by jagged, stony mountains with sharp, pointed crests. In early summer the lake may still be covered with ice, and the setting is quite impressive.

Le Boreón, Center

The one hike representing this middle section is one of the finest excursions in the region, to a very beautiful lake in a wild, lonely, silent place.

3. Lac du Mercantour

Rating: strenuous   **Total climb:** 1,040 m
Distance round trip: 9.5 km   **Time:** 3 hours 10 minutes up, 2
High point: 2,454 m   hours 30 minutes down

At the junction just beyond the artificial lake at Le Boreón, turn left (west) on D89 toward the Col de Salèse. Just beyond this junction on the right is the trailhead for Lac du Mercantour and several other destinations, including the Col de Cerise. If you are driving, park here, along D89. From here, a little paved road leads upward to a gîte d'étape, just above the D89 road. Follow this little road for a few minutes, then turn right onto the "*Sentier*," so indicated by a sign and a red and white blaze on a rock. Soon you reach another signpost marking the entrance to the park. At the signposted junction here, turn left (northwest) for Lac du Mercantour and walk up on a good path, blazed white and green, through the forest. This path is signposted several times. After 1 hour of hiking, at 1,800 meters, bear right (northeast) on the upper of two trails. Soon after starting on this trail there are several white blazes.

As you climb, reach a stream coursing down a steep bed to your left. Cross this stream on rocks. Then, at about 2,200 meters, start up a steep talus slope; the route ascends on switchbacks through these boulders. There is a sort of channel through the boulders, as well as cairns, and it is easy to see the way. Above this steep section and off the boulders the trail levels out, turning a hump to the left. Here, walk along the left side of a narrow valley with a high crest to your left and talus slopes to your right. In another 20 minutes, reach little Lac de Cerise. Above to the left you can see the small, rounded notch of the Col de Cerise.

About 3 hours from the start of the hike, at 2,320 meters, signpost No. 376 points left (northwest) for the Col de Cerise, right (northeast) for Lac du Mercantour. The route crosses a stream on rocks, then zigzags up, traversing a small section of boulders; there are cairns for markers. The stream you crossed below cascades down on your left. In 10 more minutes, reach Lac du Mercantour. The lake is almost surrounded by a cirque with steep, rocky walls, topped with a serrated crest of jagged peaks. Across the lake are the Cimes de Cerise (2,714 meters) and, to the right, the Cime du Mercantour (2,772 meters).

Le Boreón, East

At the junction just beyond the artificial lake at Le Boreón, continue straight ahead on D189 (instead of crossing the bridge and turning left onto D89, the road to the Col de Salèse). D189 proceeds through the woods past several picnic sites; at the end are two parking areas, a lower and an upper one. It is 2.5 kilometers on a narrow, paved road from Le Boreón to the lower *Parking Inférieure* and another kilometer on a very rough, unpaved road to the upper *Parking Supérieure*. The two are also connected by a footpath that starts at signpost No. 419 and passes the stone buildings of the old *vacheries*, or dairies, no longer in use. It takes about 20 to 25 minutes on the footpath to hike up to signpost No. 422 from the upper parking lot. This path has both yellow and orange blazes and is steep in sections. The road, although longer, is more gradual.

The hikes to various destinations at the eastern end of the Le Boreón valley have a common beginning, diverging after an hour's hike, more or less, through the woods above the parking areas.

From the upper parking lot, a broad path leads at first east and then northeast. Stay on this path, ignoring a narrower one that heads off to the left. The broad path proceeds at a moderate grade with a stream visible to your left. In 20 minutes, reach a shallow pond. Cross a little wooden bridge over the pond and continue with the stream still on your left. The trail then veers right (north-northeast) away from the stream, narrows, and climbs more steeply for about 5 minutes. Thirty minutes from the start, reach a more level stretch where the trail gets broader again. At 1,838 meters there is a junction (signpost No. 422) as the GR 52 enters from the left (west), with its red and white blazes. If you turn left here onto the GR 52, you can walk back to Le Boreón. Soon after this, there are two stream crossings, both on bridges. Emerge from the woods into a rock-strewn meadow, from which you can see the big tooth of La Cougourde (2,921 meters) and other mountains.

The trail then crosses a few shallow rivulets on rocks and another bridge to reach a junction at 1,900 meters, about 1 hour 30 minutes from the lower parking lot, or about 1 hour from the upper one. At this junction (signpost No. 424), turn left (northwest) for Les Lacs Bessons, or right (northeast) for Lac de Trécolpas and the Refuge de la Cougourde.

4. Les Lacs Bessons

Rating: very strenuous
Distance round trip: 9 km
High point: 2,541 m

Total climb: 1,000 m
Time: 4 hours 10 minutes up, 2 hours 40 minutes to 3 hours down

This is a very demanding hike, not only because it is long and often steep, but because some route-finding skills may be needed. It's a good excursion for hikers who feel fit, want a challenge, and have good weather. The destination is a pair of lakes in a high, barren cirque, below the Collet des Lacs Bessons. In early summer there can be steep snow-fields that must be climbed; trekking poles are then advisable, and crampons can also be useful.

At the junction of the trails for Les Lacs Bessons and Lac de Trécolpas (signpost No. 424), turn left (northwest). The trail climbs steeply, passing some slabby rock to your left. The way is marked by cairns and occasional white blazes. It crosses a small talus slope, then ascends a deep gully, and about 30 minutes above the junction (at 2,150 meters) you are pretty much above treeline. After another very steep climb of 60 meters the trail levels out into a narrow valley (the Vallon Sangué) with a fine view. There is a lovely stream to your left as well as a couple of big mountains closing off the upper end of this narrow valley, the Cime Guilié (2,999 meters), and to the right, the Tête de la Ruine (2,984 meters).

Here the way becomes more difficult to follow, as the blazes cease and there are only occasional cairns.

The trail crosses this upper stream twice: first crossing to its right bank—you can see the trail there—then crossing again to its left. There are no bridges for either crossing, and the current can be swift. If you prefer, you can avoid these two crossings by some scrambling guided by a few small cairns, so that you stay on and above the stream's left bank. Cross-ing back the second time or else staying on the left bank is the key to this hike. If you stay on the right bank you may see occasional traces of path and a few cairns, but this way leads north-northwest, climbing steeply to Lac de Baissette. The way to Les Lacs Bessons is up along the tributary stream that enters the main stream from the north-northeast, to your right, as you hike along the main stream.

Then, at about 2,270 meters, the route turns right (northeast) to ascend the side valley, the Vallon des Lacs Bessons. Soon you will see a small brook on your right. Stay on its right bank and follow a trail marked by some cairns. This route then leads you northward; in another 10 minutes (at 2,340 meters), you will see a cascade running down a small rock face about 50 meters high. Fifteen minutes beyond that, at 2,390 meters, cross the brook to its left bank and follow traces of path with occasional cairns. The route swings left and ascends a stony couloir at 2,410 meters, bearing northwest. At 2,500 meters ascend a very wide chimney, then bear right (east) at the top.

Reach the lakes 4 hours 10 minutes after the start, at 2,541 meters. The wild, desolate scene is typical of the high Mercantour: no soft meadows, but forbidding, jagged walls enfold the basin of the two lakes.

5. Lac de Trécolpas and the Refuge de la Cougourde

Rating: easy
Distance loop trip: 10 km
High point: 2,150 m
Total climb: 470 m

Time: 1 hour 10 minutes from the upper junction to the lake, then 30 minutes to the hut, from which 1 hour down

The trip to Lac de Trécolpas and to the only French alpine club hut near Le Boreón can be combined to make a loop trip, or they can be visited separately. Either combined or separate, they are pleasant hikes and fairly easy.

At the junction of the trails for Les Lacs Bessons and Lac de Trécolpas (signpost No. 424), take the fork to the right for Lac de Trécolpas, the Refuge de la Cougourde, and the Pas des Ladres. In about 10 minutes there is another junction (signpost No. 425): left (north) goes to the Refuge de la Cougourde, and right (south and then east) goes to Lac de Trécolpas. Take the route to the right. The trail leads through an open, grassy area and then over a bridge. Red and white blazes indicate that this is now part of the GR 52. One hour past the Bessons/Trécolpas junction, reach the junction of a second trail to the hut, marked by signpost No. 427, which turns left here (northwest). Continue to the right (east) on the trail to the lake. Reach the lake in about 10 more minutes. Around it is a semicircle of rock peaks, with the Pas des Ladres—the pass leading over the mountains to the Madone de Fenestre—visible as a notch on the skyline.

You can either retrace your steps to the upper Le Boreón east parking area or descend to the junction at signpost No. 427 and take the trail now to your right (northwest) to the hut. To reach the hut requires a half-hour traverse, crossing several talus slopes and marked by occasional cairns or blue blazes. The hut is a long, one-story metal shed painted bright yellow, with a pleasant little terrace where hikers can pause for a drink or snack. Dominating the view is the big rock dome of the Caïres de Cougourde, known locally as La Cougourde (2,921 meters). From the deck, with your back to the hut, the trail for the descent is to your right. It leads directly down the slope to signpost No. 425.

Walks from La Madone de Fenestre

The road up the valley of La Madone de Fenestre, D94, begins at St.-Martin–Vésubie. Like Le Boreón, the name Madone de Fenestre refers both to the valley and to the tiny cluster of buildings near its upper end, 12 kilometers from St.-Martin–Vésubie. At the end of the road there is a little square with several buildings. To one side of the square is the Refuge de la Madone de Fenestre, an alpine club hut that is highly unusual because you can drive up to its door. At the back of the square stands a small church, the summer home of a twelfth-century statue of the madonna, Notre-Dame de Fenestre, for whom the valley is named. Although the present church is 200 years old, a sign explains that this place has been dedicated to Marie la Madone de Fenestre for a thousand years and advances several explanations as to the origin of the name of this

Twelfth-century statue of Marie la Madone de Fenestre

place. According to one theory, it is so named because of a hole in a rock above the sanctuary, through which you can see the sky as if through a window. *Fenêtre* means "window" in modern French. The circumflex over the second *e* takes the place of the former *s* in archaic French. Another theory proposes that the name derives from the Latin *Finisterrae,* meaning "end of the world," which this place may have seemed to be in the Middle Ages. The inhabitants of St.-Martin–Vésubie still bring the statue up to this place at the beginning of July and take it down again in mid-September. Around the upper walls of the little church are painted all the names given to the Virgin Mary.

This valley has a wilder aspect than that of Le Boreón. The little cluster of buildings at Madone de Fenestre is at 1,900 meters, considerably higher than the settlement at Le Boreón (1,473 meters). While all the walks from the valley of Le Boreón begin in the woods and require a walk of an hour or two in the forest before reaching treeline, those here all start in the open.

Beyond the square the ground drops away to the river of La Vésubie, across which is a *vacherie,* a simple alpine dairy where cheese is still being made and sold.

6. Lac de Fenestre

Rating: easy
Distance round trip: 4.5 km
High point: 2,266 m

Total climb: 380 m
Time: 1 hour 30 minutes up, 1 hour down

From the parking area just before the Refuge de la Madone de Fenestre, a sign points to Lac de Fenestre, the Col de Fenestre, and, on the GR 52, the Pas des Ladres. The trail, broad but rocky, heads northeast for these destinations, climbing at a moderate grade. After 35 minutes (at 2,060 meters), come to a junction and signpost No. 368. To the left (northwest) the GR 52 climbs to the Pas des Ladres, while the trail to Lac de Fenestre continues to the right (northeast). The Pas des Ladres is the pass leading to Le Boreón, where the GR 52 descends to Lac de Trécolpas.

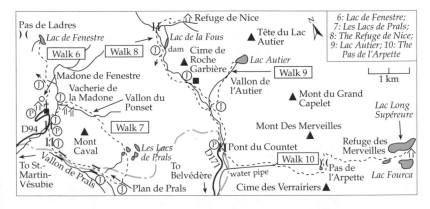

The trail curves slightly leftward then heads up to the lake, which you reach in 1 hour 30 minutes. Lower down on the trail, the Cime du Gélas (3,143 meters) dominates the view, but when you reach the lake, its pointed rock peak is hidden behind a smaller mountain. The lake is enclosed below a curved, rocky wall in a wild setting.

7. Les Lacs de Prals

Rating: easy
Distance loop trip: 7 km
High point: 2,335 m

Total climb: 650 m
Time: 1 hour 35 minutes up, 1 hour 40 minutes down

This loop trip can be made in either direction, clockwise or counterclockwise. The loop circles Mont Caval to reach a group of five small lakes, Les Lacs de Prals. If you do it in the direction I give here, you climb at the beginning rather than at the end of the hike.

Just before the last segment of road crosses a bridge and climbs up in a big switchback to the square of La Madone de Fenestre, there is a small parking area along the road, at 1,870 meters. Leaving your car in the parking area, begin the walk here; a signpost points the way along the left bank of the river. Continue on what is now a broad jeep road and in 10 minutes reach the Vacherie de la Madone, a simple, rather rough alpine dairy where cheese is still made. The milk is cooked in a huge cauldron, and the cheeses, called *Tomme de Pays,* are laid out on shelves for 40 days. Beside the *vacherie* is a footbridge over the river, connecting with a path up the hillside to the square above.

Walk to the left of the *vacherie;* a signpost indicates the GR 52 and the Pas du Colomb, and a red and white blaze shows that you are on the GR trail. This leads to the right, to cross a tributary stream on a little bridge and then a rivulet on a few stones; reach a junction (signpost No. 367, at 1,910 meters) in another 5 minutes. Take the fork to the right (east), identified on the sign as the direction for the Baisse des Prals. The trail then climbs steeply for a short stretch through a band of larches and rusty alpenrose growing amid outcrops of rock, with a stream to your right. You may have to use your hands for a boost at one or two places. After 20 minutes reach a hanging valley where the trail becomes more gradual as it ascends a boulder-strewn meadow. Then it climbs steeply again, passing a rocky tower on your right. There are blazes of various colors, red and white, green and white, or sometimes just green.

Above this steep section reach another grassy shelf (2,120 meters) at the base of an old cirque. The meadow is partially surrounded by a low wall of natural rocky towers. The trail, which heads south, is almost level here. Cross a tiny stream on rocks. A network of little trails switchbacks up the low wall to the south, then follows the ridge line to the left (southeast). Reach the little notch at the top of this ridge about 1 hour 30 minutes after the start of the hike. From here you can see Les Lacs de Prals below to the south, in a big grassy bowl—an ideal picnic spot.

The lakes are strewn among hillocks in this vast meadow called the Plan de Prals, ringed by rounded mountains. Some cows or goats may be grazing here, attended by a shepherd. To resume the tour, start at the trail indicated by signpost No. 366 and descend to the south through meadows to signpost No. 364 (at 2,120 meters), about 25 minutes past the lakes. Turn right (northwest), follow the trail to signpost No. 363 (2,070 meters), and bear right (northwest) for Madone de Fenestre. Enter an area with some larches and cross a bridge to the left bank of the stream, then later turn right (north) at signpost No. 362 to cross it again on another bridge. Ignore the hexagonal green marks painted here and there above the streambed; they are not trail blazes but rather show the boundaries of the national park. The trail climbs slightly again before reaching the road at signpost No. 361. The parking area is about a 5-minute walk up the road.

Walks from the Gordolasque

The Gordolasque is a long valley that offers striking contrasts of landscape and vegetation as it climbs into the mountains. In ascending this valley you pass from a Provençal landscape with terraced hillsides, rose bushes, and houses with red-tiled roofs up to high alpine meadows. The road up this valley, D171, begins near Roquebillière in the valley of the Vésubie. The road climbs on switchbacks to Belvédère, a picturesque village on a promontory overlooking the valley. Beyond this the road eventually straightens out and climbs less steeply. Belvédère is 5 kilometers from Roquebillière, and it's another 12 kilometers to the end of the road, where there is a parking area just before a bridge—the Pont du Countet.

Note: Strong hikers who move quickly can do hikes 8 and 9 in one rather long day, weather permitting. The disadvantage is that one has much less time to spend at either place, enjoying the view.

8. The Refuge de Nice

Rating: easy
Distance round trip: 10 km
High point: 2,232 m
Total climb: 540 m

Time: 2 hours 50 minutes up, 1 hour 30 minutes to the Lac Autier junction, then 20 minutes down

The first half of this walk may be done on either the left or right bank of the Gordolasque, the valley's stream; you can hike in on one side and hike out the other. Since the route to Lac Autier starts from the left bank of the stream, the itinerary here starts on the right bank. The lively mountain stream descending from Lac de la Fous makes this a very attractive walk, and the lake itself, which you pass on the way to the hut, is deep blue-green in color. The best views are from the valley and along the lakeshore, rather than from the hut.

From the parking area before the Pont du Countet, do not cross the bridge but instead walk northward along the right bank of the stream. In a few minutes you pass some large boulders used for practice by a rock-climbing school. Do not cross the river on another bridge you will see soon afterward. The path on the right bank, although narrower, is on the sunny side of the valley in the early morning.

The valley is very green and comely, full of rusty alpenrose, with the clear stream gurgling down its center. After about 35 minutes, switchback up a talus slope toward the upper part of the valley. To your right, the stream descends over a series of rock steps into blue pools. In another 40 minutes reach the higher valley where the stream is almost level. Here the trail from the left bank crosses on stones to merge with the trail you are on.

The trail now bends left, away from a little gorge. There are a few red smudges for blazes. Climb up another talus slope, the way marked by cairns, and then rejoin the stream at another level stretch, in a meadow. A wooden bridge extends across part of the grass. A sign cautions that this moist area is fragile and should be respected, thus requesting hikers to stay on the wooden bridge. About 2 hours from the start of the hike, at 2,173 meters, reach a junction at signpost No. 416. Continue to the right (northeast) for Lac de la Fous, the Refuge de Nice, and the Baisse du Basto. Soon after this, reach Lac de la Fous, a rather large, turquoise-colored artificial lake.

The trail follows the lakeshore to the left. Cross a tributary stream on a bridge and zigzag up to the hut, which you reach 2 hours 45 minutes from the start of the hike. The big mountain dominating the view is Mont Clapier (3,045 meters).

To return to the parking area, retrace your steps, and in 1 hour reach the junction of the right bank and left bank trails (at 2,000 meters; no signpost). Take the trail to the left, crossing the stream on rocks (it is not a difficult crossing). Soon you will pass some old stone walls, abandoned fortifications, after which the trail descends very steeply, switchbacking on small stones. There is a view of cascades. After 15 minutes the descent becomes more gradual, and you cross a shallow stream on stones. In another 5 minutes (at 1,840 meters), reach the junction at signpost No. 414 for Lac Autier, which climbs up to your left (east). To return to the parking area, however, continue descending on the main trail, heading south. This soon broadens to a jeep road and descends in 20 minutes in big, wide switchbacks to the Pont du Countet.

9. Lac Autier

Rating: moderate
Distance round trip: 6 km
High point: 2,275 m
Total climb: 600 m

Time: 1 hour 20 minutes up from the junction at signpost No. 414 on the main trail for the Refuge de Nice; 1 hour 10 minutes to return to that junction on the main trail, and 20 minutes back to the parking area

Although the route up to this lake is quite rough and difficult, the lake itself occupies one of the most splendid sites in the entire park.

From the parking area at the end of the road, cross the bridge (the Pont du Countet) and follow the broad jeep road along the left bank of the stream. This climbs in a few broad switchbacks before narrowing to a footpath. In 40 minutes, at 1,840 meters, there is a junction at signpost No. 414. Turn right (east) for Lac Autier. The trail to the lake ascends steeply up a slope covered with rusty alpenrose. There are no blazes and at first no cairns, and soon the trail peters out in places. After about 10 to 15 minutes, you will see a rock wall before you, about 15 meters high. Bear to the left here. Continue bearing left, toward and then along a narrow side valley (the Vallon de l'Autier), with a stream below on your left and a big rock wall on your right. The trail hugs this rock wall.

About 1 hour after starting up from the Refuge de Nice/Lac Autier junction, at a small cairn at 2,110 meters, cross the stream to its left bank. Climb steeply past occasional cairns and even more occasional faint red blazes. There is a big rock tower to the right. For the last few minutes of the hike the trail levels out, crossing a grassy terrace to reach the lake

Lac Autier

about 1 hour 30 minutes from signpost No. 414. The scene here is one of savage, wild grandeur. Despite the one small concrete spillway just below the lake, the effect is of untouched wilderness. All other evidence of hydroelectric power has been concealed: there are no power lines, pipes, or other signs of humankind (unless one happens to pass another hiker). The small lake, a light turquoise color, is set below a semicircle of rugged mountains with sharply serrated peaks.

10. The Pas de l'Arpette

Rating: moderate
Distance round trip: 7 km
High point: 2,511 m

Total climb: 850 m
Time: 2 hours 30 minutes up, 1 hour 30 minutes down

From the parking area, cross the bridge and follow the signposted path to the right and then to the southeast. After an initial short section on rocks, continue on a dirt trail that winds uphill at a moderately steep grade, passing some cliffs on the left. The first 100 meters up is quite steep, but then the grade becomes more moderate. On your right is a stream and also a metal water pipe, which feeds the hydroelectric station at Lac de St.–Grat below.

Climb steeply again for 400 meters; this takes about 1 hour 40 minutes. The trail levels out again. There are a few larches on the way up, but mostly you are in the open and can see the higher bowl ahead that you must reach. The trail passes under the water pipe, climbing to reach the high shelf strewn with boulders that you could see on the way up. Jagged walls enclose this area to the left and right; the stream is to your right. Occasional yellow and green blazes mark the way. The trail crosses the stream, heading up along its left bank through an open area of grass, rusty alpenrose, and juniper. The trail turns east and ascends another rocky area. It gets steeper on a final section of scree, bearing northeast and then north to reach the pass 2 hours 30 minutes after the start of the hike. There is a tiny pond at the saddle, and a view down to the Refuge des Merveilles and its nearby lakes. A signpost here points the way down to that hut and the Vallée des Merveilles.

NORTHEASTERN MERCANTOUR

This extraordinary valley at the eastern end of the Parc National du Mercantour combines great scenic splendor and anthropological interest. Remote and wild, completely uninhabited except for two nearby alpine club huts, it is an outdoor museum of Neolithic and Bronze Age art on a grand scale. Incised on rock walls, outcrops, and boulders strewn about its slopes are more than 100,000 rock engravings. A visit to the Vallée des Merveilles provides not only some excellent hiking but also the rare chance to see such prehistoric images in the wild alpine setting in which and for which they were created, rather than under glass in a museum. The effect of these mysterious, ancient rock engravings in their desolate, mountainous landscape is thrilling.

Celtic petroglyph, Vallée des Merveilles

Scientists believe that the Vallée des Merveilles was the site of cult ceremonies practiced by an ancient Celtic people who did not live or pasture their animals here, but who made special journeys up into this high valley to carve images into the great smooth slabs of schist found here and to practice their rites. The general orientation of many engravings toward Mont Bégo (2,872 meters), the highest of the surrounding mountains, suggests that it may have been an object of worship. Some scholars have speculated that the violent electrical storms that sometimes enshroud the region during warm afternoons, when lightning strikes the highest peaks, may have contributed to such a deification of Mont Bégo.

A few of the images are anthropomorphic, including one figure with a sort of halo around its head and zigzag arms that look like lightning bolts. This figure has been popularly dubbed "Le Cosmonaut," because the circle around its head resembles a space helmet with an antenna. Other famous human images are the so-called "Chef de Tribu" (Chief of the Tribe), who wears some sort of hanging ornament on his chest; "Le Sorcier," brandishing daggers above his head; and a three-eyed face called "Le Christ," or "Le Mage Christiforme" (the Magus with a Christ-like form), whose broad forehead, narrow jaw, and beard resemble a conventional image of Christ. Far more of the images, however, are nonhuman. Many represent the heads of bulls, sometimes crowned with long, twisting horns. Some scholars speculate that they reflect the ancient mythology and cult of the bull that was once spread around the Mediterranean basin.

There are also many carvings of daggers, scythes, and plows as well as squares and circles covered by a grid of lines, thought to represent the earth or land holdings. Suns and stars are also depicted.

The Vallée des Merveilles, once part of King Victor-Emmanuel II's private hunting reserve, belonged to Italy until 1947 when it was given as war reparations to France. Even now, cut off as it is by mountains on every side, the closest approach by motorable road is generally made through a small section of Italy. Except for those few who come in by jeep, the valley must be reached by hiking into the mountains on trails in France. There are two French alpine club huts, the Refuge des Merveilles and the Refuge de Valmasque, at the southern and northern ends, respectively, of the valley. Because it takes several hours to hike into the valley and at least several hours more to see the engravings (or some of them, to be more precise), it is best to plan to stay for one or two nights, or more. Strong hikers, however, walking in from Lac des Mesches, can see some engravings and return to Mesches in the same day.

Just outside the Refuge des Merveilles is a set of information tables offering short explanations of the region's geology and natural history and some analysis of the petroglyphs.

The Vallée des Merveilles is a protected area; it is forbidden to stand on or deface the engravings or to write on or scratch the rocks.

The Refuge des Merveilles is certainly the most popular point of departure for tours of the Vallée des Merveilles. Organized, guided group tours leave from the Refuge des Merveilles during the main season, approximately the first weekend in July to the first weekend in September. There are also tours on weekends and holidays during the last 3 weeks of September and the first 2 weeks of October. There is a small fee for adults and children under eighteen; the tour is free for children under seven. Reservations can be made at the hut or through the Office du Tourisme de Tende (tel. (1) 93 04 62 64) or at the Chalet de la Minière (tel. (1) 93 04 68 66). You can also hire a private guide, or *accompagnateur,* through the Bureau des Guides et Accompagnateurs de la Vallée des Merveilles, BP 12, 06430 Tende, France (tel. (1) 93 04 62 64). These private guides offer more extensive tours, including 2-day tours, than organized group tours. Several *taxi-accompagnateurs* in St.-Dalmas–de–Tende provide both taxi-jeep trips up to the hut and also guided tours.

From Nice, St.-Dalmas–de–Tende can be reached by train, and from St.-Dalmas–de–Tende it is possible, although rather expensive, to take a taxi-jeep up to the Refuge des Merveilles. Another way to reach the Refuge des Merveilles is by hiking from the valley of the Gordolasque over the Pas de l'Arpette, and then on to the Refuge des Merveilles. The route between the Gordolasque and the Pas de l'Arpette is described in hike 10, The Pas de l'Arpette.

The nearest approach by car, and the easiest hike up to the Vallée des Merveilles, is made from Lac des Mesches, about 10 kilometers above the small town of St.-Dalmas–de–Tende, which is southeast of the Vallée des Merveilles. To reach St.-Dalmas–de–Tende, take route 20 (E74) north from Vintimiglia, an Italian town on the *autoroute* along the Riviera between Nice and San Remo. Crossing the border into France, it becomes N204. St.-Dalmas–de–Tende can also be reached by a more mountainous, tortuous, secondary road through Sospel that stays, for the most part, inside French territory. From St.-Dalmas–de–Tende, the road climbs to the artificial lake at Mesches, where there are several parking areas. Beyond this you must walk.

There is one main trail up the Vallée des Merveilles, with no signs pointing to the rocks with engravings on them, nor are all the engraved rocks next to the trail. It's exciting and a great deal of fun to hunt for them, like going on a great outdoor treasure hunt in rugged terrain. The people who made the pictures used rocks with an orange or green patina (oxidized schist, containing iron or copper), and after a while you learn to spot the rocks that are likely to have petroglyphs. But by hunting alone you are not likely to find some of the more famous images. This is the advantage of having a guide. It would be well-nigh impossible without a guide to find "Le Cosmonaut," which is quite high in the mountains and very far from any trail.

Although close to the Mediterranean coast, the Vallée des Merveilles is at a fairly high altitude, with the main valley between about 2,200 and 2,500 meters high. Consequently, there may be snow over the passes and in parts of the valley into June, when some of the engravings may be concealed under snow. The huts, however, are much less crowded in June and also on weekdays during September. A small party of two or three people need not write for hut reservations during the high season, but a group of four or more should do so. For the Refuge des Merveilles, write to M. Claude Baringo through June 1 at Le Roc Blanc, Impasse des Sables, Chantemerle, 05330 St.-Chaffrey, France; tel. (1) 92 24 16 28. After June 1 at 06430 St.-Dalmas–de–Tende. It is not possible to telephone the hut for reservations.

Lac Long Supérieure

11. Lac des Mesches to the Refuge des Merveilles

Rating: moderate
Distance round trip: 17 km
High point: 2,111 m

Total climb: 760 m
Time: 3 hours up, 2 hours 10 minutes down

There are five parking areas near Lac des Mesches. Some are on the road just before the lake and some are above the lake. From the western edge of the lake, take the signposted trail to the Refuge des Merveilles. The trail, heading west, is broad, gradual, and well marked, leading at first through lovely woods. About 20 minutes up the trail, pass a smaller lake, Lac de la Minière. Accommodations are available here. In another 1 hour 25 minutes, signs announce that you have entered the national park. There are several signposted junctions; continue southwest on the main trail (*par la piste*) to the Refuge des Merveilles. The trail crosses a little stream on a bridge and climbs above treeline to a wild valley strewn with rocks, with a stream to your left. There are both green and white and also some yellow blazes. Pass between two small tarns, one on each side of the trail. Cross a second bridge, passing a dam wall with sluicegates. Reach the hut soon after this on the southern shore of Lac Long Supérieure.

12. The Vallée des Merveilles Trail

Rating: easy
Distance round trip: 9 km
Total climb: 500 m
High point: 2,549 m

Time: 2 hours up from the Refuge des Merveilles to the Baisse de Valmasque, 1 hour 30 minutes down, but add a minimum of 3 hours to look at petroglyphs

The Refuge des Merveilles is not actually in the valley with the engravings, but it is close. The trail starts to the west of the hut on the GR 52 and continues along the south shore of the lake. After 20 minutes, there is a junction. The fork to the left (west) climbs to the Pas de l'Arpette (see hike 10, The Pas de l'Arpette); the one to the right (north) climbs gently to a

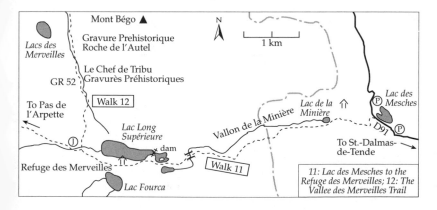

11: Lac des Mesches to the Refuge des Merveilles; 12: The Vallée des Merveilles Trail

Hunting for petroglyphs, Vallée des Merveilles

little notch, the entrance to the Vallée des Merveilles. Here you continue on the GR 52. Despite faint traces of other paths, which disappear soon after leaving the main path, this broad, very visible trail is the only one up the valley, with the stream on your right. The valley narrows, walled in by mountains on the left and right. On the west side are the Mont des Merveilles (2,720 meters) and, beyond it, the Mont du Grand Capelet (2,935 meters); on the east, Mont Bégo (2,872 meters). The trail passes a few smaller lakes and leaves the zone in which the petroglyphs are found. It climbs northward to the Baisse de Valmasque (2,549 meters), a saddle from which you can look down to the bigger Lac du Basto. Just beyond and below the saddle is the junction for the trail to the Refuge de Nice, which descends to the left (northwest). The continuation of the main trail is to the right (northward) to the Refuge de Valmasque.

PARC NATUREL RÉGIONAL DU QUEYRAS

Until the 1980s the Parc Naturel Régional du Queyras (pronounced "kay-rah") was scarcely known, even among the French. On a map, the region appears as a small bulge into Italian territory, yet this alpine upland is distinctively French, a region with its own cultural character and its own unique and interesting history.

The geological features of the Queyras region are deceptive. With only the remnants of a few glaciers and mountains that for the most part are bare of snow in summer, the countryside seems of a lower elevation than that of the alpine regions to the north. Yet St.-Véran, at 2,040 meters, is reputed to be the highest village in the Alps that was traditionally populated year-round. (At 2,320 meters, the new French ski resort, the Val Thorens, is even higher, but it is an artificial creation, "purpose-built" for skiing, rather than a true village.) The Queyras is a rugged, mountainous upland and truly alpine in its vegetation and animal life as well as its culture. Because many of its peaks and the ridges that connect them are free of snow in summer, one of the characteristics of this region are *crête* (crest) walks that snake along these connecting ridges, or crests. These routes would require mountaineering gear and experience were they covered with snow or ice. The general absence of glaciers and snowfields opens much more territory for hiking, so there is a larger network of trails here than in, for example, the Ecrins.

This little pocket of French territory, almost tucked away out of sight, has a political and religious history disproportionate to its modest status. In the twelfth century, the lord of the Briançonnais, whose lands included the Queyras, married an Englishwoman and for some unknown reason gave his son the surname Dolphin—Dauphin in French—which became the name of his dynasty and later the title for the eldest sons of the Kings of France (see the introduction to the Parc National des Ecrins).

Humbert II, the lord who ruled this territory in the early fourteenth century, found himself in severe financial difficulty, unable to raise funds. He gave his people a great deal of personal freedom in return for the loan of a large sum of money. The people thus became true *francs-bourgeois* (free men); their liberties were set forth in a *Grande Charte,* reminiscent of the Magna Charta. It is still kept in the town hall of Briançon. The count of the Briançonnais renounced his rights as a lord, feudal service was abolished, and the people gained the right to freedom of assembly and to elect their own leaders. A curious historical note: The Queyrassins were henceforth allowed to pay homage to their lord, the Dauphin, by kissing his ring or the palm of his hand, instead of his thumbs, as had been customary for peasants. A point of environmental interest is that under the

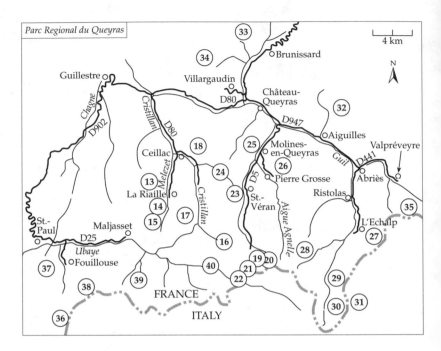

Grande Charte, the aristocracy could no longer cut trees in the forests, which the people understood caused floods, earthslides, and avalanches.

The Queyras thus gained a measure of real democracy in the fourteenth century. Leadership rotated among the heads of each family and an assembly decided all matters and assigned collective tasks, such as irrigation and road-building. As for Humbert, despite this infusion of cash, his troubles continued and he was later forced to cede his territory to King Charles V of France. The king's elder son took the title *Dauphin* and ruled over the Dauphiné, extending from Grenoble over all the southern Alps. Thus, the Queyras officially became French.

The religious history of the region is more troubled. A medieval movement of religious dissenters, the Waldensians, attracted many followers among the rural poor of the Queyras. Ultimately, in the sixteenth century, the Catholic church sent an army to suppress the Waldensians, and a religious and civil war ensued, with excesses committed by both sides. Many Protestant families fled to Switzerland. By the time of the French Revolution when freedom of conscience and worship were granted, the movement had been largely repressed, although small "temples," as the Protestant churches are called, many of which appear abandoned, are still seen in villages throughout the Queyras.

Perched above the Guil River in the center of the region is a walled, fortified medieval castle, Château-Queyras, resembling a small version of the great fortress of Carcassonne, which was besieged during the religious wars. Open daily from June to September, from 9:00 A.M. to 7:00 P.M., it is a nice excursion for castle buffs and families with children.

A distinctive feature of the region is its sundials, or *cadrans solaires,* painted with folk art motifs and inscribed with moral or religious epithets, seen on the walls of many churches and houses. The Queyrassins, it is said, needed clocks but were too poor to buy them, although perhaps the impulse behind many of the sundials was simply decorative. The Queyras is also famous for its wood carving; its craftsmen sell objects carved in wood, *en bois sculptés,* ranging from children's toys and small kitchen articles to chests and tables.

The Parc Naturel Régional du Queyras was created in 1977 and covers 650 square kilometers. The twenty-six regional natural parks of France are differentiated from the national parks essentially in that the regional parks are inhabited. No one lives within the national parks year-round. The purpose behind the creation of the regional natural parks, however, was not to stop development, as was the case with the national parks, but to help the indigenous people live in their own environment in harmony with nature. Hunting, for example, while outlawed in the national parks, is allowed under close restriction in the regional natural parks. Dogs are also allowed, although they must be leashed. It is recognized that human presence and human agricultural activity has been a part of this landscape for centuries. The aim in creating the regional natural parks, therefore, was to conciliate economy and ecology. The parks are administered to favor the development (or rather, these days, the survival) of agriculture, and also of handicrafts and commerce, while protecting the quality of the environment, and to accept and welcome tourism without spoiling the region and overturning the lives of its inhabitants.

Rules for visiting a regional natural park are much less stringent than for a national park, and there is no schedule of fines for violations. Visitors are instead requested to show courtesy and respect for the environment and to farmers and their livestock. Guidelines ask visitors not to trample crops and meadows, not to disturb herds and flocks, not to obstruct irrigation channels, and not to leave trash behind. Visitors are also asked not to pollute lakes and rivers or allow children to build little stone dams in the brooks. Some places request that hikers keep to the trails and not take shortcuts, which cause erosion. Visitors should not make unnecessary loud noises that will disturb wild animals, and dogs should be kept on a leash. The guidelines also urge visitors not to pick protected wildflowers or gather minerals and to be careful with campfires and in extinguishing cigarettes.

Guillestre, at the head of the river Guil, where it flows into the Durance, is the market town of the Queyras and serves as its entry point. It is reached by taking N94 south from Briançon and then turning east on D902 for 3 kilometers. It's an attractive place, set in a large, sunny bowl, and because the Queyras is a small area, nearly anyplace in the region can be reached from Guillestre in an hour or a little more at most. Hikers, however, will probably want to be based closer to the trailheads, and several villages are more conveniently located. The majority of the walks covered in this book are south of the Guil, and the villages of Ceillac, St.-Véran or Molines-en-Queyras, and Abriès or Ristolas make the best bases from which to hike. There are several walks north of the Guil; these can easily be reached from these same villages or from Arvieux or La Chalp, north of the river. It is a curious fact that architectural styles differ from one Queyras village to another.

To change money from various currencies, one must go to Guillestre or to the St.-Véran post office.

VALLEYS OF MÉLEZET, CRISTILLAN, AND ALBERT

Reach Ceillac by traveling northeast of Guillestre on D902, and then east on D60. From the road, the first view of Ceillac is dominated by the belltower of Ste.-Cécile, an abandoned fifteenth-century church set amid the fields just outside the village. In the center of Ceillac is the sixteenth-century church of St.-Sébastien amid a cluster of old stone houses whose arched entrances lead into groundfloor barns and stables. A scattering of new vacation chalets lies above Ceillac, but the architectural harmony of the central village has not been spoiled. There is a good gîte d'étape and a hotel in the village. Another hotel is very attractively situated a little farther up the valley at the Pied du Mélezet, about 2 kilometers southwest of the village on D60.

Ceillac gives access to walks in several upper valleys whose streams, the Torrent du Mélezet, the Torrent du Col Albert, and the Cristillan, join near the village.

Lac Ste.-Anne and the Col Girardin

Lac Ste.-Anne is the most popular destination in the area and, indeed, one of the most popular itineraries in the Queyras. Its only drawback is that there are always many hikers here, whereas on other routes you will see very few people. From above, Lac Ste.-Anne looks like a turquoise brooch set in the meadows. Above it tower the Pics de la Font Sancte (3,385 meters), a row of serrated rock peaks streaked with the remnants of a few glaciers and, early in the season, covered with snowfields. On the lakeshore is the tiny Chapelle Ste.-Anne, focus of an annual pilgrimage every July 26.

Several legends with the theme of water are associated with this place. It is said that a young shepherd girl suffered from thirst in the high meadows. Then she noticed that a white goat from her herd went every day to a certain place, disappeared into a cleft in the rock, and reemerged a few minutes later. Following the goat one day she found a clear spring issuing from a perfectly circular hole. She asked to be buried nearby to keep the memory of this miracle, and the site was named Font Sancte in archaic French, or "holy fountain." Since then, during periods of drought, the peasants have climbed up here with their priest to pray for rain and drink the water of the sacred spring.

Some suggest that the annual pilgrimage of prayer for the harvest dates back to the Roman era, the procession dedicated not to Ste.-Anne but to Ceres, goddess of grain and the harvest, or a similar pagan goddess. As for the chapel, it is said that a young shepherd girl (perhaps the same one?) took a boat out onto the lake but could not return to shore; her frightened parents promised to build a chapel if she was able to return.

There are two different approaches to Lac Ste.-Anne.

13. Lac Ste.-Anne via Lac Miroir

Rating: moderate   **Total climb:** 730 m
Distance round trip: 12.5 km   **Time:** 2 hours 45 minutes up, 1 hour
High point: 2,415 m   55 minutes down

Walk or drive southwest on D60 from Ceillac (the GR 5 runs along the road). After 2 kilometers bear right at a fork in the road, and in 0.4 kilometer reach the Pied du Mélezet and a parking area. Facing the parking area is a footbridge. Cross this bridge; a signpost on the other side marks the trailhead to the two lakes. The GR 5 switchbacks up, steeply at first, leveling out after an hour's climb. You'll cross another bridge and reach Lac Miroir (2,214 meters) about 1 hour 30 minutes after starting.

Upon reaching this shallow, brownish-green lake, follow the trail along its eastern shore, and then turn left (east); a few blazes on a big rock to your left show the way. Descend a few meters into a hollow, then climb again. About 35 minutes beyond Lac Miroir you'll join a broad track under a ski-lift cable, one of the very few in the Queyras. Reach Lac Ste.-Anne about 1 hour 10 minutes after leaving Lac Miroir.

14. Lac Ste.-Anne from Chaurionde

Rating: easy   **Total climb:** 448 m
Distance round trip: 4.5 km   **Time:** 1 hour 15 minutes up, 50
High point: 2,415 m   minutes down

This is the route taken for the annual pilgrimage on July 26, a centuries-old tradition when villagers and vacationers march behind the banner of

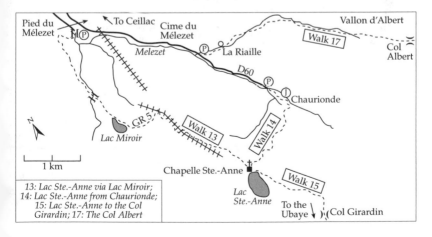

13: *Lac Ste.-Anne via Lac Miroir;*
14: *Lac Ste.-Anne from Chaurionde;*
15: *Lac Ste.-Anne to the Col
Girardin; 17: The Col Albert*

Lac Miroir

Ste.-Anne to the chapel above for an outdoor mass, followed by picnic lunches (bring your own) and various games and races.

In the Middle Ages, the pilgrims began their march from the village; today, they assemble at the parking area at Chaurionde.

Walk or drive southwest from Ceillac on D60 as for the start of hike 13, Lac Ste.-Anne via Lac Miroir. At the fork after 2 kilometers, bear left (you'll soon see a hotel on your right) and continue for 3.2 kilometers to the parking area at the end of the road, at Chaurionde. The trail begins at the southern edge of the parking area.

Five minutes beyond the trailhead, at a signposted junction, turn right for Lac Ste.-Anne. The trail climbs at first through the woods. You'll pass a waterfall and climb to a shelf. After about 1 hour from the start of the hike, emerge above treeline. A sign requests hikers to stay on the path, to protect resown meadows. The trail climbs at a moderate grade to a rim, from which the trail drops a few meters to reach this vivid turquoise lake about 1 hour 15 minutes after starting.

15. Lac Ste.-Anne to the Col Girardin

Rating: moderate   **Total climb:** 284 m
Distance round trip: 4 km   **Time:** 1 hour up, 50 minutes down
High point: 2,699 m

From Lac Ste.-Anne, follow the GR 5 trail from the Chapelle Ste.-Anne. The trail curves around the northern shore, heading southeast. After about 30 minutes the trail becomes steep and switchbacks up on scree; some passages are eroded and narrow. From the col there is a view of the snowy peaks of the Ecrins and of the Ubaye. (From the col the GR 5 descends southward to the Ubaye.)

Banner of Ste.-Anne at the annual pilgrimage in Ceillac

Other Walks in the Area

16. Tête de la Cula

Rating: strenuous
Distance round trip: 11 km
High point: 3,121 m

Total climb: 965 m
Time: 3 hours 10 minutes up from L'Etable des Génisses, 2 hours down

The wild upper valley of the Cristillan is quite unfrequented. This hike takes you to the top of a mountain at the head of the valley, with excellent views of some of the highest peaks in the neighboring Ubaye. Note: If there is snow on the final section of trail to the top of the mountain, this becomes a technical climb. To find out about snow conditions, call the Office du Tourisme in Ceillac: tel. 92 45 05 74.

Many of the signposts for this walk point to the Pas de la Cula, but that route is difficult to find. The route suggested here is much easier to follow.

From Ceillac, take the Route de Cristillan: this road leads northeast from the little square in front of the church of St.-Sébastien in the village center. After 7 kilometers (just past the sign for Le Bois Noir, where you must bear right for a few yards) is a sign for the Col du Cristillan and the Pas de la Cula to your left. From here, however, the trail is difficult to find and fades out. Instead, drive another 0.5 kilometer. Either park where the road crosses a wooden bridge and walk 1.5 kilometers to the end of the road at L'Etable des Génisses, where there is a house and an old barn, or drive this last 1.5-kilometer section on unpaved road and park at L'Etable des Génisses (9 kilometers from Ceillac).

A sign points right to the Col du Cristillan and Lac de Clausis; turn left, however, and take an unsigned narrow track down through the woods to the stream and cross a bridge. The trail begins on the opposite bank, slightly above the stream; after you cross the bridge there are two ways to connect with it.

After crossing the bridge, turn left (northwest) and take a narrow track that leads back in the direction of Ceillac. This peters out in a few minutes, but climb about 20 meters up the slope, off trail; you'll connect above with a broad track through the grass. Turn right (east) onto this track; from here, the trail is clear. You'll see a white and red blaze and then, painted on a rock, a sign indicating the Col Ceillac, the Col Nord du Cristillan, the Col de la Cula, and the Col Longet. (The bridge you crossed 10 minutes early can be seen below to your right, a few yards ahead—southeast—of this spot.) Soon after this there is a signpost for the Pas de la Cula and the Col du Cristillan.

Alternatively, turn right after crossing the bridge, walk along the right bank of the stream, and then climb up on a small track that leads to the trail and signpost above.

From the signpost follow the trail, marked by occasional yellow or red and white blazes, as it turns into the wider upper valley. At a signpost for the Pas de la Cula, cross the stream; there is no bridge, but it is not a difficult crossing. The trail climbs another step to a shelf above. This higher valley, lined on the right by craggy peaks, gradually narrows. At a signposted junction, turn left (northeast) for the Tête and Pas de la Cula.

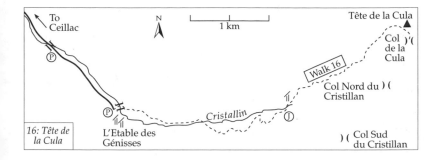

The blazes disappear but there is a clear track. Cross the stream again (easy), then ascend to a stone cabin, an old customs hut, on the slope above.

As the track climbs, you'll see a large area filled with stones and boulders to your right. Cairns set amid this stone slide indicate the route to the Col de la Cula, but they are very hard to spot against the general background of stones; the track to the left of the stone slide, however, is clearly visible. It rises steeply to the ridge line, where a very distinct path leads to your right, up to the top of the Tête de la Cula.

17. The Col Albert

Rating: very strenuous
Distance round trip: 8 km
High point: 2,846 m

Total climb: 946 m from La Riaille
Time: 3 hours up, 2 hours 55 minutes down

The Vallon d'Albert, like the Vallée du Cristillan, is uninhabited and wild. This offers a bit of route-finding challenge in the mid-section, although the way is quite easy to find when you know what to look for. The meadows of the upper Vallon d'Albert are quite beautiful, and hikers may prefer to stop there, since the final climb to the col is very difficult. It is extremely steep, rising on sand and scree, so footing is poor (trekking poles are a godsend here).

From Ceillac, take the D60 road to the Cime du Mélezet, but continue until you see the sign "Ceillac par la route forestière," 4.4 kilometers from the village; park here. Walk up the road for a minute or two, and turn left at the sign for La Riaille and the Col Albert. At the hamlet of La Riaille, about 0.5 kilometer away, turn right (northeast) for the trail to the Col Albert, indicated by a signpost. The trail climbs at a moderate grade through a meadow and then crosses a streambed (dry in late summer) and continues up through the woods along its left bank. It crosses the stream again, and then climbs along the right bank through meadows. About 1 hour 15 minutes after starting the hike, cross a rivulet to your right. "Col Albert" is painted on a stone to your left. Twenty-five minutes after this the trail gets indistinct, although a trace can be seen through the grass heading southeast. In 10 minutes, turn left to cross a dry streambed; cairns mark the way. A huge hump with a sheer rock face above is before you, to the east, and a long, jagged rock wall, the Montagne de la Riche, is to your right. You must now ascend on a trace of path between these landmarks, keeping the large hump to your left. The scenery is lovely here, and the most difficult part of the hike is ahead, so this is a good place to stop if you don't want to climb up to the col.

Cross the dry streambed once again. As you climb, you'll see a large boulder field to your left. At about 2,480 meters the trail swings to the right of the huge hump; cairns mark the way up the stony slope, which is extremely steep, especially above a few large outcrops of yellowish rock at 2,600 meters. From the col there are splendid views of the Ubaye and the distant Ecrins. Retrace your steps to return; the descent is necessarily slow.

18. The Col de Bramousse and the Col Fromage

Rating: moderate
Distance loop trip: 11.5 km
High point: 2,582 m

Total climb: 942 m
Time: 3 hours 30 minutes up, 2 hours down

From Ceillac, this route climbs to the relatively low Col de Bramousse, then threads its way along the Crête des Chambrettes to reach the Col Fromage, and returns to Ceillac.

At the northern entrance to Ceillac, there is a large signboard and map. From there, follow the sign to La Clapière, northwest, turning left (west) at the fork for the church of Ste.-Cecile. This takes you in about 10 minutes to the church of Ste.-Cécile, where you turn right (north), uphill. A sign points the way, initially along a cart road, to the Col de Bramousse. The GR 58 trail starts to rise into a narrow, wooded valley with rocky outcrops to your right; it switchbacks steeply through this ravine, then emerges from the woods and levels out into a meadow about 1 hour 30 minutes from the start of the hike. Turn right and walk a few meters; from the edge of the meadow, there is a good view of the Pics de la Font Sancte. From here you'll see a clear trail that climbs beside a lift line; turn left (north) and follow this trail to the upper end of the valley. The gradient is moderate.

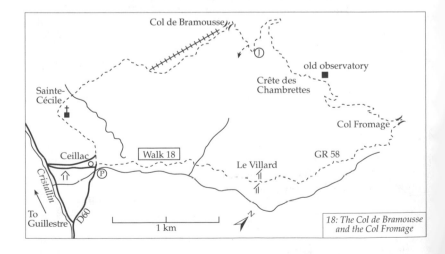

18: The Col de Bramousse and the Col Fromage

Lunchbreak at the old observatory between the Col de Bramousse and the Col Fromage

You'll soon reach the Col de Bramousse at 2,251 meters, where a sign points straight ahead to the Chalets de Bramousse and the lower hamlet of Bramousse. Here, turn right (east), leaving the GR 58; there is no sign for the Col Fromage, to which you are now headed. Ascend toward the ski lift to your right; the trail is distinct. At another junction, follow the switchback to your left (north). The trail now traverses along the *crête*; it's exposed on one side, but the trail gives level footing, has a good surface, and is about 2 feet wide. The space at 2,582 meters near a small ruined building said to be an old observatory is a popular lunch spot. You reach this about 3 hours 30 minutes from the start of the hike.

From here, follow the descending trail eastward to reach the Col Fromage (2,301 meters) in about 40 minutes. Here you rejoin the GR 58; turn right (south) and reach a farm road about 1 hour below the col. Turn right (southeast), passing the little cluster of houses at Le Villard, and follow the road down to Ceillac.

THE VALLEYS OF L'AIGUE BLANCHE AND L'AIGUE AGNELLE

Le plus haut village d'Europe où l'on mange du pain, the highest village in Europe where bread is eaten, is how St.-Véran describes itself. The village is spread along a sunny slope facing south (*l'adret,* in local dialect; the

Croix de la Passion, St.-Veran

slope in shade is *l'ubac*), and its southern exposure was surely a factor that enabled the community to survive at this altitude. The slope is so steep that the village grew laterally, in two tiers; its two streets, an upper and a lower one, extend for about 1 kilometer across the slope.

The villagers made good use of their southern exposure. Their living quarters, on the ground floor, are built of stone, but the upper parts of the houses are wooden haylofts and granaries several stories high and open to the air to dry the hay that may have been brought in damp from the fields in case of early snow. Only a few houses older than 200 years have survived because of devastating fires that swept through these wooden houses stuffed full of hay. The village once actually consisted of five *quartiers*, each with its own oven and outdoor fountain. The separation of the village into different quarters was in part an attempt to limit the destruction of such fires.

Near the church, on St.-Véran's upper street, is a house bearing the sign *"Ici Habitat d'Autrefois"* (a home of yesteryear), which an elderly lady shows to the public on afternoons. Her family once lived in the ground floor room at the back of which are four mangers. Cows and one pig were kept there, as their bodies helped warm the room in winter. The animals stood on a dirt floor; the front part of the room, with a plank floor, served as bedroom, dining room, kitchen, and workroom for such tasks as making and resoling boots and shoes. On the lower street another house offers an exhibit of old furnishings.

The porch of the church of St.-Véran is supported by two columns resting on the backs of recumbent lions, who hold little figures between their paws. These Romanesque lions are a characteristic motif of the Queyras, appearing in several churches. One interpretation of the motif is that the lions are not about to devour prey but, rather, that this is an illustration of the prophecy of Isaiah (11:6) that "the wolf shall dwell with the lamb, and the leopard lie down with the kid."

Another folk art tradition is the "Croix de la Passion," or Cross of the

Passion, of which there are several in St.-Véran. Large outdoor wooden crucifixes are decorated with carved images, each symbolizing an element of the crucifixion story.

Picturesque St.-Véran is no longer completely unknown; on a sunny day in August it is full of visitors, most of whom drive up just for the day. It has several gîtes d'étape and several attractive hotels. There are parking areas outside the village; only local people and guests staying in St.-Véran are allowed to drive into the village. You can reach St.-Véran from Guillestre by driving northeast on D902 and then D947 to Ville-Vielle, and then turning southeast on D5.

Several attractive smaller villages nearby also offer pleasant accommodations. Molines-en-Queyras, on D5, is located near the confluence of the two streams L'Aigue Blanche and L'Aigue Agnelle, which flow together as L'Aigue Agnelle into the Guil. Above Molines-en-Queyras, in the valley of the upper L'Aigue Agnelle, are several even smaller villages, on D205: Pierre Grosse, Le Coin, and Fontgillarde. There are two hotels at Molines-en-Queyras, one hotel at Le Coin, and two gîtes d'étape at Molines-en-Queyras and one at Pierre Grosse. (Beyond Fontgillarde, the road continues over the Col Agnel, crossing the border there into Italy.) All these villages are close enough to one another so that any of them makes a good base for day hikes.

Walks from St.-Véran

There is only one road that continues past St.-Véran, making initial directions for these walks simple and straightforward. From St.-Véran, the road continues southeastward for several kilometers. The end of the road is the starting point for several good walks, but no traffic is allowed on the road during July and August. Instead, the village has set up *navette,* or shuttle, service for hikers. A small bus picks up passengers just past the southeast end of the village and takes them out about 7 kilometers to a spot just past an old marble quarry, marked on maps as *"ancienne carrière de marbre."* The ride takes 15 minutes, and the *navette* leaves the village every morning at 6:30 A.M., 7:30 A.M., and 8:00 A.M. and every 30 minutes thereafter until noon. In the afternoon there are departures at 2:00 P.M. and 3:00 P.M., and then every 30 minutes until 6:00 P.M. Each *navette* returns to the village after dropping off passengers at the quarry. The fare is about 20 francs for a *trajet simple* (one way) or about 35 francs for an *aller/retour* (round trip). Guests staying in St.-Véran get a reduced fare by obtaining a special ticket at their hotel. An *abonnement,* or discount card, gives you ten trips for about 100 francs. You can also walk to the trailhead, either along the road or on the GR 58, which begins at the same point and runs along the left bank of L'Aigue Blanche.

Hikes 19 through 22 all begin from the *navette* stop at the end of the road.

19. The Col de St.-Véran

Rating: easy
Distance round trip: 7.2 km
High point: 2,844 m

Total climb: 536 m, plus 300 m if you leave from St.-Véran
Time: 1 hour 40 minutes up, 1 hour 20 minutes down

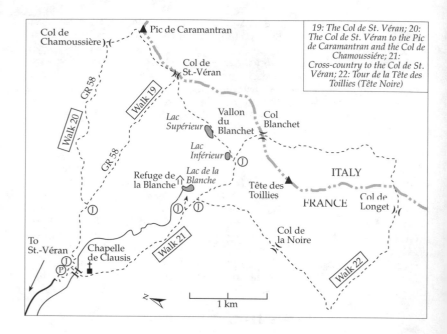

19: The Col de St. Véran; 20: The Col de St. Véran to the Pic de Caramantran and the Col de Chamoussiére; 21: Cross-country to the Col de St. Véran; 22: Tour de la Tête des Toillies (Tête Noire)

One of the most popular walks in the area is an easy hike out to the Col de St.-Véran on the Italian border. From there, if you continue northward along the ridge, you can climb a very small mountain, the Pic de Caramantran, descend to the Col de Chamoussière, and then rejoin the main trail. The latter itinerary is described below as hike 20, The Col de St.-Véran to the Pic de Caramantran and the Col de Chamoussière.

From the *navette* stop continue up the road and reach a signposted junction in about 10 minutes. This is the fork for the trail to the Col de St.-Véran to the left (east), and to the Col de la Noire or the Col Blanchet to the right. The upper end of the valley is a broad, wedge-shaped, undulating meadow, contained within the walls of the ridges that bound the valley to the north, south, and east.

About 35 minutes after starting, reach a signposted junction and keep to the right (east) for the Col de St.-Véran. After another 45 minutes reach another signposted junction and continue straight ahead (again, east) to reach the col in another 20 minutes. Retrace your steps to return, or continue on hike 20.

20. The Col de St.-Véran to the Pic de Caramantran and the Col de Chamoussière

Rating: moderate
Distance loop trip: 5.4 km
High point: 3,025 m

Total climb: 241 m from the Col de St.-Véran
Time: 30 minutes up, 1 hour 15 minutes down

From the Col de St.-Véran, turn left (north) onto the trail along the ridge. The Pic de Caramantran is the small peak directly above you; several steep trails lead to its top and you can take either the one to the left or to the right. The trails become a little indistinct but the way is always clear—up! Reach the top in about 30 minutes.

Descend westward, just to the right of the small marker on top of the Pic de Caramantran. Stay close to the center of the ridge's spine; do not stray too far to the right as you descend. There are a few exposed steps where you may want to use a hand to steady yourself by holding the rocky ridge to your left; this section is just a few meters long. The rest of the descent is easy and on a good path, down to a saddle in the ridge. Follow the path down through scree and reach the Col de Chamoussière, at 2,884 meters, in 20 minutes. (At the little saddle you'll see another small peak before you that you can ascend in 5 minutes, but it's a dead end; you must return to the same path to descend to the Col de Chamoussière.)

If you do this itinerary in the reverse direction and wish to climb the Pic de Caramantran from the Col de Chamoussière, no sign points the way; take the small but clear path to the south that ascends the shaly slope. Above you is a high ridge with a cairn visible to the left: that is not the Pic de Caramantran. From below, as you look up, you can see quite clearly that the end of the ridge, to the right, is the higher point: that is the Pic de Caramantran. It is both higher and rounder on top, whereas the peak to the left has a sharper profile. Therefore, when you reach the little saddle between the two peaks already mentioned, turn right (south).

The Col de Chamoussière is signposted for the Refuge Agnel and St.-Véran. In descent from the Pic de Caramantran, turn left (west) at the col; this is the GR 58, and from this trail the view of the upper valley is lovely. In a few minutes, reach a signposted junction for the trails to the Col de St.-Véran or the Cols de la Noire and Blanchet. Continue straight ahead (west). A few blazes and also wooden wands mark the way, although the path is clear. About 50 minutes below the Col de Chamoussière, turn right (west) at a signposted junction. When you see the small Chapelle de Clausis below to your left and the bridge and road, leave the blazed GR 58 and take the little trail that descends to the road; you'll reach the *navette* stop in 1 hour 15 minutes below the Col de Chamoussière.

21. Cross-country to the Col de St.-Véran

Rating: moderate
Distance loop trip: 8 km
High point: 2,920 m

Total climb: 612 m
Time: 3 hours up, 1 hour 20 minutes down

This is a more adventurous route to the Col de St.-Véran that passes a few small lakes and requires a little route finding. It ascends through a narrow valley marked "Vallon du Blanchet" on maps.

Begin as for hike 19, The Col de St.-Véran, but a few minutes after the *navette* stop, cross a bridge; a signpost here indicates that you are crossing over the GR 58. You will pass the little Chapelle de Clausis, to your left. At first, you are headed for the Col Blanchet, although later you diverge from that trail. Nearly 1 hour after starting the hike, continue straight ahead (east) through a signposted junction (from here, the Refuge de la Blanche is to the left, the Col de la Noire to the right) and then through a second junction, signposted for the same destinations. As a landmark, call this the second junction. From here you can see the Refuge de la Blanche to your left. Continue eastward, toward the Col Blanchet.

Cross a brook (very easy) and continue toward the long cliff in front of you; there are some yellow blazes to guide you. Ascend steeply to the right of the cliff. The last part of this section takes you up a very shallow streambed. About 45 minutes past the second junction, a small path diverges off the trail to your left (northeast) alongside a rivulet and close to the eastern edge of the cliff. (The trail to the Col Blanchet, continuing southeast, is marked by a yellow blaze.)

Turn left onto the small path; the rivulet is to your left, and there are some red and yellow blazes. You will reach the first small lake, Lac Inférieure, in about 15 minutes. From here, continue between the rocky ridges to your left and to your right: you are walking through a notch between them. Cross an area covered by large boulders. There is a trace of trail beyond them. Reach the second lake, Lac Supérieure, 20 minutes beyond the first one. Continue past this second lake, ascending to the left of the rocky hump rising above its farther shore. Go halfway around the lake, which is to your left; after 10 minutes, at about 2,840 meters, follow a faint trail that turns right. Climb a stony slope toward a higher ridge. In about 15 minutes you will see the Col de St.-Véran on the ridge below and the Pic de Caramantran just beyond the col, to the north. Cross an area of scree to reach the ridge line. Follow a trail that extends along the ridge line to your left (north), and in another 15 minutes descend to the Col de St.-Véran.

From the col, turn left (west) and return to the *navette* stop (see hike 19, The Col de St.-Véran).

22. Tour de la Tête des Toillies (Tête Noire)

Rating: very strenuous
Distance loop trip: 14 km
High point: 2,955 m
Total climb: 700 m

Time: 7.5 hours (2 hours to the Col de la Noire, 1 hour 35 minutes to the Col de Longet, 1 hour to the Col Blanchet, 3 hours back to the *navette* stop)

This grand and scenic walk circles a mountain with two names—Tête des Toillies, or Tête Noire (3,175 meters)—that stands above the French–Italian border like a dark tower. It crosses two cols, taking you into the edge of the Ubaye region and also briefly into Italy. It is strenuous but is one of the most scenic itineraries in the Queyras. It should not, however, be undertaken in bad weather—snow, rain, or mist. It can also be done as a 2-day walk with an overnight stop at Chianale, on the Italian side.

Begin as for hike 21, Cross-country to the Col de St.-Véran. From the *navette* stop, follow the signs for the Col de la Noire. After about 50 minutes, reach the last signposted junction; turn right (south) for the Col de la Noire. The trail starts up a rocky slope with a shallow stream to your left and a few yellow as well as yellow and red blazes. A few minutes after turning onto this trail, cross a stream (easy). Soon after this, blazes point you southeast. The trail becomes steep, crosses a short grassy area, and then rises by very steep switchbacks over black scree to the col, at 2,955 meters. You will reach it in about 2 hours.

From the Col de la Noire, the trail descends to an oval blue-green tarn, and you can see larger lakes in the beautiful valley below to the southeast. Passing the tarn, the trail bends to the right (southwest) and disappears for a time. Do not try to follow this trail; instead, continue downward through the meadows. About 35 minutes below the col at about 2,750 meters, watch for a narrow path to your left. As you turn left (southeast) you will see that there are actually many little tracks across the meadow. Follow them toward the larger lakes that you saw from above. Any of the paths will lead you down to a 5-meter-long section of rocky ledge on which you must use your hands. Continue on a path that then descends to join a wide trail on the valley floor below. (This section of trail is followed in hike 40, The Col de Longet, in the upper Ubaye valley; it connects Maurin with the Col de Longet.) Turn left (east) when you reach this wide trail, about 1 hour 10 minutes below the Col de la Noire.

Heading east toward the Col de Longet up this wild, handsome valley you will pass several lakes; the last one is a lovely blue-green. The trail up to the Col de Longet is very gradual. Reach this col (2,660 meters), with its commanding view, about 25 minutes after joining the wide trail through the valley.

From the Col de Longet, take the trail that descends at first east, then northeast. (Do not take a trail that climbs to the left, past the ruined stone cabin you can see from the col.) About 10 minutes below the col a red blaze on one rock marks the way and "Col Blanchet" is painted on another rock, indicating a turn to the left (northeast). The small path crosses a brook (easy), then begins to ascend, and soon connects with a broader trail and turns left; some red blazes mark this. Cross another brook (easy); there are red blazes on a big rock to your left. The final ascent to the Col Blanchet is steep. Reach the Col Blanchet (2,897 meters) 1 hour after leaving the Col de Longet. Here you'll find a stone marker with the *fleur-de-lis* of France on one side, the cross of Savoy on the other, and a notch across the top—the French–Italian border.

Cairns show the way down, although the path is distinct. The descent is steep and a little rough over some rocks at first. Cross a shallow stream, following yellow blazes, and then descend on a dirt trail that hugs the slabs of cliff to your right. You can see Lac de la Blanche below. The grade of the descent eases, and the trail leads you northwestward back to the *navette* stop, which you reach about 2 hours after leaving the Col Blanchet.

23. Crête de Curlet and Croix de Marron

Rating: easy   **Total climb:** 500 m
Distance round trip: 8 km   **Time:** 2 hours up, 1 hour down
High point: 2,350 m

Hikes 23 through 25 are on the slope opposite St.-Véran. Hikes 23 and 24 begin from the Pont du Moulin. To reach this, drive down from the village toward La Chalp; 0.3 kilometer past the Hotel des Etoiles (on your right, as you descend), turn sharply left on a narrow road between two

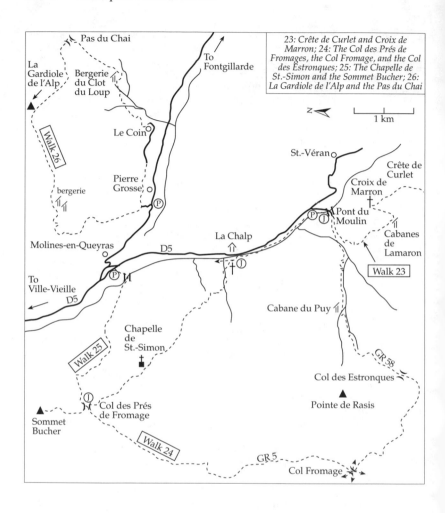

23: Crête de Curlet and Croix de Marron; 24: The Col des Prés de Fromages, the Col Fromage, and the Col des Estronques; 25: The Chapelle de St.-Simon and the Sommet Bucher; 26: La Gardiole de l'Alp and the Pas du Chai

pink houses that belong to Union de Centre de Plein Air (UCPA), an organization for outdoor activities. However, the UCPA sign, which is on the larger house, can be seen only as you approach from the direction of La Chalp and Molines-en-Queyras. This narrow road to the Pont du Moulin is 1.4 kilometers below the large signboard with a map of the village at the entrance to St.-Véran. If you are coming from Molines-en-Queyras, it is 0.2 kilometer from the road sign for Le Raux to the UCPA house. This road leads across a bridge to the Pont du Moulin parking area, the starting point for several hikes.

This is an easy and quite popular walk, with a good view of St.-Véran and the upper valley. Although there is no trail for part of the way, it is obvious which way you should go.

A broad trail ascends from the Pont du Moulin parking area; 5 minutes after starting up this, bear left (south) at a junction where an old sign indicates the Crête de Curlet. A cart road climbs through the woods; turn left, following yellow blazes, onto a path that cuts across the loops of the cart road. After about 50 minutes, emerge into a meadow in which there is a ruined stone cabin. You can see two narrow paths and the ridge line. Continue up through the grass, soon passing another cabin that is intact. As you reach the two narrow paths, take the one to the left and start climbing northeast up the grassy slope. The trail peters out, so you must work your way up by the easiest slope to reach the ridge line. You will find a trail running along the spine of the ridge—this is the Crête de Curlets—with good views. Reach the ridge line about 1 hour 30 minutes after starting the hike. To your right (south) is the Pic Cascavelier. (You can follow the ridge line trail for 15 or 20 minutes to the base of this small peak at about 2,390 meters, but I do not recommend climbing it because there is a lot of loose rock and scree.) When you reach the ridge line, turn left (northwest) and follow the trail to a big wooden cross, the Croix de Marron (2,301 meters), on which is a small plaque with a date and fourteen names. This was erected by grateful parents whose child had disappeared in the mountains. The names honor a search party of villagers who combed the area until they found the missing child.

Return by the same route, since there is no other real trail from the cross.

24. The Col des Prés de Fromage, the Col Fromage, and the Col des Estronques

Rating: very strenuous
Distance loop trip: 20 km
High point: 2,651 m
Total climb: 900 m

Time: 6 hours 40 minutes total (2 hours 35 minutes to the Col des Prés de Fromage, 1 hour to the Col Fromage, 1 hour 20 minutes to the Col des Estronques, 1 hour 45 minutes down to the Pont du Moulin)

This tour is long but very lovely, offering some of the most varied scenery of any itinerary in the region.

Begin as for hike 23, Crête de Curlet and Croix de Marron, at the Pont du Moulin parking area, but instead of ascending on the broad trail through the woods, follow the signposted way (a dirt farm road) along the left bank of the stream, northwest: the signs indicate Gîte le Monchu and La Chalp. In 25 minutes reach a signposted junction where you turn left (northwest) for the Col des Prés de Fromage. Just beside this junction is a large cross inscribed "1685–1985: Retour en Queyras qu'ils soient un." This cross, proclaiming the unity of all Queyrassins, was erected to commemorate a great gathering of the descendants of the Protestants who were forced to flee, mostly to Switzerland and Germany, during the religious wars in France 300 years earlier.

Follow this path, turning left in 10 minutes just before a small brook. The trail ascends at a moderate grade into a narrow cleft and then crosses the brook (easy). A yellow blaze marks the continuation of the path,

Sundial near St.-Veran

which now switchbacks steeply up a grassy slope. After 45 minutes, the trail nearly levels out through woods. Emerge in 15 minutes into meadows; there are occasional yellow blazes along the path. Follow this to the west. It becomes a track through grass, descends a little, and enters the woods again. You will see a small chapel to your right, the Chapelle de St.-Simon (see hike 25, The Chapelle de St.-Simon and The Sommet Bucher), 2 hours 20 minutes from the start of the hike.

From the signposted junction at the Chapelle de St.-Simon continue staight ahead (northwestward), and in 15 minutes reach the Col des Prés de Fromage (the Pass of the Cheese Meadows—an appropriate name, as the cows that create the milk to be made into cheese are strewn about the grass, busily munching or digesting). This is a low pass (2,146 meters) and a pretty spot rather than a grand viewpoint. Turn left (south) here at the signposted junction and head for the Col Fromage on a broad dirt road. After 1 hour reach a ridge with fine, extensive views, and follow the trail (you are now on the GR 5) to the left (south) along the ridge line, a sort of *sentier balcon*. The cone-shaped craters beside the trail are eroded pockets of gypsum, a white, powdery substance. One hour past the Col des Prés de Fromage, reach the Col Fromage (the Cheese Pass) at 2,386 meters, overlooking the valley of Ceillac.

The next part of this tour requires close attention. Your next destination is the Col des Estronques, but the signposted junction at the Col Fromage does not include that direction. From the Col Fromage, take the unblazed, unsigned track that diverges to the left at a 45-degree angle from the main trail. (Do not climb up to the small, ruined stone cabin or down on the red and white blazed trail, the GR 5 and GR 58, to Ceillac.) The unblazed track up to the left crosses a scree slope and enters a ravine. A moment later come to a fork where you must climb up to the left (east). Do not continue on the level path to the right. Traverse the slope on another *sentier balcon*, after which the trail switchbacks steeply up through meadows. To your right there is a grand view of the Pics de la Font Sancte. Reach the Col des Estronques (2,651 meters) 1 hour 20 minutes beyond the Col Fromage.

You are now on the GR 58. The descent is steep at first. Cross a shelf, then descend steeply again down a ravine with a stream to your right. About 45 minutes below the col the path swings left to another gully. Reach the Pont du Moulin parking area 1 hour 45 minutes beyond the col.

Walks from Molines-en-Queyras and Pierre Grosse

25. The Chapelle de St.-Simon and the Sommet Bucher

Rating: moderate
Distance round trip: 13 km
High point: 2,554 m

Total climb: 804 m
Time: 2 hours 10 minutes up from the bridge below Molines-en-Queyras, 1 hour down

This pleasant itinerary leads up past the Chapelle de St.-Simon to a panoramic viewpoint atop a conical hill, the Sommet Bucher. If you are in the area on August 6 you can join the annual pilgrimage to the chapel. According to local legend, shepherds saw the saint's name on an image in the fields. They brought the image to the village, but the next day it disappeared. When they led their flocks up the mountain again, they found it had reappeared, and so they built a chapel on the spot. Villagers and vacationers march up together for an outdoor mass, followed by a picnic and perhaps some wine or an aperitif offered by the parish on this holiday. The traditional food is *croquants,* crisp, sweet biscuits. Unlike the annual *pèlerinage* at neighboring Ceillac on July 26, there are no games or races after the picnic.

You could begin this walk at the Pont du Moulin, as in hike 24, The Col des Prés de Fromage, the Col Fromage, and the Col des Estronques, and follow that route to the Col des Prés de Fromage. At the col, a signpost points straight ahead (northwest) to the Sommet Bucher, which you reach 20 minutes beyond the col, 3 hours after starting the hike.

The pilgrimage, however, begins at the bridge just below Molines-en-Queyras. There is a signpost about 200 meters southeast of the junction for the road up to Molines-en-Queyras. Descend from the road and cross the bridge, at 1,750 meters. The trail starts on the far side of the river. The trail bends to the right and continues up a broad farm road. After 1 hour 20 minutes at a signposted junction, turn left for the chapel, but turn right (northwest) if you want to go directly to the col and the Sommet Bucher. To reach the chapel from this junction, turn left on a forest path marked by a small yellow blaze, but no sign, where the farm road turns sharply right (west). Reach the chapel in about 10 minutes, 1 hour 35 minutes after starting the hike. There is a signposted junction just before the chapel. To hike from the chapel to the Sommet Bucher, continue westward and reach the Col des Prés de Fromage in 15 minutes.

At the col, turn right (north); several trails ascend to the Sommet Bucher. The easiest one is a cart road that swings around the Sommet to the left. Then climb up a narrow path marked by a few blazes, or take an unmarked path to the right, about 50 meters past the col; this is a steeper but more direct route. Reach the top in about 20 minutes. From the top you can see some of the big peaks of the Ecrins, and orientation tables explain the skyline. Note: Just beyond the Sommet Bucher is another, lower hill with a radio transmitter on top—that is not the Sommet Bucher.

26. La Gardiole de l'Alp and the Pas du Chai

Rating: strenuous
Distance loop trip: 12 km
High point: 2,805 m
Total climb: 890 m

Time: 2 hours 40 minutes up to La Gardiole de l'Alp, 1 hour 30 minutes down from the Pas de Chai to Pierre Grosse

A somewhat adventurous hike, this route ascends through trackless meadows to a good viewpoint, then takes you along a ridge line, or *crête*, and descends on a trail. The hike should be taken in the direction described here because it is safer to ascend than to descend through grass. Wet grass, in particular, is slippery. This walk should only be taken in good weather. The route is quite exposed on the ridge line, and if there were snow or the threat of a thunderstorm, it would be dangerous.

Drive to Molines-en-Queyras and continue on D205 to the hamlet of Pierre Grosse. Turn left at the first hairpin turn as you enter the hamlet and drive toward the last houses; park along the road. A sign on your right as you drive toward the last houses points up to La Bergerie and La Gardiole. Hike up this paved road to the northwest. After a few minutes, pass under a power line; the route becomes a dirt farm road, climbing north. After 50 minutes, a sign points right (east) to La Gardiole; here briefly enter the woods. Emerge onto open meadows, and in another 10 minutes reach the *bergerie,* which consists of a small stone cabin and a stable. There is a picnic table beside the house. If you have small children along and go no farther than this place, you would still have a nice outing with good views from here. Follow a track that can be seen climbing north between (and behind) a little stone outhouse and the stable. When it peters out, you must make your own way up the slope to the high point on the ridge line above, La Gardiole de l'Alp—the destination is clear, and as you get close you can see the cross on top. Reach the top (2,786 meters) and a grand, panoramic view about 2 hours 40 minutes after starting the hike.

From La Gardiole, turn right (east) and follow the trail that snakes along the ridge line, rising and falling slightly as it traverses the cusps of the ridge. This is a *crête* walk, quite exposed, especially to the north. The trail climbs to a point a little higher (2,805 meters) than La Gardiole. After about 1 hour on this traverse, descend to the Pas du Chai, a notch at 2,660 meters. Here, turn right (south) and descend from the ridge line on a visible path through meadows. About 35 minutes below the col, pass a small cabin, the Bergerie du Clot du Loup. The path turns into a broader track, and you can see the hamlet of Le Coin below. Reach a cart road and turn right to reach Le Coin, about 1 hour 10 minutes below the Pas du Chai. Return to Pierre Grosse by the paved road to the right (west). There is also a trail through the meadows that avoids the road, but it is not easy to find. If you wish to try to find it, go to the large house at the western edge of Le Coin and take a small track westward across the fields, then find a small path that descends beside a little irrigation canal to Pierre Grosse. Either way should take about 20 minutes.

THE VALLEY OF THE UPPER GUIL

The giant of this region is Monte Viso (3,841 meters), but although its profile dominates the French skyline, the mountain itself is on Italian territory. The Guil, the central watercourse of the Queyras, originates in the massif surrounding Monte Viso. The valley of the upper Guil offers a selection of very attractive walks and a variety of views of "the Viso."

Abriès is a pretty little town at the confluence of the Guil and the Bouchet, with several gîtes and a few simple hotels. Reach Abriès from Guillestre by driving northeast on D902 and then D947. Three kilometers beyond Abriès is the small village of Ristolas, with an attractive hotel and a gîte d'étape with partial hotel service; in addition to the usual gîte dormitories, it has a wing containing private rooms and baths. There is also a gîte at La Monta, a tiny hamlet about 2.5 kilometers southeast of Ristolas on D947.

One might expect that the history of such a lovely, quiet, sparsely populated valley would be serene. Not so. Ristolas was the only community in France to be occupied by the Italians under Mussolini during World War II. In retreat, the invaders burned every building in the village except for the church and one or two houses. (Mussolini's troops also marched on Abriès, destroying part of the town.) It is said that some friendly, anti-Fascist Italian neighbors from just across the border came to Ristolas after the war to help rebuild it.

Another tragedy struck the valley a few years later when terrible snow avalanches destroyed La Monta and L'Echalp, two neighboring hamlets. The survivors subsequently moved to Ristolas. La Monta and L'Echalp have since been declared *Zone Rouge:* no one is allowed to live in them in winter, but farmers still mow the fields there in summer.

27. The Col Lacroix

Rating: moderate
Distance loop trip: 10 km
High point: 2,299 m

Total climb: 638 m
Time: 2 hours 10 minutes up, 1 hour
15 minutes down

This walk takes you from the hamlet of La Monta to the nearby hamlet of L'Echalp and then up to the Col Lacroix on the Italian border. It brings you down again to La Monta by a different trail.

Park at La Monta at the parking area beside the road; you can't miss it. Although you can walk or drive up the road from La Monta to L'Echalp, it is more pleasant to take the gravel path across the river. Walk up the road (southeast) toward L'Echalp for a minute, then turn right and cross a bridge. Turn left (southeast) and follow the gravel road along the river; do not turn off it, and in about 15 to 20 minutes you'll see a bridge and L'Echalp across the river. Turn left and cross the bridge and then the road; a few more minutes' walk will bring you into the hamlet. There is only one church here and it is very easy to find; a sign in front of the church points you right (east) for the Col Lacroix.

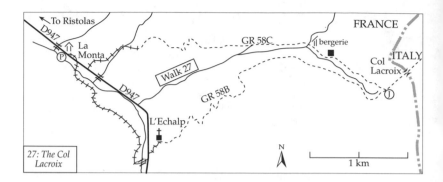

The trail ascends the grassy slopes, then passes through a fine larch wood. About 1 hour above L'Echalp, emerge into the open. The valley is narrow with steep, green slopes, and rises by a moderate grade to a bowl. The way is always obvious and also is marked by a few yellow blazes. Cross a brook (easy), then a rivulet, and then pass the junction of the trail from La Monta. Continue upward, and 5 minutes later reach the col (2,299 meters) on the Italian border, 1 hour 35 minutes beyond L'Echalp. Follow the trail down for 5 or 10 minutes on the Italian side for a view, weather permitting, of Monte Viso.

The descent follows part of the GR 58 and is marked by red and white blazes. Turn right at the junction just beyond the col: the names "La Monta" and "L'Echalp" are painted on some rocks. You'll pass the ruins of one of the old Refuges Napoléons, built with money Napoleon left in his will for a series of refuges in this region because the people turned out to welcome him upon his return from Elba. A little lower pass an old stone *bergerie*. Below this the trail descends by a network of switchbacks, marked by both yellow blazes and white blazes. A short section of trail runs along ledges with some exposure, but the trail is good. Cross a brook (easy) and almost at once turn left (south) onto a gravel cart road, which takes you down to the paved road, D947. Turn right (northwest) and reach La Monta in 5 minutes.

28. The Lacs Egorgeou and Foréant and the Col Vieux

Rating: strenuous
Distance round trip: 9.5 km round trip to Lac Egorgeou, 13.5 km round trip to Lac Foréant, 16 km round trip to the Col Vieux

High point: 2,806 m
Total climb: 1,105 m
Time: 4 hours to the col, 2 hours 40 minutes down

This long walk is one of the most popular in the region, which means that you will meet many other hikers on the trail, but it is a lovely itinerary, passing two lakes of stunning color and clarity. You can stop the walk at the first or even the second lake if the col seems too far.

The trailhead for this walk is just across the bridge below L'Echalp, where you can park. A signpost to "Les Lacs" points left (south), but in 10 minutes the trail swings to the right and begins to ascend. There is a red and white blaze on a rock to your right, indicating that you are on the GR 58, and a sign announcing that fishing is allowed. A network of trails switchbacks up through woods and then emerges onto a pleasant meadow with a view of Monte Viso. Cross the meadow on a path to your left, or take the parallel trail through the woods. Descend about 40 meters to cross a dry streambed, then ascend to a shelf above and a sort of saddle of rock. The trail bends to the right to rise steeply around this. Reach Lac Egorgeou (2,394 meters) 2 hours 30 minutes after starting the hike. This utterly clear, blue-green lake appears against the backdrop of the Crête de la Taillante, a high ridge covered with slabs of bare rock that look like plate armor.

To continue to Lac Foréant, follow the trail south. Cross a stream with a cascade above it, continue up a moderately steep grade to cross a low ridge, and then descend a few meters to reach Lac Foréant (2,618 meters), 1 hour 15 minutes past the first lake. Its waters are a brilliant blue; the color shows best from a slight distance above the lake. Above its eastern shore are the huge gray slabs of the Crête de la Taillante, and across its southern end is Le Pain de Sucre (sugarloaf; 3,208 meters). If you wish to hike to the col, continue southward. The trail climbs at a moderate grade to the broad Col Vieux (2,806 meters), which you reach about 40 minutes beyond Lac Foréant. Just above to your left (east) is Le Pain de Sucre,

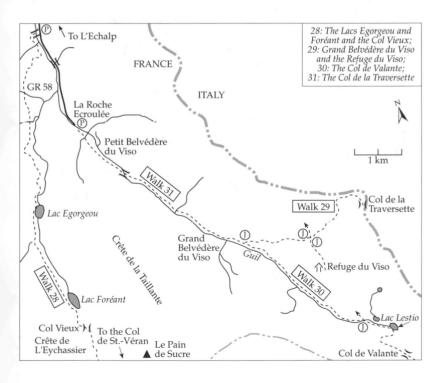

28: The Lacs Egorgeou and Foréant and the Col Vieux;
29: Grand Belvédère du Viso and the Refuge du Viso;
30: The Col de Valante;
31: The Col de la Traversette

while behind the Crête de Taillante appears as a conglomeration of massive, tilted slabs of rock. The view across the col, however, is less extensive, being partly blocked by the range of mountains along the Italian border and the ridge across the valley of L'Aigue Agnelle. The GR 58 crosses the pass, descending to the Refuge Agnel and then crossing the Col de Chamoussière (St.-Véran; hike 20, The Col de St.-Véran to Pic de Caramantran and the Col de Chamoussière).

Note: You can walk from St.-Véran over the Col de Chamoussière, with an optional overnight stop at the Refuge Agnel, then walk past the lakes and end up at L'Echalp, but arrange for a taxi-van from St.-Véran to pick you up at the trailhead there to take you back to St.-Véran.

29. Grand Belvédère du Viso and the Refuge du Viso

Rating: easy
Distance round trip: 15.5 km (10.5 km round trip to the Grand Belvédère; from there, 5 km round trip to the Refuge du Viso)
High point: 2,133 m at the Grand Belvédère, 2,460 m at the Refuge du Viso

Total climb: 350 m to the Grand, Belvédère, 677 m to the Refuge du Viso
Time: 1 hour 35 minutes up to the Grand Belvédère, 1 hour 20 minutes down; 2 hours 45 minutes up to the Refuge du Viso, 2 hours 10 minutes down

Two walks that approach Monte Viso from different sides diverge from this *belvédère,* or viewpoint. You can stop at the *belvédère,* which offers a good view of the mountain, or continue across the meadows to the Refuge du Viso. Some trail signs merely display a picture of Monte Viso's distinctive profile to indicate the way.

The Monte Viso parking area is about 6.2 kilometers beyond Ristolas. There is a first parking area beside La Roche Ecroulée, a gigantic rock that tumbled down from the heights. Most hikers drive a little farther, crossing a wooden bridge to the second parking area just before the trailhead. There is also a small information office here.

From this second parking area, hikers can proceed either by the old road (only farmers and personnel for the Refuge du Viso are allowed to drive on it) or by the trail. The trail begins at the far end of the parking area where a sign marks the trailhead. (Maps indicate *navette,* or shuttle bus, service, but that has been discontinued.) The trail climbs along the left bank of the Guil, while the road proceeds above its right bank. After about 30 minutes the trail descends to cross a bridge over the river and briefly joins the road on the other bank, but soon you can take sections of trail to cut across the loops of the road. The Grand Belvédère du Viso is a small, somewhat level area with a fine view across the meadows of the mountain. To continue to the Refuge du Viso, sometimes marked on signs and maps as Refuge du Balif Viso, follow the signposted trail to the left (east) across the meadows. Turn right in about 50 minutes at a signposted junction, and reach the hut (2,460 meters) in about 20 minutes.

30. The Col de Valante

Rating: strenuous
Distance round trip: 12 km
High point: 2,815 m
Total climb: 742 m from the Grand Belvédère

Time: 2 hours 50 minutes up from the Grand Belvédère, 1 hour 40 minutes down to the Grand Belvédère

This walk brings you quite close to the north face of Monte Viso, offering the best view of the mountain when approached from France. Along the way, the trail passes little Lac Lestio, beyond which the terrain becomes much more difficult. Lac Lestio has a very scenic location, and some hikers may prefer not to go beyond the lake. Note: The Col de Valante faces north, and snow is likely to linger above Lac Lestio on the approach even in late summer. Be prepared, or ready to turn back if necessary.

Begin at the Grand Belvédère du Viso, described in hike 29, Grand Belvédère du Viso and the Refuge du Viso. About 5 minutes beyond it at an unsignposted junction are two trails. Take the trail to the right (southeast), which descends to the stream along the center of the valley. (This route is more direct than the other trail, which passes the Refuge du Viso.) The trail follows the right bank of this lovely stream; the valley walls are lined with waterfalls. A few yellow blazes mark the route. After about 30 minutes two strands of the same trail merge to climb above the stream, and you can see the Refuge du Viso above to your left. After another 25 minutes, the trail from the hut joins the one you are on. Cross a brook (easy), and reach Lac Lestio in another 15 minutes, about 1 hour 40 minutes beyond the Grand Belvédère. This blue-green tarn is an attractive destination in its own right.

From the lake, the notch you can see above is not the col, which is a little higher than the notch and also hooked around to the west, out of sight.

For the Col de Valante, continue along the right (south) side of the lake and look for a big yellow arrow painted on a rock and some yellow and also some red and white blazes. These mark the path that ascends at first to the west. This path is quite good for about 30 minutes, but then it becomes steep, and narrow in a few places. Cross a boulder slide and follow the route—path or snow track—southeast to reach the col on the Italian border, about 1 hour 10 minutes beyond Lac Lestio. For the best view, descend a short distance on the Italian side for a splendid, close look at Monte Viso and the mountains beyond.

Note on hikes 30 and 31: If you wish to take both of these walks, they can be hiked on consecutive days with an overnight stop between them at the Refuge du Viso, thus eliminating the need to repeat the long approach via the Grand Belvédère. These two walks are part of a 3- or 4-day circuit around the mountain, Tour du Mont Viso; you can write to the park for information on this tour; see Appendix 1 for the address.

Lac Lestio

31. The Col de la Traversette

Rating: strenuous
Distance round trip: 7.2 km
High point: 2,947 m
Total climb: 844 m from the Grand Belvédère

Time: 2 hours 25 minutes up from the Grand Belvédère, 1 hour 25 minutes down to the Grand Belvédère

This is a rugged hike because the upper approach to the Col de la Traversette crosses many boulder slides. The view of Monte Viso is not as close or as spectacular as the one obtained from the Col de Valante, but there will likely be less snow on this itinerary than on that one.

Follow the signposted trail east from the Grand Belvédère toward the Refuge du Viso. After 50 minutes, turn left (north) for the col at a signposted junction. In 5 minutes, keep to the right (east) at a second signposted junction. A yellow blaze marks the way. After this, follow cairns up to a brook; ascend at first along its right bank, then cross the brook. As you climb, you will lose sight of Monte Viso. At about 2,760 meters, 1 hour 45 minutes beyond the Grand Belvédère, follow a yellow blaze to the right (southeast). The way continues north through passages littered with boulders and reaches the base of a wall of cliffs, their rocky faces all scored and broken. The route turns right (east), climbing along the base of these cliffs to the notch between them and the stony peak to your right. On the way, pass two stone walls with a space between them. This is the remains of a tunnel built in the fifteenth century to facilitate the transport of salt from Provence. Soon after this reach the col, from which there is a view of Monte Viso and the lower hills behind it. This is the Italian border, and at the col is a rock on which are chiseled several dates, including 1798, with the French *fleur-de-lis* and the cross of Savoy.

The descent—back the way you came—is slow, since you must watch your footing over the many boulder slides before reaching the meadows below.

32. Lac le Grand Laus

Rating: strenuous
Distance round trip: 16 km
High point: 2,585 m

Total climb: 1,045 m
Time: 3 hours up, 2 hours 40 minutes down

This walk to Lac le Grand Laus, which is the largest of three lakes known as the Lacs du Malrif, is a long but varied one. (Signs often indicate Lac Malrif instead of Lac le Grand Laus, but following these signs will indeed bring you to Lac le Grand Laus.) As mentioned later, hikers who want a shorter walk can make their destination Les Bertins, the attractive meadows in the upper valley of the Malrif stream. Although the directions given here are from Abriès, hikers can also begin from the town of Aiguilles, then drive or walk to the hamlet of Le Lombard, and follow a trail from there to the lake.

Begin this walk in Abriès, near the bridge over the Bouchet River just before it enters the Guil. You should be on the river's right (west) bank, along which are many parking spaces. Find the footbridge (but do not

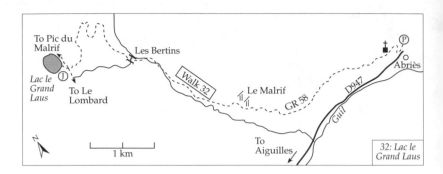

To Pic du Malrif

Les Bertins

Lac le Grand Laus

To Le Lombard

Walk 32

Le Malrif

GR 58

D947

Guil

Abriès

To Aiguilles

N

1 km

32: Lac le Grand Laus

cross back to the left bank); just opposite the footbridge, across the road, is a passageway with a metal railing between the houses. Walk up this; on the next street above there is a fountain with a wooden roof to your right. Do not turn toward the fountain, but continue up a flight of stone steps and, above that, up two flights of wooden steps. Above the last flight is a wooden post with some Parc Naturel Régional du Queyras information on it—this is the trailhead and here you pick up the GR 58. Other than this, there is no sign here for Lac le Grand Laus.

The broad GR 58 trail ascends beside some shrines (stations of the cross) and passes an old chapel with a steeple, now closed. Start along a sort of *sentier balcon* overlooking the Guil and the road below. The trail gradually curves to the right (northwest), away from the Guil valley below. After about 1 hour, pass a few old stone houses, some in ruins. These are the remains of the hamlet of Malrif. Some signposts for Lac Malrif include the destination "Les Bertins," which is the name of the meadows in the upper valley.

The trail rises by a moderate grade into the narrowing upper valley of the Malrif, a lovely stream to your left. One hour 45 minutes after starting, pass a signpost indicating that you are at "Les Bertins." This is a very pleasant place, a long, serene meadow, at the edge of the woods, with bare, green slopes all around, and some hikers or families with young children may wish to end the walk here.

The sign at Les Bertins points you straight ahead (northwest) to Lac le Grand Laus. Follow the blazed trail, crossing the stream on a bridge. The trail hooks around to cross over some rocky ledges and then climbs the slope to your left (west) on steep switchbacks. Following red and white blazes, watch for the main trail and avoid the shortcuts, which are very steep. At about 2,400 meters, 1 hour above Les Bertins, the trail is exposed for a few minutes. Just beyond here, continue to the right (northwest) at a little fork, and in another 5 minutes reach Lac le Grand Laus, 1 hour 15 minutes above Les Bertins. It's a blue-green lake, with a view of Monte Viso.

It is possible to continue northward on the GR 58 and climb the Pic du Malrif, 2,906 meters, which overlooks the lake.

Walks North of the Guil

As the region is fairly compact, hikers making their base in Ceillac, St.-Véran or Molines-en-Queyras, or Abriès or Ristolas can easily reach these trails. There are also accommodations, however, at the villages of Arvieux, Brunissard, and La Chalp. These villages are all located on D902 after that road turns northwest from the bed of the Guil River, just west of Château-Queyras.

33. Lac de Néal

Rating: moderate
Distance round trip: 11 km
High point: 2,509 m

Total climb: 615 m
Time: 3 hours up, 1 hour 30 minutes down

This walk takes you past some old chalets and farmers' huts to a large area of high, spacious meadows and several small lakes.

From the northern end of Brunissard on D902 (on the approach to the Col d'Izoard), turn left at a sign for Les Esquirousses and Camping Le Planet. Walk or drive past Le Planet campground. There is a small parking area near a signpost pointing left (west) off this road to the Chalets de Clapeyto and Lac de Néal. You can drive another 0.3 kilometer up to another, larger parking area, but there is no trail sign there (although the trail is very visible) and the road beyond is limited to local use. The GR 5 trail cuts across loops of the road but sometimes continues on the road.

After about 40 minutes, at the Chalets de L'Eychaillon, turn left (south) at a signposted junction, leaving the GR 5. Follow a gravel road with some orange-pink blazes and some yellow ones. In another 30 minutes reach the Chalets de Clapeyto, another cluster of houses, some quite old and picturesque, with darkened timbers. At the upper end of the group of chalets, a sign points left (southwest) off the gravel road onto the trail for Lac de Néal; a red arrow painted on a rock also points that way.

Ascend gently to a huge green bowl, surrounded by rugged, craggy forms, and then climb to a higher meadow in a very spacious landscape.

33: Lac de Néal

You'll pass several small lakes and, about 1 hour 20 minutes beyond Clapeyto, ascend at a moderate grade to a low ridge with a cairn. This is the Col de Néal (2,509 meters), from which you can see Lac de Néal below on the other side. Descend to the right on traces of trail, marked by a few blazes, to the lake (2,453 meters).

34. Chalets de Furfande

Rating: moderate
Distance loop trip: 12.5 km
High point: 2,293 m

Total climb: 610 m
Time: 2 hours up to the Refuge de Furfande, 3 hours down

The chalets of the Furfande are the only alpages, or mountain farms, in the Queyras that cannot be reached by road.

From the road between Guillestre and Château-Queyras, turn north onto D902, the road toward the Col d'Izoard. After 0.8 kilometer, turn left onto the road that reaches Villargaudin in another 3 kilometers. Drive through this hamlet and continue on a narrow road that is paved for the first kilometer and then becomes a dirt road for 3.3 kilometers) to the parking area at Le Queyron, where the road ends.

The trail begins at Le Queyron with a sign pointing southwest to Furfande. After 15 minutes on this trail, stay right (west) at a signposted junction. After passing through a small wood, the trail becomes a *sentier balcon* along the side of some rocky outcrops. One hour 15 minutes after starting the hike, there is a junction, but the signpost can only be seen if approached from the opposite direction. Take a right at the junction and continue westward, now on the GR 58, switchbacking up a slope. The trail passes to the left of a rocky crest, rising over a little pass, the Col de la Lauze (2,076 meters), into the valley of the Furfande. About 2 hours after starting the hike, reach the Refuge de Furfande, beyond which a few old chalets and alpages are scattered up the meadow. (From here, you can turn right to follow the GR 58 up to the Col de Furfande, at 2,500 meters, and then retrace your steps or descend by Les Granges de la Furfande to rejoin the trail below. Although I didn't take this route, I'm told the trail is good.)

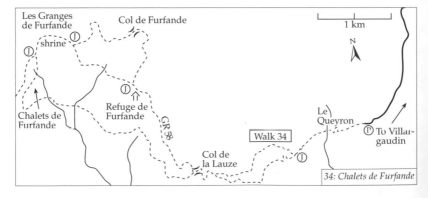

34: Chalets de Furfande

Follow the trail, blazed red and white, or yellow, westward. It curves left (south) around the upper end of the valley, passing to the right of a little stone shrine. At a partially signposted junction, turn left (southeast) onto the path with no sign (the signposts at this junction point only to the Col Garnier and the Col St. Antoine). Cross a brook (easy) and some rivulets, and enter the woods you saw from above. The trail then turns leftward (east), passes between some alpages, and crosses a brook (easy). Just beyond the last farmhouses, the trail, marked with a yellow blaze, begins to climb. It loops around and brings you back to the junction below the Col de la Lauze that you passed earlier. Bear right (east) and descend to Le Queyron.

35. The Col de Malaure

Rating: moderate
Distance round trip: 9 km
High point: 2,536 m

Total climb: 685 m
Time: 2 hours 15 minutes up, 1 hour 30 minutes down

The country above Valpréveyre is quite wild and attractive. Rather than the hike outlined here, you could instead make a circuit by crossing the Col de Bouchet into Italy and returning over the Col de Malaure. This, however, is a tricky route in mist, which is, unfortunately, quite common. The French side can be clear and sunny, while the Italian side is socked in with fog. This is perhaps because of warm air rising from the Po valley that is blocked by the steeper slope of the mountains on the Italian side. The same phenomenon can be seen on the border cols above St.-Véran.

From Abriès on the east side (left bank) of the Bouchet River at the Pont du Bouchet, follow the D441 road 3.9 kilometers to the junction at the edge of the hamlet of Le Roux. Here a sign points right (southeast) to the even smaller hamlet of Valpréveyre, another 2.3 kilometers. There is a large parking area at the road's end beside a campground. As you enter Valpréveyre, turn right and cross a bridge. Here, at a signposted junction, turn left (east) for both the Col de Bouchet and the Col de Malaure. The trail climbs through woods above the stream's left bank. After 20 minutes emerge into a pleasant, broad meadow with high slopes ahead. The trail, nearly level here, soon crosses the stream (easy) and starts upward again,

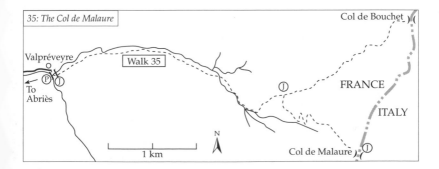

Below the Col de Malaure

becoming steep. About 30 minutes after crossing the stream, at 2,200 meters, there is a cairn and a trail that turns abruptly to the right. There is neither a sign nor a blaze, but this is the way to the Col de Malaure. (The trail heading left—northeast—climbs to the Col de Bouchet.)

Turning right at the cairn, climb steeply to a grassy bowl below the green slopes of an old cirque. The col is above and to the right. After a brief level stretch across this bowl, climb steeply again to reach the col on the Italian border. A stone marker there bears the *fleur-de-lis* of France, the cross of Savoy, and the date 1823.

THE UBAYE

The Ubaye (pronounced "u-bye") was once one of the most god-forsaken corners of France: no one ever came here, and many of its inhabitants, who were few and poor, left to seek better lives elsewhere. It is even now one of the most remote and unknown regions of France—more so than the Queyras today—yet hikers have been finding their way to it. The upper Ubaye is a small wedge of mountainous country between the Queyras and the Mercantour and is sometimes viewed as a sort of lower appendage to the Queyras. The few inhabitants of this high valley consider it wilder, more authentic, more *perdu* than the Queyras: more "out of the way," although *perdu* literally means lost. For centuries, villagers from the upper Ubaye crossed the Col Girardin on a trail that is now part of the GR 5 for the annual pilgrimage to Lac Ste.-Anne, where they were joyfully greeted by the people from Ceillac. The upper Ubaye fits as closely into the alpine range as a well-cut piece fits into a jigsaw puzzle. For these reasons, and because its beautiful terrain and very good hiking deserve to be better known, it is included in this chapter, although it has no park.

The landscape of the upper Ubaye is more rugged and craggy than that of the Queyras upland, giving it a more traditional alpine appearance. Its valleys are deeper and narrower, and it is also somewhat drier.

The charming little town of Barcelonnette, east of the town of Gap on D900, is the gateway to the Ubaye. It derives its name from its thirteenth-century founder, the Comte de Provence et Barcelone. The town has another Hispanic connection: in 1821, when Barcelonnette was a poor place, three of its young men departed to seek their fortune in Mexico, where they enjoyed a commercial success beyond anyone's expectation. This led to a virtual emigration of people from Barcelonnette to Mexico. Some returned to spend their last years in Barcelonnette, building sumptuous villas at the edge of the old town. Family connections have been maintained, and there is still a flow of visitors and commerce between the descendants of the "Barcelonnettes" in Mexico and the people of Barcelonnette.

Attractive as Barcelonnette is, it would take about an hour from there, each way, to reach most trailheads. Hikers will therefore probably wish to stay in the high country above Barcelonnette, where villages are few and poor, and the choice of accommodations very limited, but pleasant. St.-Paul-sur-Ubaye is a simple village at the entrance to the upper valley, with the only grocery of the upper Ubaye and a little museum of the regional rural life. To reach St.-Paul, drive north from Barcelonnette on D900 and then D902. However, the best accommodations as well as the trailheads are still farther, and many hikers find it more convenient to stay at either Fouillouse or Maljasset. Past St.-Paul on D25 and just beyond the hamlets of Petite and Grande Serenne, the road forks, turning right (east) for Fouillouse or continuing to the left (northeast) for Maljasset and Maurin. The distances are not great, and hikers can make their base at either Maljasset or Fouillouse.

A historical note: In these wild, remote mountains one can see sections of the Maginot Line, the chain of fortifications that was built across France after World War I in order to deter any future German attack. At a lonely meadow near Fouillouse, gun turrets protrude slightly from the hillside (see hike 36, The Col du Vallonet and the Col de Mallemort). While it is well known that the Maginot Line did not hold off the Germans (they attacked from the north, where the line had not been extended), it is much less known that one of the Maginot forts succeeded in its job. The defenders of the fort of Roche LaCroix in the upper Ubaye drove back an invading Italian army in 1940. You can visit this subterranean fortress, which is still intact. There are guided tours on Wednesdays and Fridays. To sign up, call or visit any tourist office in the region a day or two in advance.

Walks in the Vallon de Fouillouse

The road to Fouillouse crosses the Pont du Châtelet, a narrow stone bridge that spans a rock-walled gorge 100 meters above the Ubaye River, with one audacious arch. From the road junction, it is 3 kilometers to the hamlet of Fouillouse on a narrow, twisting road that is exposed in several places. People are mindful of this and drive very carefully, slowly, and even courteously.

Fouillouse has one hostelry, a very charming gîte d'étape, with a few private rooms in addition to the dormitories. Because it is on the GR 5 it is much frequented, and many local people drive up here on Sunday afternoons for dinner in its pretty dining room, a converted fourteenth-century *bergerie*, and perhaps a walk. The owners of the gîte are very accommodating to hikers; if you ask them the evening before, they will obtain bread for your next day's picnic lunch or make you a packed lunch.

All hikes from Fouillouse (hikes 36 through 38) begin from the church, which is at the eastern end of the hamlet.

36. The Col du Vallonet and the Col de Mallemort

Rating: moderate to the Col du Vallonet; strenuous to the Col de Mallemort

Distance round trip: 16 km total (10 km round trip to the Col du Vallonet; from there, 6 km round trip to the Col de Mallemort)

High point: 2,524 m at the Col du Vallonet, 2,558 m at the Col de Mallemort

Total climb: 625 m to the Col du Vallonet, 1,108 m to both cols

Time: 2 hours 30 minutes up to the Col du Vallonet, 1 hour 10 minutes down; 1 hour 30 minutes up from the Col du Vallonet to the Col de Mallemort, 1 hour 10 minutes down from the Col de Mallemort to the Col du Vallonet

This is both an interesting and an attractive walk, combining relics of history with a lovely, wild landscape. If you only go as far as the Col du Vallonet, this is still a fine walk.

Old wooden signs beside the church at Fouillouse direct you straight ahead (east) for these cols. Continue on this trail (the GR 5 and also the GR 56); cross a small bridge, but do not turn right at a sign pointing to the Col du Vallonet, *rive gauche* (left bank). The trail rises gently into a broad valley, and after about 1 hour pass a few concrete ruins and the entrance of a tunnel, with 1935 chiseled into its capstone, that burrows into the slope. These are ruins of the famous Maginot Line (see the historical note in the preceding section), marked on the map as Fort de Plate Lombarde. You can peer into the tunnel entrance and see the hooks for the soldiers' coats.

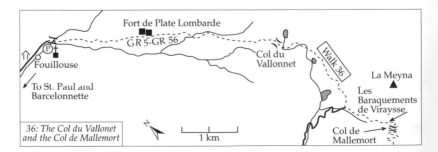

Fort de Plate Lombarde
GR 5-GR 56
Fouillouse
To St. Paul and Barcelonnette
Col du Vallonnet
Walk 36
La Meyna
Les Baraquements de Viraysse
36: The Col du Vallonet and the Col de Mallemort
1 km
Col de Mallemort

Fort de Plate Lombarde, Maginot Line

And if you leave the trail and walk up the slope you will find the old gun turrets above, set into concrete and steel a foot thick. (The Germans did, in fact, reach this valley later in the war and occupied Fouillouse.) Now wildflowers grow in front of the tunnel entrance, and there is absolute silence on the hillside except for the song of birds and the humming of crickets in the long grass.

Continuing southeastward along the trail, pass a *bergerie* and cross a brook (easy), and then cross another on a bridge. About 1 hour 30 minutes after starting the hike, bear right (southeast) at a junction signposted for the Col du Vallonet (this signpost also points left—northwest—to "Chambeyron par la Couletta," but this is incorrect because that trail does not connect at this point). Fifteen minutes later, keep to the right at a junction with no sign. The trail to the col is marked by a red and white blaze. Switchback up a moderately steep slope and reach the Col du Vallonet (2,524 meters) 2 hours 30 minutes after starting the hike. The pointed rocky tower before you is La Meyna (3,067 meters), set in a wild and rugged landscape.

To continue to the Col de Mallemort, descend to the south, then turn left (east) to go around a rocky hump about 20 meters high. Some red and white blazes show the way. The trail continues to the west of La Meyna and joins a jeep road, where a sign points you left (southeast) to the Col de Mallemort. You will pass a large ruined fortified barracks, a remainder of a different era, built in the nineteenth century to protect the border country from a feared invasion by Italians and Austrians. (Another fort is visible on the ridge above.) The trail loops around the southeastern end of this lower fort. From here, a broad gravel road switchbacks gently up to the Col de Mallemort (2,558 meters).

37. The Col de Mirandol

Rating: easy
Distance round trip: 9 km
High point: 2,433 m

Total climb: 535 m
Time: 2 hours 15 minutes up, 1 hour 15 minutes down

This is a very agreeable walk and a fairly easy one—not long and never very steep—leading up to a beautiful, broad meadow with excellent views.

From the church at Fouillouse, head east on the GR 5 and in 10 minutes cross the bridge to your right; a signpost here indicates the Col de Mirandol. Almost immediately cross a second bridge. Walk up the slope about 20 meters (there is a yellow blaze) and immediately turn sharply left (southeast) where several tracks can be seen through the meadow. Walk toward the band of trees along the stream just ahead and to your left, and take the track along the stream's left bank. This takes you to a jeep road; follow it upward. Soon, a signpost points right (south) to the Col de Mirandol. Follow this road upward, past a road barrier and through a woods. Although sections of trail, marked with yellow blazes, cut across the loops of the road, some are steep and a little overgrown, and it is better to take the jeep road.

As you ascend the jeep road, about 1 hour after starting the hike, you will see a sign pointing left to the col. Follow that trail upward and after 15 minutes emerge into an open meadow with extensive views behind you of the Aiguille de Chambeyron (3,412 meters) and the Brec de Chambeyron (3,389 meters) and of La Mortice (3,169 meters) across the Ubaye valley. In the meadow are several yellow blazes on a rock. Follow the track on the left (east) across a vast meadow, marked by occasional yellow or blue blazes. The scene is both gentle and wild. A series of cairns and some more blazes mark the way up to the col with wide-ranging views in several directions.

37: The Col de Mirandol

38. The Refuge du Chambeyron and the Col de la Gypière

Rating: very strenuous
Distance loop trip: 17.5 km
High point: 2,927 m
Total climb: 1,200 m

Time: 3 hours 40 minutes to the Col de la Gypière, 3 hours down by Pas de la Couletta

This is the classic itinerary from Fouillouse, with close views of the two mountains that dominate the Vallon de Fouillouse, the Aiguille de Chambeyron and the Brec de Chambeyron, and the lakes below them. The best-known of these is Lac des Neuf Couleurs (lake of nine colors).

The walk presented here can be shortened by stopping at the Col de la Gypière and returning the way you came. (This hike can be done as a 2-day tour, returning via the Col de Stroppia, but that is said to involve a very steep, rough descent.)

Just past the church at Fouillouse, turn left (north), following the sign for these destinations. At a junction reached in 45 minutes a small wooden sign placed very low to the ground points right (east) to Chambeyron. The trail switchbacks up the slope. In another 45 minutes it joins a broader trail that enters from the left. After a long traverse, taking about 30 minutes, reach the Refuge du Chambeyron at 2,626 meters, about 2 hours 10 minutes after starting the hike. Beside the hut is an azure tarn, Lac Premier, over which towers the Brec de Chambeyron.

From here the trail continues northward, but in a few minutes, turn right (east) at a partially signposted junction. A few cairns and blazes show the way, although it is very clear. Reach another azure lake, Lac Long, and turn left at its southern end where a sign points left (northeast) for Lac des Neuf Couleurs, and right for the Pas de la Couletta (the descent for this itinerary). From here, the trail follows the west shore of Lac Long, then climbs up through a narrow defile. Beyond this, take either trail at an unsigned junction—they merge ahead. As you climb, the long,

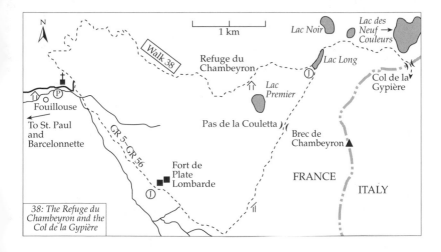

38: The Refuge du Chambeyron and the Col de la Gypière

Homemade apple tarts at the gîte d'étape *in Fouillouse*

sand-colored rock wall of the Aiguille de Chambeyron is to your left, and the tower of the Brec de Chambeyron is to your right. There is a small lake 1 hour beyond the Refuge du Chambeyron; here, take the trail up to the right and continue to a larger lake, Lac des Neuf Couleurs. The trail to the Col de la Gypière is marked by red blazes and starts from the southern edge of the lake, switchbacking up to the southeast on scree. Reach the col (2,927 meters), on the Italian border, 1 hour 30 minutes beyond the Refuge du Chambeyron. The view is good, although not necessarily the best view on this walk.

To return by the Pas de la Couletta, descend back to Lac Long and turn left (southeast) at the signpost. Cairns and a few blazes mark the way, which is a little rough and rocky, but distinct. A trail joins this one from the right (west), and then another trail joins it, coming up from the Refuge du Chambeyron. Thirty minutes beyond Lac Long, reach the Pas de la Couletta (2,752 meters) and descend to the south.

Cross an area of boulders—it will take about 5 minutes to cross it—and descend to a concrete cabin, a *bergerie*. Below this the trail turns right (northwest) to descend the slope on a gradual traverse; you will be able to see the GR 5-GR 56 trail below. Intersect the GR trail near the Fort de Plate Lombarde—the Maginot Line gun emplacements (see hike 36, The Col du Vallonet and the Col de Mallemort)—turn right (northwest), and reach Fouillouse about 2 hours past the Pas de la Couletta. Note: The 1:50,000 map marks this incorrectly; the trail does not descend to the Vallon de Plate Lombarde.

Walks in the Upper Ubaye Valley

From the junction for the road to Fouillouse, turn left on D25 to reach the upper valley of the Ubaye. This is an easier road than the one to Fouillouse, wider and not exposed. After 8 kilometers reach the hamlet of Maljasset, where there is a pleasant gîte d'étape and an alpine club hut, the Refuge du Maljasset, almost next door to each other and both only a few steps from the road. About 0.5 kilometer farther is the hamlet of Maurin; the tall bell tower of its church is a local landmark. After another 0.5 kilometer there is a parking area, beyond which only residents may drive. This parking area is the starting point for two hikes that show different faces of the upper Ubaye.

39. The Col de Mary, the Col de Marinet, and the Lacs de Marinet

Rating: strenuous
Distance loop trip: 17.6 km
High point: 2,787 m
Total climb: 915 m

Time: 2 hours 50 minutes up to the Col de Mary, 40 minutes up to the Col de Marinet, 30 minutes down to the larger Lac de Marinet, 2 hours down

This is a popular walk with a lot of variety, through meadows, over two cols, and past lakes, with a view of one of the few glaciers remaining in the southwestern Alps. It also has historical interest as it takes you along a section of clearly visible Roman road, which linked Rome with ancient Gaul nearly 2,000 years ago. You can, of course, choose to walk only part of the itinerary for a shorter trip, either to the cols and back or to the lakes and back.

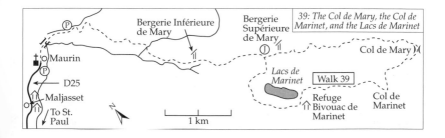

From the parking area across from the church at Maurin, descend on the road (marked by a sign) that leads to the river. Cross the bridge and continue east and southeast along a rough, dirt road bordered with larches. Parking is also allowed down here, and many hikers leave their cars near the river. There is no signpost. The dirt road begins to climb, and you will emerge from the woods into a meadow, where the road becomes a trail. There are scattered red blazes and yellow blazes. Ascend through a narrow valley that widens as you rise into a broader, sloping meadow. Cross a stream (easy). A sign cautions you not to feed the horses as they may bite; horses are kept at a cabin ahead. About 50 minutes after starting the hike, reach a signposted junction; bear left (southeast) for the Col de Mary (the trail to the right—southwest—leads directly to the Lacs de Marinet). Just beyond the cabin is a straight section of regularly placed stones. This is part of the Roman road. Climb a moderately steep section with large boulders strewn around, then emerge into a higher, broad meadow with the Col de Mary in sight ahead, to the southeast. From here, there are sections of Roman road all the way to the col (2,641 meters) on the Italian border, which you will reach about 2 hours 50 minutes after starting the hike.

A signpost points right (west) for the Col de Marinet. The trail ascends along the border ridge, marked by a few red and blue blazes. Cross one section, perhaps 2 meters long, on a very narrow ledge, but the footing is mostly good and there is not much exposure. Reach the Col de Marinet (2,787 meters), also on the border, 40 minutes beyond the Col de Mary.

From the Col de Marinet, you can see the Lacs de Marinet below and to the right (northwest), but there is no signpost. Descend about 5 meters and turn right onto a trail that traverses to the first, and larger, lake. It's a long traverse and the slope becomes shaly; it would be difficult in snow. At the end there is a steep descent. Reach the lake about 30 minutes from the Col de Marinet. Despite the appearance of a track along its eastern shore, the trail passes along the south end of the lake. At the southwestern corner is a small stone cabin, the Refuge Bivouac de Marinet. The trail then passes to the west of the lake and reaches the second, smaller Lac de Marinet. Continue along its eastern shore, then along the right bank of a stream strewn with rocks. Looking back you can see a small glacier, high in the mountain behind you. The trail curves to the right, descends a steep, rocky slope, and crosses the stream below (easy to moderate crossing); in a few more minutes reach the junction for the trail to the Col de Mary. Turn left (northwest) and reach the parking area 2 hours from the larger lake.

40. The Col de Longet

Rating: strenuous
Distance round trip: 24 km
High point: 2,660 m

Total climb: 800 m
Time: 4 hours 30 minutes up, 3 hours 30 minutes down

This is a very long walk—so long that many hikers will only want to do part of the walk—but you can still get a good view if you cut short your hike. The very last segment of the walk is the same as that part of hike 22,

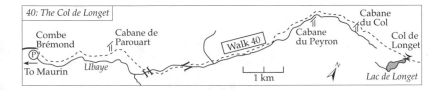

Tour de la Tête des Toillies (Tête Noire), from St.-Véran after the descent from the Col de la Noire to the valley below.

From the parking area across from the church in Maurin, continue farther down the same road, eastward (do not descend to the bridge and river below). In about 7 minutes reach the hamlet of Combe Brémond, where the road ends, becoming a trail; there is no signpost. Continue on this trail, marked by a few yellow blazes. Below to your right is the Ubaye River. After a stony area, cross a bridge to your right. Turn sharply left (northeast) and continue above the left bank of the stream. The trail now passes through a narrow defile, traversing the slope, which is eroded in places; the delicate part of the traverse takes about 10 to 15 minutes. After this, the trail emerges into a broad, upper valley. About 45 minutes after starting the hike, a sign points left (northeast) for the Col de Longet. Cross a bridge to your left, and turn right, continuing up the right bank. The valley is long and deserted, but you'll pass a few stone cabins and some ruins. Alongside the trail are rocks with initials and dates carved into them, such as 1864, 1867, and 1808—made, perhaps, by the shepherds who once watched their flocks here. (Sheep are still brought here to graze.) The trail climbs at a moderate grade, curving to the east. "La Noire" is blazed on a rock to your left; above to the north is the Col de la Noire, from which hikers on hike 22 from St.-Véran descend into this valley. About 4 hours after starting the hike, reach the first of the series of lakes that extend to the col, about 30 minutes farther. Even from the first lake, there is a very good view of the mountains across the col.

PARC NATIONAL DES ECRINS

The largest national park in France, although virtually unknown in the United States, the Ecrins contains some of the glories of the French Alps. The country's three highest mountains outside of the Mont Blanc massif are found here in the Dauphiné Alps amid an abundance of other peaks and glaciers. Until France annexed the Savoie in the nineteenth century, gaining Mont Blanc in the process, the highest French mountain was the Barre des Ecrins (4,102 meters). La Meije (3,983 meters) is only a few meters short of the magic alpine number 4,000, but it is more celebrated in the history of mountaineering than many other peaks that top the 4,000-meter mark. It was the last of the great alpine peaks to be climbed in the nineteenth century during the golden age of mountaineering. Mont Pelvoux (3,932 meters) completes the trio.

With its narrow valleys scooped out below huge mountains ringed with glaciers, the Ecrins presents a true high-alpine landscape. The park is unusual not only for the height of its peaks but also for the sheer extent of these glaciers: 12,000 hectares are covered by ice. It is the most southerly area in the entire alpine chain with such extensive glaciation.

The areas within the Dauphiné Alps to which hikers are drawn are also largely unspoiled. La Grave, the only community mentioned in this chapter that is larger than a village, is a small, quiet alpine town with none of the slickness of a fashionable ski resort.

Created in 1973, the park's 91,700 hectares extend across the crown of the Dauphiné Alps. The title Dauphin, which literally means "dolphin," was used for the first time (no one knows why) by a lord of this region in the Middle Ages, and his lands became the "Dauphiné." Eventually, a descendant burdened with debts sold the territory to the king of France. The title was thereafter used for the king's eldest son—the Gallic Prince of Wales.

Since the heart of the Ecrins is a dense cluster of massive peaks and glaciers, no road or even hiking trail traverses the entire park. Only a trained alpinist, equipped for ice and rock, can cross from one valley to the next. The central Ecrins can, however, be approached by road from the south, west, north, and east. You can make a base in any or each of the valleys that enters the park from these directions and take numerous day trips into the mountains. The valley that extends along the southern Ecrins is the Valgaudemar; to the west is the Vallée du Vénéon; to the north, the Romanche; and to the east, the Vallouise. In each valley, there are villages or hamlets where accommodations are available.

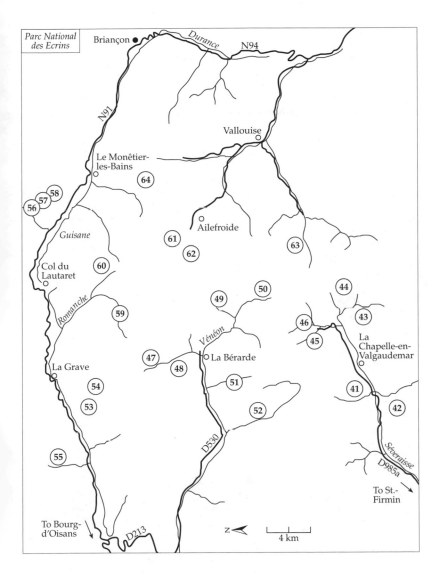

SOUTHERN ECRINS

The Valgaudemar evidently bears the name of Gaudemar, a Burgundian chieftain of the sixth century A.D. The river that drains this valley is the Séveraisse; it has cut an exceptionally deep bed, so the valley walls rise some 2,000 meters above it. Lionel Terray, the celebrated French guide and climber, called it "the lowest valley of the high mountains."

St.-Firmin, just off N85, is at the entrance to the Valgaudemar. From there, D985a extends northeast to La Chapelle-en-Valgaudemar. Several small, quiet villages along the lower part of the valley offer accommodations, yet most guests stay in La Chapelle-en-Valgaudemar, itself a simple, modest village with a hotel on its main street. Although La Chapelle-en-Valgaudemar is essentially a farming village, not a resort, vacationers are drawn here by several large camping areas, its position as the highest village in the valley, and its unassuming charm. There is also a gîte d'étape in the village and another somewhat farther up the road, D480, at Le Casset. There is cross-country skiing but not downhill skiing in the valley, a factor that has certainly preserved its quiet charm.

A few of the distinctive, traditional Valgaudemar farmhouses have survived the principal destructive forces of fire, avalanches, and floods. The houses are large, rectangular structures made of fieldstone, with living quarters, barn, and stable all under the same steeply pitched, thatched roof. A large arch shelters the front door, next to which exterior stairs lead up to the hayloft. A small raised panel in the roof protects the steps and the loft entrance.

You can walk or drive the 2 kilometers directly south of La Chapelle-en-Valgaudemar up the small Vallon de Navette to the hamlet of Les Portes, a tiny, sweet, and simple place where you can see a few of these traditional houses. A sign here announces that you are inside the Zone Périphérique of the national park and that picking mushrooms and gathering snails are forbidden. Just past the hamlet is Les Oulles du Diable, where an arched stone bridge spans the stream that charges tumultuously

La Chapelle-en-Valgaudemar

through a narrow channel. Be careful to stay on the path; the slopes are steep, and the rocks above this torrent are very slippery.

The paved road, D480, continues eastward beyond La Chapelle-en-Valgaudemar along the right bank of the river and past a tiny cluster of houses at Le Casset. A bridge leads across the river to another hamlet, Le Bourg. The main road, however, continues eastward along the right bank and climbs to Le Gioberney, which you reach in about 20 minutes (9 kilometers) from La Chapelle-en-Valgaudemar. Past Le Casset the road becomes narrow (although two cars can certainly pass each other) and steep, with no railing or barrier for much of the way, and there is an increasingly steep drop to the valley below. Mindful of the dangers, everyone I saw drove very carefully. Part way up the road along the inside shoulder is a space for parking for the Refuge du Xavier-Blanc (Le Clot). There is a much larger parking area nearly at the end of the road.

Walks from La Chapelle-en-Valgaudemar

41. The Refuge de l'Olan

Rating: strenuous
Distance round trip: 4 km
High point: 2,345 m

Total climb: 1,250 m
Time: 3 hours 30 minutes up, 2 hours 30 minutes down

This route is quite simple—it goes almost straight up from the valley to the hut. Start early since the trail is in the sun all day and can be very warm. There is no particular difficulty on the trail; it is strenuous because of the unrelenting climb.

The trailhead is about 300 meters outside La Chapelle-en-Valgaudemar on D480, the road toward Le Gioberney. The parking area is just past the second bridge beyond the village, on your left (the northern side of the valley), marked by trail signs. The way starts up along the left bank of the

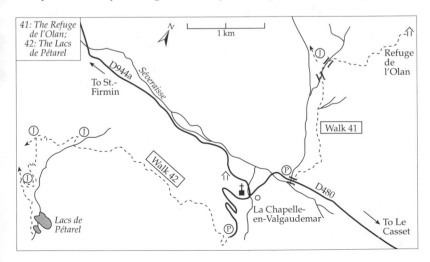

41: The Refuge de l'Olan; 42: The Lacs de Pétarel

stream, toward a vigorous waterfall that you can see above. At the sign indicating the park boundary, the trail begins to switchback up the slope, staying on the left bank of the stream. A signpost points to the Refuge de l'Olan. More cascades can be seen to the right, above. After 1 hour 20 minutes cross a bridge below a thundering waterfall. It takes about 10 minutes to cross a section of trail covered with small, round stones. About 1 hour 30 minutes after the start of the hike, come to a junction, the only one on this route; take the fork to the right (northeast), signposted for the hut and the Pas de l'Olan.

As the trail continues its steep climb, views open up of the mountains on the other side of the Valgaudemar. Cross a tributary stream on a bridge: there is another waterfall just above to your left. The trail continues to switchback up through the grassy slopes, crossing occasional rocky ribs and ledges, but you never have to use your hands and the trail is not exposed. For the last half hour of the hike you can see the hut above you, a long stone building with a flat roof. The trail bears to the right around a rocky promontory, but soon a wooden sign bars this little path and informs you that you are not on the path for the hut and that you should make a half-turn and follow the white arrows. This requires you to climb up a bit on rock. You can, instead, go around to the left, following traces of a trail and a few cairns, and end up just above the roof of the hut. By taking a few steps to the left, you can walk down to the hut. It is situated on a long ledge facing the Valgaudemar, with a view up the Vallon de Navette to Le Vieux Chaillol (3,163 meters). Since the hut is built into the slope (for protection against avalanches), you have to walk back up behind it to see the broad cirque and the mountains above it. The big rocky mountain is the Pic de l'Olan (3,564 meters) and the pointed one to the right (east) is the Cime du Vallon (3,409 meters).

42. The Lacs de Pétarel

Rating: moderate
Distance round trip: 11.5 km
High point: 2,090 m

Total climb: 845 m
Time: 3 hours up, 2 hours 35 minutes down

This walk faces the Pic de l'Olan, across the valley. It is also possible to ascend to the Lacs de Pétarel from Les Andrieux, just west of La Chapelle-en-Valgaudemar, but more of that trail is in woods, whereas this itinerary gives you a good view of the upper Valgaudemar. The Lacs de Pétarel are two small lakes, one above the other, in a wild setting. When you reach the lakes, however, the view of the upper valley is closed off.

There is only one road through La Chapelle-en-Valgaudemar, but it is identified by two numbers: it is D944a to the west of the village, and D480 to the east of it. Heading eastward into La Chapelle-en-Valgaudemar, turn right just before the bridge that is in the center of the village and pass a church; a sign indicates Les Portes and Pont des Oulles. A narrow, paved road climbs 1.4 kilometers to the hamlet of Les Portes; there is a small parking area just before the first houses.

From here, a signpost points right (west) to the lakes. The path climbs moderately steeply through meadows for about 25 minutes and then traverses through woods and again through meadows. It is occasionally narrow, crossing a few exposed ledges, but never very delicate. About 1 hour 40 minutes after starting the hike, turn left (southwest) at a junction; a signpost indicates the lakes. Ascend a ridge line through woods to a signposted junction, at which you turn left (east) for the lakes (the trail to the right leads to La Muande). Switchback up out of the woods; there is a somewhat faded blaze on a rock to your left after you leave the woods. After passing a shortcut that ascends the slope, keep climbing upward in the same direction toward which the shortcut pointed, and reach the lakes.

Walks from Le Clot (Xavier-Blanc) and Gioberney

The finest walks in the Valgaudemar begin at the upper end of the valley road, D480. You can start the walks to the Refuges de Vallonpierre and Chabournéou from either Le Clot or Gioberney.

Near the upper end of D480 is a CAF hut, the Refuge du Xavier-Blanc, now officially called the Refuge du Clot. The change of name came about because the CAF altered its policy and no longer allows huts to be named after people. It is important to mention both names here, however, as some people still call it Xavier-Blanc, and you may see it under either name on maps and signs and in telephone directories. About 7 kilometers to the east, past the bridge leading out of La Chapelle-en-Valgaudemar over the Séveraisse, there is a widening in the road, which serves as the hut parking area. From there, take the gravel trail down from the road and reach the hut in 10 minutes. It is quite charming, both indoors and out, in a very pretty location on a bank above the Séveraisse. The dining room has a little stone fireplace and red-and-white-checked tablecloths. The guardians, M. and Mme. Pochon, have arranged all the hut shoes on shelves according to size so you do not have to rummage for two that are the same size. Here we were served not the standard four-course hut meal but five courses, including a tuna-tomato salad between the soup and the meat.

After the turnoff for the Refuge du Clot, the road switchbacks steeply upward to a larger parking area next to a trailhead and then terminates at a large structure, the Chalet-Hôtel du Gioberney. Its location is spectacular, surrounded by four high valleys, with the big, multi-turreted peak of Le Sirac (3,440 meters) to the south, Les Bans (3,669 meters) to the east, Les Rouies (3,589 meters) to the north, and the Pointe de la Muande (3,315 meters) to the west. Nearby is a beautiful, high waterfall, Le Voile de la Mariée (bridal veil). Many tourists and hikers who are not staying here come up for the view or to enjoy a drink on the terrace.

Four stories high, the Chalet-Hôtel du Gioberney is unlike any other refuge in the Alps. It was built in 1942 by the Vichy government so that young men could avoid being sent to work in Germany. The road up, however, was only built in 1960. The French government gave it to the Touring Club de France in 1967, but it went bankrupt. In 1980, the government let its Ministère de la Jeunesse et des Sports (Ministry of Youth and Sport) run the place; it was again contracted out to a private group who let the facility run down until it became a virtual dump. The people of the district were unhappy with this state of affairs, and when the French government changed in 1992, the people of the Valgaudemar were allowed to take it over. They have thoroughly cleaned it and are now completely renovating the building, which will be finished in 1995 or 1996; all private rooms should be ready by 1994 and all dormitories by 1995. Since they are doing one section at a time, some accommodations will be available throughout this period, and the dining room is also open. In the future, guided hikes and tours will be run from here.

43. The Refuge de Vallonpierre

Rating: moderate
Distance round trip: 10 km
High point: 2,280 m

Total climb: 930 m
Time: 3 hours 15 minutes up, 2 hours 15 minutes down

The Refuge de Vallonpierre (on some maps spelled "Vallompierre") enjoys a spectacular location facing the whole range of mountains along the southern edge of the Ecrins. It can be reached either from the Refuge du Clot, or from the trailhead next to the parking lot below the Chalet-Hôtel du Gioberney. Although the directions given here start from and return to the Refuge du Clot, you can also do this hike from the Chalet-Hôtel du Gioberney or start at the Refuge du Clot and end at the Chalet-Hôtel du Gioberney, or vice versa. Note: Some hikers traverse between the Refuge de Vallonpierre and the Refuge de Chabournéou on a connecting trail, but this is considered dangerous when there is snow on the route.

From the Refuge du Clot, walk out the door and turn left. A level path leads northeast along the right bank of the Séveraisse. In 15 minutes cross a bridge. On your left is a stone ruin. Soon, a wooden sign points left to the GR 54, which you join here. The trail proceeds along the edge of a big meadow. Stone walls on your left are the remains of the hamlet of Le Clot, destroyed by fire in 1934. Continue southeast on a track through this meadow, with a very fine view of Les Rouies glacier above to your left. As the valley narrows the slope steepens and the meadow disappears. After

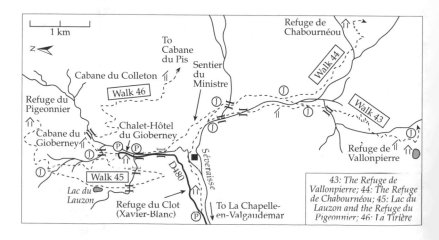

43: The Refuge de Vallonpierre; 44: The Refuge de Chabournéou; 45: Lac du Lauzon and the Refuge du Pigeonnier; 46: La Tirière

Refuge de Vallonpierre

30 minutes you are facing Le Sirac, a multi-turreted peak whose name means six dents—six teeth—in local dialect. There are wonderful views of that and other mountains along the trail. (At 1,522 meters, a path comes in from your left—southeast—that connects to the Sentier du Ministre. This is one of two ways to the Chalet-Hôtel du Gioberney from the Le Clot–Vallonpierre trail.)

About 35 minutes after the start of the hike, reach a junction. The path to the left (southwest) climbs up to the Cabane de Pis, the Glacier d'Aupillous, and the Refuge du Chabournéou. Continue straight ahead (south) along the right bank of the stream. A short section of the trail here is eroded and narrow. Forty-five minutes from the start of the hike, cross a bridge and continue through lovely meadows full of rusty alpenrose. The trail soon dips a little to cross another bridge to the left bank, along which the trail continues on a fairly level stretch through the meadows, with a cliff to your right. Then the trail begins to climb at a moderate grade.

Pass a stone hut to the right (1,650 meters) belonging to the park warden. Behind you and to the left is a view of Les Aupillous. At 1,670 meters, come to a junction; a sign points left (northeast) to the Chalet-Hôtel du Gioberney, or right (southeast) to the Refuge de Vallonpierre. As the trail climbs gently, a splendid broad cirque appears on your left below Le Sirac. Cross the stream on another bridge and climb generally south. About 1 hour 15 minutes beyond the warden's hut, at 2,050 meters, cross the stream on stones. Then switchback up the fairly steep slope. At 2,200 meters, pass another small stone hut on your right. Reach a beautiful meadow with a sign pointing right to the Refuge de Vallonpierre, left to the Refuge de Chabournéou. Turn right here and cross the meadow to reach the hut, beside a tiny pond. The view is splendid, a skyline full of alpine peaks, including the peak and glacier of Les Rouies, the Pic du Says, the Pic des Aupillous, and the Pic Jocelme.

44. The Refuge de Chabournéou

Rating: moderate   **Total climb:** 620 m
Distance round trip: 11 km   **Time:** 2 hours 10 minutes up, 2 hours
High point: 2,150 m   down

The Refuge de Chabournéou and the Refuge de Vallonpierre are at opposite ends of the curving wall of mountains that culminates in Le Sirac with its multiple peaks, but these two huts offer a different visual perspective. The Refuge de Chabournéou gives a view that is closer in to the mountains but less panoramic than the view from the Refuge de Vallonpierre.

Start at the parking lot at 1,580 meters, just below the Chalet-Hôtel du Gioberney, and cross the stream on a bridge. The trail descends a little, then traverses a narrow, rather exposed section to reach a junction in 25 minutes. (The trail to the right descends sharply and leads to the Refuge du Clot.) Continue on the trail to the left and cross a second bridge. After a fairly level stretch through broad meadows the trail turns left to begin a long traverse along the east side of the valley, climbing gently. This section is not exposed although it climbs at a moderate grade, sometimes on stones. Fifty minutes after the start of the hike come to a signposted junction (1,660 meters); take the upper trail to the left (southeast). (The lower trail heads right, southwest, to the Refuge de Vallonpierre.) Soon afterward the trail curves gently southeast into the valley of the stream descending from Le Sirac; there is a fine view of the broad north face of that mountain. One hour 30 minutes after the start of the hike, cross the stream on a bridge. The trail then switchbacks upward at a moderate grade to reach the hut, perched on a promontory. It offers a splendid view of Le Sirac, a big mass with its crest of six teeth. A few small glaciers cling to its upper reaches.

There is a grand but different view from a charming meadow about 70 meters higher. Take the little trail behind the hut, which climbs past a ruined stone cabin. In 15 minutes reach this meadow on a high shelf, offering a better view of the Pic Jocelme, the Pic du Loup, and the Pic Verdon. Moreover, from here you can see the Pic du Chabournéou, which you cannot see from the hut. However, you cannot see Le Sirac from this shelf.

45. Lac du Lauzon and the Refuge du Pigeonnier

Rating: easy to Lac du Lauzon, moderate on continuation to the Refuge du Pigeonnier
Distance loop trip: 8 km
High point: 2,070 m at Lac du Lauzon, 2,400 m at the Refuge du Pigeonnier

Total climb: 500 m to Lac du Lauzon, plus 380 m to the Refuge du Pigeonnier
Time: 1 hour to Lac du Lauzon, another 2 hours 15 minutes to the Refuge du Pigeonnier, 2 hours down

This excursion climbs first to a lake above the west side of the valley, then traverses to a hut above its east side and returns to the Chalet-Hôtel du Gioberney. The traverse to the hut has a few difficult passages with exposure. You can do either section alone, however, as a round trip.

Just behind the Chalet-Hôtel du Gioberney are signposts marking the park boundary and the trailhead. Take the trail first to the north, then left (west) to Lac du Lauzon. The trail is well signposted. The trail switchbacks up the western slope of the valley at a moderate grade. After 30 minutes cross a stream on a bridge. About 25 minutes later reach a broad meadow. The lake cannot be seen at first, so continue northward toward the big wall of mountains. Cross a stream on another little bridge and follow the dirt track. To the left is a magnificent rock wall streaked with waterfalls. Soon you will reach Lac du Lauzon, at 2,010 meters. The view here is spectacular, as you are surrounded by snow-streaked mountains—literally, 360 degrees around you.

The trail continues past the lake toward a shoulder. Head north toward a splendid cirque, climbing up to 2,070 meters, then descending a little. At 2,020 meters, 25 minutes after leaving the lake, there is a junction; go left (north) for the Refuge du Pigeonnier. You could also turn right (south) here to descend to the Chalet-Hôtel du Gioberney. Several large snow bridges cover the stream here, and a sign warns you to be careful and not linger on the *pont de neige*. The lower snow bridge normally disappears by the end of July; later in the season you must hop across this stream on stones. The hut keeper told me that a park warden checks the thickness of the snow bridge before it collapses and throws more rocks into the stream if necessary to create more stepping points. The path continues up on switchbacks. You will come to a stream and see a little path across on the other side. Do not take it; instead, keep climbing up on the right bank of the stream. The trail ascends steeply first north, then east. About 30 minutes beyond the snow bridges, at 2,160 meters, cross a tributary stream on stones. There is a beautiful cascade just above you to your left. Continue upward; in another 40 minutes, just below the hut, there is a big slab of rock at 2,390 meters. The trail, quite exposed, passes to the right of the large rock; exercise care here. (You can also climb directly over this rock.) Reach the hut at 2,400 meters, in another 10 minutes. The view from the hut is not actually as good as the one from Lac du Lauzon, with its 360-degree view of mountains.

Shepherd near the Chalet-Hôtel du Gioberney

After about 65 minutes of descent reach the junction after the snow bridges (at 2,020 meters); take the lower trail, to the left, to return to the Chalet-Hôtel du Gioberney. The trail switchbacks down quite steeply and is a little rough, eroded, and narrow in places.

46. La Tirière

Rating: moderate
Distance round trip: 8 km
High point: 2,251 m

Total climb: 640 m
Time: 2 hours 10 minutes up, 1 hour 15 minutes down

This trail departs from the Chalet-Hôtel du Gioberney in a southwesterly direction and climbs the shoulder of Le Colleton. At the top of the trail is an abandoned stone hut, the Cabane du Colleton. This hike can be made into a loop trip by continuing past this hut; the trail beyond it descends southwest toward the Cabane du Pis. It reaches a streambed, the Ravin de la Beaumette, then turns west, descending to a section of trail called the Sentier du Ministre. The trail turns northwest and leads to the Chalet-Hôtel du Gioberney parking lot. Just past the Cabane du Colleton, however, is a short (20 meters) but very badly eroded, tricky section of trail; this section is not marked. After that it improves, and the Sentier du Ministre, although narrow, is a good trail. If you should take this route beyond the Cabane du Colleton, count on 2 hours 30 minutes for the return trip.

From the trailhead directly behind the Chalet-Hôtel du Gioberney, take the signposted trail to the right, above the right bank of the stream. In about 20 minutes, there is a signposted junction; turn right (east) for La Tirière. This descends and crosses the stream on a bridge. Once across, do not take the very clear trail that descends through larch woods along the stream's left bank, back toward the Chalet-Hôtel du Gioberney. Take an upper trail instead, heading southeast; if you find yourself in the larch woods, you are on the wrong trail. This junction may be churned up by sheep for about 20 meters, so you must look carefully for the way: do not go toward the wall of mountains upstream, and do not go through the larches next to the stream.

The trail, once established, rises over a grassy shoulder with masses of rusty alpenrose. The shoulder offers a good view behind you of Les Rouies and before you of Le Sirac. The path, sometimes a track through the grass, winds around the shoulder. About 1 hour 35 minutes from the start of the hike, the trail crosses a small talus slope and traverses toward Le Sirac. The trail is good although only wide enough for one person, with the slope falling steeply away to your right. After another 20 minutes the slope becomes less steep as you reach a meadow. Climb a few switchbacks, passing the stone ruins of some shepherds' huts, and in another 10 minutes reach the Cabane du Colleton, a small stone cabin with a tin roof. The scene is wild and the views lovely.

WESTERN ECRINS

The Vallée du Vénéon cuts deeply into the center of the Ecrins, offering the closest approach to its highest mountains from the west. The star attraction is La Bérarde, a tiny hamlet at the upper end of the valley and one of France's premier mountaineering centers. From La Bérarde, climbers can reach nearly every one of the highest mountains in the Dauphiné Alps, and hikers can get a good view of most of them.

The road up the Vénéon valley, D530, begins at Le Clapier, a small town at the western end of the Romanche valley a few kilometers east of Bourg-d'Oisans. The entire road is 26 kilometers long, and it takes about 50 minutes to drive to the end. If you are driving, you should fill your gas tank in Bourg-d'Oisans, since there is no gas station on the road up the Vallée du Vénéon. There also is no bank in the valley.

There are several villages and hamlets along the valley, many of which offer accommodations. Perched up on a slope near the entrance to the valley is the picturesque village of Venosc, with its narrow streets and fourteenth-century belltower. Several artisans have opened attractive little shops in Venosc. Just below Venosc, on the road, is Le Bourg d'Arud, where a small seventeenth-century château has been turned into a hotel. The road at first runs along the riverbank, but then the valley narrows and the road begins to climb alongside the valley's northern wall. Halfway up the valley is St.-Christophe-en-Oisans, the highest village here accessible in winter, and the birthplace of Père Gaspard, sometimes called Gaspard de la Meije, the famous mountain guide who led the first successful climb of La Meije. A memorial in front of the church commemorates St. Christophe's most famous son. In the little graveyard behind the church, several fallen alpinists are buried.

Beyond St.-Christophe the road narrows down to one lane, with tremendous exposure to one side—a long, sheer drop to the valley floor below. Along this stretch are numerous "garages," meaning lay-bys, places where you can pull in to allow another car to pass. These are indicated by signs. The road is gradually being improved and when the work is completed it will be two lanes wide all the way to the end. Perhaps people will then relax their guard a little and the road may become more dangerous; at present, everyone drives slowly and very cautiously.

Finally the road levels out as it meets the streambed with a large campground on its grassy bank, beyond which is a pleasant gîte d'étape with a restaurant. Just past the gîte a bridge leads into La Bérarde, where the road ends. The hamlet consists of a couple of small, simple hotels and restaurants, a tiny grocery/general store, a church, a small information center, and a guides' office. At the end of the little street is a Poste de Secours and next to that, the Centre Alpin du CAF (also called the CAF Centre de la Bérarde, or the Club Alpin de la Bérarde), one of the handful of alpine club huts that can be reached by road. Many hikers and climbers spend a night here upon arrival before heading up to the huts in the mountains. For those who are thinking of making the Centre Alpin their base, note that guests are limited to three overnights. If you drive into La Bérarde, bear right for the large parking area at the southern edge of the hamlet, beside the stream.

For hundreds of years, La Bérarde was a year-round village, dependent on its dairy cattle, sheep, and goats, and on the oats, barley, and rye that could be grown at this altitude. Now the road is left unplowed once the snow begins to fall and only one old shepherd still lives in La Bérarde through the winter. Tiny as this place is, a visitor feels the weight of its mountaineering history. Plaques along the outside wall of the Centre Alpin du CAF recall the passage of Edward Whymper, celebrated for the first ascent of the Matterhorn, and his companions through this valley. The young Whymper was blazing his way into the annals of alpinism. On June 23, 1864, Whymper along with two friends and a pair of Swiss guides made the first traverse of the Brèche de la Meije, thus crossing from La Grave to La Bérarde. On June 25 they made the first ascent of the north face of the Barre des Ecrins, crossing from La Bérarde to Vallouise, and 2 days after that, the first traverse of the East Col of Les Bans, bringing them back from the Vallouise area to the Vénéon valley.

"Notre Dame des Glaciers, Protégez les Voyageurs," reads the plea above the door of the little chapel at La Bérarde, and the walls, inside and out, are hung with plaques. One commemorates the first ascent of La Meije, which was made from La Bérarde (not La Grave) in 1877, by a French team consisting of E. Boileau de Castelnau and J. B. Rodier, led by two guides from St.-Christophe, Pierre Gaspard and his son. Numerous other plaques memorialize less-successful climbers who died on these mountains.

The Poste de Secours is a mountain rescue station. In Switzerland alpine rescues are performed by guides, but in France they are carried out by special units of both the national police (CRS) and the gendarmerie, a quasi-military force, that perform rescues at the government's expense. At La Bérarde the two units alternate at this task.

You can reach La Bérarde from Grenoble by bus. From early July to early September, Autocars VFD offers a connection between Grenoble and the hamlet, with a stop at Bourg-d'Oisans.

47. The Refuge du Châtelleret

Rating: easy   **Total climb:** 580 m
Distance round trip: 7 km   **Time:** 2 hours 25 minutes up, 1 hour
High point: 2,232 m   50 minutes down

Few walks in the western Alps as easy as this one yield such a splendid sight: the grand south face of La Meije. Seen from La Grave to the north, La Meije is a pinnacled crest of rock rising above steep hanging glaciers; from here in the south, with more of its rock exposed, it presents a mass of awesomely sheer, stark walls.

You can get onto the trail to the Refuge du Châtelleret from both ends of La Bérarde. For the main point of departure, cross the bridge on the only road leading out of La Bérarde toward St.-Christophe. The trailhead is just past the bridge, to the right, and the directions given here are from this starting point. You can also connect with the main trail by taking a path behind the chapel. A signpost for it is attached to the little wood

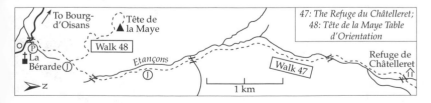

cabin beside the chapel, which serves as the guides' office (Bureau des Guides du Vénéon).

The broad trail just past the bridge switchbacks up along the right bank of the Torrent des Etançons, beside a few old stone walls. In 10 minutes pass a signpost for the Refuge du Châtelleret and also the Refuge du Promontoire. The stream, to your right, flows through a small gorge. Enter the park in another 10 minutes. Continue up on switchbacks; about 35 minutes from the start of the hike is a signposted junction. Take the trail to the right (northwest); the way to the left (west) climbs to the Tête de la Maye (see hike 48, Tête de la Maye Table d'Orientation). The trail soon descends a few meters to cross the stream on a bridge, then turns left (north). There is no signpost here. Proceed at an almost level grade along a lovely, grassy bank with a few small white birches, alders, juniper, and rusty alpenrose. Despite rock walls to each side, the valley is broad enough to be sunny, and the scene is very agreeable. About 1 hour from the start of the hike, the other path from La Bérarde joins this one, from the right.

As you approach a cascade on the wall to your right, the trail skirts below a talus slope and begins to climb gently. Cross a little sidestream on a bridge. One hour 15 minutes from the start of the hike (1,980 meters), at another bridge, a sign points right (north) to the hut. Follow more gentle switchbacks through a talus slope. You can now see La Meije ahead; it takes some concentration not to trip over a stone as you enjoy the increas-

On the route to the Refuge du Châtelleret

ingly grand view of the mountain. Moreover, to the sides of the trail are hanging valleys crowned with snowy, sharply pointed peaks. Almost 2 hours from the start of the hike cross the stream on a bridge to its right bank (signposted to the hut). Climb a stony but broad trail of gentle grade, cross another bridge, and reach the hut in a minute.

The hut faces down the valley with its back to La Meije. You can walk a little farther behind it toward the mountain on traces of trail until they disappear. La Meije here is a multi-turreted peak with great, vertical rock walls and a broad skirt of glaciers. You can spot the Refuge du Promontoire perched on a rocky ledge and accessible only by some climbing.

48. La Tête de la Maye Table d'Orientation

Rating: strenuous
Distance round trip: 5 km
High point: 2,517 m
Total climb: 830 m
Time: 2 hours 30 minutes up, 2 hours 30 minutes down

This itinerary is popular because it leads to the top of a small mountain, La Tête de la Maye (pronounced "mye"), via its east face. A second route, via the south face, is a climb.

This small mountain is just sufficiently isolated so that it gives a completely panoramic view of all the mountains around La Bérarde. The view is indeed excellent, and other hikers or local people may tell you that the hike is a "must." This route is different, however, from every other hike described in this book. Not just one but several sections require a little climbing—scrambling—and there are fixed cables or metal rungs bolted into the rock to assist you. One step near the top has no fixed cable, although it should. Some French hikers would deny that there is any serious difficulty on this route as long as one is careful. All would agree, however, that it should not be done in wet weather or by persons subject to vertigo. When they want to dismiss the suggestion of difficulties on a route, they often say that even children do it, and this is a prime example of what we have come to call a *même les enfants* route.

How dangerous is this route? I attempted to find out by inquiring at the Poste de Secours in La Bérarde. A gendarme checked his record books listing every mountain accident for the last 32 years and reported nothing more serious than a scratch or graze. But that was only half the story; the gendarmerie and the CRS keep separate record books and neither agency has access to the other's. The next morning the CRS arrived for their week on duty. A CRS man did not check their books but said he'd heard of a few serious accidents and observed that he would not take a child up that route, or would do so only if the child were on a short rope.

Wet rock is dangerous, and this is obviously not a route to take on a day when the weather looks threatening. Note also that the descent will take as long as the ascent.

On top of the mountain is an orientation table, identifying all the peaks visible (and some that are not visible) from this perch. Some signposts for this route therefore say "Tête de la Maye Table d'Orientation," to distinguish it from the climbing route up the mountain.

Start as for hike 47, The Refuge du Châtelleret. After about 20 minutes you will pass a Parc National des Ecrins sign; a moment after that, reach a signposted junction at 1,920 meters. Turn left here for La Tête de la Maye Table d'Orientation. After this there are no more junctions and so this cannot be confused with any other route.

After about 25 minutes of hiking steeply upward, reach the first difficult section on rock, about 50 meters long, which may take 25 or 30 minutes. If you have any doubts about your abilities, turn around here. You must watch for red blazes, which are sometimes rather faded. After this section on rock, resume hiking on trail. In about another half hour, you must scramble up ledges for about 20 meters; there is a bit of chimney here, and a fixed cable. Another section of trail is followed by yet another scramble on rock. About 2 hours 15 minutes from the trailhead, reach a shoulder with a sign pointing west to Tête de la Maye Table d'Orientation, indicating that this is 10 minutes away. The trail rounds the shoulder for a few meters, then rises; there's a little more scrambling before you reach the summit.

49. The Refuge Temple-Ecrins

Rating: moderate   **Total climb:** 700 m
Distance round trip: 6 km   **Time:** 2 hours 45 minutes up, 2 hours
High point: 2,410 m   5 minutes down

Another fine walk but with a steep climb at the end, this gives superb views of the big peaks and glaciers south of La Bérarde.

Walk out of La Bérarde past the CAF refuge, heading southeast on a broad, level, easy trail along the right bank of the Vénéon. Cross a small tributary stream on a little bridge and soon come to a junction; a bridge leads to the left bank of the river and an alternative route to the Refuge de la Pilatte. Stay, however, on the right bank, which is the main route to that hut as well as the only way to the Refuge Temple-Ecrins. A few minutes later come to a broad place with a sign that says "Plan du Carrelet, Alt. 1881." This is the confluence of several valleys, with big, triangular rock peaks standing at the corners. About 10 minutes beyond here is the pri-

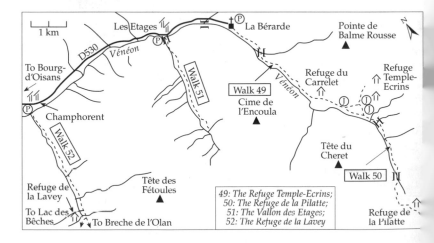

vately owned Refuge du Carrelet; it takes about 1 hour 10 minutes to reach this hut. The view is dominated by L'Ailefroide (3,953 meters) to the southeast and a view up the Vallon de Chardon to the southwest.

Ten minutes past the Refuge du Carrelet, come to the junction of the trails to the Refuge Temple-Ecrins (left, northeast) and the Refuge de la Pilatte (right, southeast). (You can also reach the Refuge Temple-Ecrins from a point about 15 minutes' walk farther up along the trail toward the Refuge de la Pilatte; the junction is signposted.) Take the trail to the left. Cross a bridge and begin a fairly steep ascent, soon crossing another bridge. The trail switchbacks very steeply upward. To the left, across a sort of vertical gorge, are sheer rock walls. Just before the hut the steep grade eases. The hut is on the edge of a high shelf, with the big black mass of L'Ailefroide above. Past L'Ailefroide to the right (south) is the Glacier de la Pilatte, the Pic du Says, and the Pointe du Vallon des Etages. The hut faces this spectacular view. The scene behind the hut is also impressive, a long mountain wall topped with jagged teeth, among which is the notch of the Col de la Temple, with the Glacier de la Temple at its base. Temple is said to mean "gulf" or "abyss" in local dialect and refers to the very deep trench between the peaks of L'Ailefroide, Pelvoux, and the Barre des Ecrins.

50. The Refuge de la Pilatte

Rating: strenuous
Distance round trip: 21 km
High point: 2,577 m

Total climb: 825 m
Time: 4 hours up, 3 hours 30 minutes down

This is a long walk, steep only for the last hour, without much variety for part of the way. The reward, however, is a magnificent, close-up view of a superb glacier, a scene that only really unfolds in all its glory when you arrive at the Refuge de la Pilatte.

Begin as for hike 49, The Refuge Temple-Ecrins, but continue straight ahead (south) at the signposted junction, indicating the Refuge Temple-Ecrins and the Refuge de la Pilatte, which you reach about 1 hour 30 minutes after starting. A couple of bridges take you over sidestreams, and about 20 minutes beyond the first junction reach a second one, with another trail leading to the Refuge Temple-Ecrins. There is a nice view ahead of the Glacier de la Pilatte. Cross several more sidestreams on bridges and then, about 2 hours 30 minutes from the start, cross the Vénéon; a bridge spans the main channel, but you must cross a side channel on rocks. This is moderately difficult; you may want to throw in a few more rocks to assist your footing.

After reaching the right bank of the river, follow the trail, which switchbacks up and joins a path entering from the north along this bank. Turn left at this unsigned intersection. A few blazes point to a bridge over a sidestream. Cross the bridge, then take a sharp right (west) and switchback up to reconnect with the trail after a short washed-out section. Soon a blaze points you left onto the trail again. The snout of the glacier is visible to your left, and another glacier is above to your right. Cross yet another sidestream on a bridge and then cross one on rocks (easy). The trail now traverses, following the folds of the slope, and is exposed for a very short section of trail (about 5 minutes). The last section rises in switchbacks through stones and gravel to reach the hut. The way is distinct. The front door of the hut is behind the building, facing the fantastic view: a great sweep of cascading glaciers, slashed with crevasses, easing out into a broad valley glacier below. The two black humps to the south above the icefall are the summits of Les Bans, and numerous other peaks are also visible.

51. The Vallon des Etages

Rating: easy
Distance round trip: 7.5 km
High point: 2,050 m

Total climb: 450 m
Time: 2 hours up, 1 hour down

This is a very attractive walk, fairly short and easy, leading into a wild, uninhabited valley with dramatic views.

The starting point is at Les Etages, a hamlet 2.7 kilometers from La Bérarde as you drive down D530, the road toward St.-Christophe. You can also take a path from La Bérarde to Les Etages. There is a parking area at the east end of the hamlet (the side toward La Bérarde) and a smaller parking area at the west end. Starting from the west end, turn off D530 and take the road that loops down to the river. Cross the bridge and turn left (east); a sign points to the Vallon des Etages as well as to the footpath to La Bérarde. Follow a second sign that directs you along the river, and soon cross a sidestream on a bridge. Turn right (south) at once, following the sign to the Vallon. (A left turn here would take you toward La Bérarde.)

Climb steeply on a narrow path through woods, an ascent of 200 meters. About 40 minutes after crossing the Vénéon River the trail levels out considerably and emerges from the forest. You will also enter the park near here. There is a fine view ahead of the cirque and glacier, and the sound of a torrent roars below. Occasional sections of the trail lead over boulders, and there are several cairns to mark the way. Gradually the streambed rises until it flows calmly to your right beside the trail. In a lovely, grassy section before the moraine, a few ruins testify to the former use of these meadows for pasturing. These are old foundations, fallen in—now just mounds of rocks and holes with rocks tumbled in, amid the silent meadows. The trail reaches the edge of the stream and then turns left, continuing over boulders and moraine toward the cirque. I stopped at about 2,050 meters, but you may continue to the end of the trail (in perhaps a half kilometer), although eventually you would have to hop across the stream. The view is dominated by the black tooth of the Pointe de Vallon des Etages. Looking across the valley to the mountains on the opposite side (to the north) is a strange needle of rock, the Dibona.

52. The Refuge de la Lavey

Rating: easy
Distance round trip: 9 km
High point: 1,797 m

Total climb: 370 m
Time: 2 hours 20 minutes up, 2 hours down

This high valley is longer than the Vallon des Etages and softer in appearance. As soon as you reach the entrance of the Vallon des Etages you

On the way to the Refuge du Lavey

see its big glacier cirque, whereas when you enter the Val Lavey the glacier is at a greater distance, and the valley is less savage and rough, its walls less sheer and rugged. Although it is quite wild, three houses remain as well as the Refuge de la Lavey, whereas the Vallon des Etages is now wholly deserted.

The starting point is just past the hamlet of Champhorent, 8.5 kilometers down D530, the road from La Bérarde as you drive toward St.-Christophe. Just past Champhorent on the left (as you head toward St.-Christophe) there are two wooden Parc National des Ecrins signs, one with a little pitched roof over it. Directly after these another sign announces the parking area for this walk, but since that sign faces St.-Christophe you will see only its blank side as you come down from La Bérarde. From the parking sign a ramp descends from the road to a large, excellent parking area. The trailhead, signposted, is at the east end of the parking area.

The trail descends to the river, which you cross on a beautiful old arched stone bridge. You will pass signposted junctions for the trails to St.-Christophe, to the right (west), and to La Bérarde, to the left (east). Continue straight ahead, however, switchbacking up the slope. Just above, a superb waterfall enters the river. This is the steepest part of the hike and will take about 30 minutes, after which you reach the upper valley and the grade becomes gentle. The stream now flows through a small gorge to your right. You will soon enter the national park, indicated by a sign, and cross another handsome old stone bridge, arched and cobbled like the one below.

Beyond this second bridge, at a signposted junction, keep left (south) for the Refuge de la Lavey. A plank bridge then crosses a sidestream; the house you can now see to your left is a farmhouse, not the hut. A few stone ruins bear witness to the past when there was a small village here, just as in the neighboring Vallon des Etages. Ascend a final, gradual rise, then descend a few meters to the hut.

If you wish to continue farther, cross the stream to its right bank and head toward the Fond de la Muande on a trail leading up the valley toward the moraine and the glacier. Or you can continue on the trail just past the hut, above the left bank of the stream; in about 10 minutes reach a signposted junction. The fork to the left leads to the Brèche de l'Olan; the fork to the right leads to Lac des Bêches. We did not climb up to the lake, which is in a hanging valley above the Val Lavey, but were told that the trail is quite steep for part of the way and that the views from the lake of Les Rouies and La Tête des Fétoules are very fine. It should take another 2 hours to reach this lake (an ascent of 600 meters), which is at 2,401 meters.

NORTHERN ECRINS

The Romanche is the valley that borders the northern edge of the Ecrins massif. Although only the second highest peak in the massif, La Meije (pronounced "mezh") is the more legendary, celebrated in the annals of mountaineering. During the golden age of alpine climbing when the English were "bagging" nearly every peak they could get near, La Meije defeated all attempts to reach its summit. Though English climbers buzzed around the region, La Meije was finally climbed (up its south face, from La Bérarde) in 1877 by an all-French party. Pierre Gaspard, the guide who led this first ascent, was twice defeated when he tried to climb its north face, which was not climbed until 1898 (again by a French team).

This mountain's lovely name comes from a dialect word for "mid-day"; thus, it is one of several peaks in the Alps that were once used by local people to tell the time of day. Similarly, in German-speaking countries there are "Mittaghorns." La Meije is not a snow-dome or a single pyramid, but a series of jagged points atop a mountainous wall. It has three summits: the western (and highest) Grand Pic de la Meije, the central Doigt de Dieu (the finger of God), and the eastern Meije Orientale. The mountain is framed between Le Râteau (3,809 meters) to the west and the Pic Gaspard (3,883 meters) to the east. A cascade of steep glaciers is frozen onto the wall.

The little town of La Grave sits at the foot of this impressive ensemble. From La Grave, a two-stage *télépherique* extends up the wall of La Meije to a point just below the Col des Ruillans, much closer to Le Râteau than to La Meije (oddly, the view of La Meije is much better from the middle station). La Grave is a small mountaineering center that also offers downhill and cross-country skiing. As a winter resort, however, it has been eclipsed by Les Deux Alpes and Alpe d'Huez, two high-powered ski resorts at the western end of the Romanche valley. Thus, La Grave remains unassuming, a real town with a visible history rather than an artificially created community of brand-new condominiums. The little Romanesque church in the upper (and older) part of town has a beautiful apse and a barrel-vaulted nave, very simple and austere, and is well worth a visit. (Hanging on one wall is a rather curious, primitive painting, commissioned in 1749 by a man who fell from the third story of a house and survived.) Across the walk is a seventeenth-century chapel, its apse set with cobblestones; to visit the chapel you must ask the priest, who lives beside the churchyard, for the key.

The old church at La Grave

La Grave, which makes a good base for exploring this region, is located on N91 and can be reached by bus from Grenoble or Briançon.

Note: Alongside the river below the town is an arboretum with picnic tables in a grove of trees. If you are driving past La Grave, it's a nice place for a picnic lunch. As you enter the town from the east on N91, take the first left turn just after the tunnel. The road descends to the riverbank, and you can park just outside the arboretum.

In hikes 53 and 54, there are several possibilities for hiking on the slopes below La Meije, ranging from moderate to very difficult. The two described here begin the same way. Hike 53, a fairly easy walk, takes you to the Refuge E. Chancel, and hike 54, extremely difficult and very strenuous, continues from the Refuge E. Chancel.

53. Lac de Puy Vachier and the Refuge E. Chancel

Rating: moderate
Distance round trip: 4 km
High point: 2,506 m

Total climb: 240 m
Time: 1 hour 30 minutes up, 1 hour down

Most hikers start this walk from Gare de Peyrou d'Amont, the middle station of the La Meije *télépherique*, at 2,400 meters. It is an easy walk because there is little altitude gain, but the footing between the station and the lake is rough because the route is mostly over boulders. The Refuge Evariste Chancel is called Refuge E. Chancel on trail signs.

In front of the restaurant at the *télépherique* station, as you look down upon La Grave, a sign points left (northwest) for the lake. Walk under the cablecar line; a rock blazed with a red arrow points the way, and there are subsequent red and white blazes. Descend steeply for about 5 minutes (about 70 meters) to a junction, where you bear left (west); a few sections here are very narrow. Soon a sign appears pointing to the lake and the hut. The trail becomes a route, mostly over boulders, marked by countless red blazes—one on nearly every rock. The walk is almost level. There is a long traverse across a boulder slide, with a few sections of dirt trail. Reach Lac de Puy Vachier (2,382 meters) in 50 to 60 minutes. It's a small tarn, deep azure in the sun or dark, metallic blue under a cloudy sky, amid a

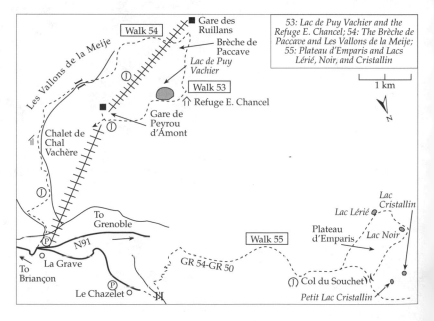

rocky wasteland with blackened cliffs above it. You cannot see La Meije from the lake; rather, the view is of the Plateau d'Emparis, the Romanche valley, and the little villages upon the valley's northern slope. From the lake a trail with much easier footing leads up for 20 minutes to the little, privately owned Refuge E. Chancel, from which you can see the summit of La Meije. Although the oldest in France, this is an attractive little hut and is now being tastefully renovated.

The return trip to the Gare de Peyrou d'Amont station takes 45 minutes, or take the trail down from the lake and descend 1,240 meters to La Grave, which takes about 2 hours 30 minutes.

54. The Brèche de Paccave and Les Vallons de la Meije

Rating: very strenuous
Distance one way: 8 km
High point: 2,836 m

Total climb: 350 m ascent
Time: 1 hour 40 minutes up, 3 hours 35 minutes down

A challenging route with spectacular, close-up views of La Meije and its glaciers, this is also the most difficult excursion in this book in terms of route finding; it is, moreover, very long. Only persons who are well conditioned and who have some experience in finding mountain routes should consider attempting this hike, and then only in good, stable weather. Start early and give yourself a lot of time. There is no clear trail that you can follow through the entire route; you will need to scout about a little from time to time to find the way.

The slope between Lac de Puy Vachier and La Meije has a long rock wall running down it like a gigantic fence. If you ride up to the top station of the La Meije *télépherique*, you will see this wall below you, and you can also spot the Brèche de Paccave, a U-shaped gap in the wall with a little signpost at the center. The word "bréche" means a breach, gap, or notch. This route takes you up from the Refuge E. Chancel to this notch, and then down along the lower slope of La Meije into the "Vallons" (small valleys) de la Meije.

Begin at the Refuge E. Chancel, as described in hike 53, Lac de Puy Vachier and the Refuge E. Chancel. If you have not already spotted the Brèche de Paccave from the *télépherique*, you may wish to ask the hut keeper to point it out to you so that you clearly know what you are aiming for. From the eastern edge of the hut (the side closest to the lake), ascend a sort of rough staircase and reach a level area on which is laid a circle of stones that are painted white for helicopter landings. To the left of this circle is a cairn and a trail. Follow this upward; at times there are only traces of a trail or route among the boulders. You will reach a sign at about 2,670 meters that reads "Chancel, Peyrou d'Aval." Looking up toward the wall of rock that divides this slope from the slope directly below La Meije, you can clearly see the shallow notch of the Brèche de Paccave. From here, however, you cannot take the shortest, most direct route to the Brèche because a cliff is in the way. You must instead continue to climb upward, bearing right, as you need to reach a point (about 2,850 meters) as high or even higher than the Brèche, and then descend to it. Keep near the ridge just before you reach the Brèche, which may be about 1 hour 30

La Meije from the Brèche de Paccave

minutes after you leave the Refuge E. Chancel. At the Brèche itself there is a signpost.

You are now poised above the slope of La Meije, and the views are superb. The first 100 meters of descent are very steep. There are traces of trail and a few cairns. Descend over rocks and boulders and reach a level shelf below. Look right (southeast) toward the glaciers for a signpost that reads "Les Vallons de la Meije, le Clot de la Cola." Pass under the *télépherique* cable to reach the sign. From here, there is a phenomenal, close view of the glacier below Le Râteau. Do not cross the stream here; look for cairns and cross it lower down at about 2,520 meters, where a group of three cairns in a row point across the stream. Continue down along the side of the moraine, with the stream now to your left (east). At about 2,400 meters reach a small level area. The stream exits from this flat place through a narrow notch, and the trail climbs a little above it. A few blazes mark the way. Climb up to a knife-edge moraine ridge, then descend to the stream and cross it; the way is marked by a blaze and a signpost for Les Vallons de la Meije and Le Clot des Sables. (You can avoid the knife-edge moraine ridge by making your way along the side of the stream, with the knife-edge ridge just above to your right; the footing here, however, is a little rough.)

Descend to a bridge at about 2,000 meters; it may take up to 5 hours from the Refuge E. Chancel to reach this. Cross this bridge and turn left. About 20 minutes later, cross a stream (easy) on stones, and at about 1,900 meters reach grassy slopes and an old alpage. An hour after crossing the bridge, reach a signposted junction at about 1,600 meters; the name of this place is marked Les Vallons de la Meije, La Lauzette. The signpost at this junction points left (southwest) to the Refuge Chancel or straight ahead to Chal Vachère. Continue straight ahead, descending. In 15 minutes reach a dirt road with a signpost pointing to the Brèche de Paccave, Lac de Puy Vachier, Chal Vachère, and Les Vallons de la Meije. Turn right and follow the road down; cross the bridge over the Romanche, and climb up to reach La Grave.

You can also take a route down from the Gare de Peyrou d'Amont *téléphérique* station into Les Vallons de la Meije, and join the trail that descends to the river and La Grave.

55. Plateau d'Emparis and the Lacs Lérié, Noir, and Cristallin

Rating: moderate
Distance loop trip: 18 km
High point: 2,430 m
Total climb: 850 m

Time: 1 hour 50 minutes to the junction for the lakes, 4 hours and 15 minutes for tour of the lakes and return

This is a three-star walk, among the most scenic in the Alps. The Plateau d'Emparis (Plateau de Paris on some maps) is a high, open, rolling plateau above the north side of the Romanche valley. It thus directly faces La Meije and the mountains west of it, Le Râteau and the Pic de la Grave, with the broad expanse of glaciers below them, and the views are spectacular. It is finer than the walk along the *balcon* facing Mont Blanc in that there is no sprawling Chamonix in the valley below to spoil the effect.

How should d'Emparis be pronounced? Well, either way. In local dialect, the final s is spoken ("dahm-par-*eess*") but in standard French it is left off, so that the name is pronounced like that of the capital of France ("dahm-par-*ee*"). M. Paul-Louis Rousset, who is both a mountain guide and a local historian, told me that he now believes that this curious place name derives from the phrase *entre les parois,* which means "between the walls," although he said that when he wrote his book on the history of the country of La Meije he had accepted another scholar's theory that the name derives from a Celtic word meaning *ensoleillé,* or "in a sunny place."

The GR 54-GR 50 crosses the plateau in a west–east direction. Scattered about the plateau are several small lakes, but they are off this main trail. You can climb up to the plateau and hike along the GR 54 as far as you wish, then retrace your steps to return. Alternatively, you can depart from the GR 54 to hike around the little lakes, then rejoin the main trail for your return. Although there is a track to Lac Lérié, after that it fades out and you must cast about and find the other lakes yourself. It's like a treasure hunt—find the lakes! This is quite safe as long as the weather is clear, because as the terrain is utterly open, you can always orient yourself and find your way back to the main trail.

Several picturesque, very simple old villages are perched on the north slope of the Romanche above La Grave: Les Hières, Ventelon, Les Terrasses, and Le Chazelet. They offer good viewpoints of La Meije and are worth visiting for their own sake. The trail to the Plateau d'Emparis begins from Le Chazelet, the most western of the four.

As you drive out of La Grave heading eastward, there is a tunnel. Immediately upon exiting from the tunnel you must turn right onto D33, the road for Le Chazelet. Note: There is no sign indicating that you are approaching this junction. From the post office in La Grave, it is 5.6 kilometers to Le Chazelet; you will pass Les Terrasses on the way. Just as you arrive at Le Chazelet, you will find a parking area. From there, walk straight along the unnamed street through the parking area (most of the village will be below, to your left). Follow this street as it curves right and then leads you down to the bridge on the other side of the village, which you reach in 10 minutes. Cross the bridge; a signpost for the GR 54 directs you leftward, up the slope. A network of paths (some are occasionally blazed) switchback up this slope toward the southwest, bringing you to the top in about 1 hour 15 minutes.

Once on the plateau, the network of paths resolves itself into one main trail, the GR 54-GR 50, which makes its way generally northwest across the broad, open meadows. The view of La Meije is beautiful. After about 1 hour on this trail, at 2,300 meters, come to a signposted junction; unless it has been repaired by now, the signpost is broken and lying on the ground, but it is oriented in the correct direction. If you are headed for Lac Lérié, turn left (southwest) on a quite visible track across the meadow, or con-

Lac Noir

tinue to the right (northwest) if you wish to stay on the GR 54. The two big green humps to the north, Le Petit Têt and Le Gros Têt (also called the Cime du Rachas), are useful landmarks.

The track through the grass becomes a dirt trail, and in about 25 minutes reach Lac Lérié, from which there is a grand, panoramic view of La Meije, Le Râteau, and the Glacier de la Girose. To continue to Lac Noir (black lake), take the little dirt track on the west side of the lake, which heads southwest, and climb up the shoulder to your right, still going southwest. Look for traces of a path: the trail veers to the west and later northwest to reach Lac Noir, about 20 minutes beyond Lac Lérié. Despite its name, Lac Noir is blue if the day is sunny, and it occupies a beautiful, wild, open place amid green meadows, with sweeping views all around.

Lac Cristallin is quite dry by midsummer, but if you wish to find it anyway, continue around the west side of Lac Noir to its northwest corner and find a path going west. There are many huge cairns scattered about to your left (west), but they do not indicate the way. The path passes a few metal poles topped with solar panels: they should be to your right, above a very tiny pond. A sign explains that this is a project to study the snow and requests that you not stand within 6 meters of the poles. Continue to the north, with only traces of a path to show the way, then northwest. You must not go too far west, for there is a steep drop. From Lac Cristallin (or even if you don't find it) ramble northeast toward Le Gros Têt and you will intersect the GR 54-GR 50. The return trip across the Plateau d'Emparis is also stunning, since you are now facing toward the mountains and the broad sweep of the Glacier de la Girose, which shines over the meadows. After a while (if it's a sunny day), your eyes may become dazzled by looking at so much emerald and white.

■

Le Grand Lac and Tour des Arêtes de la Bruyère

Above L'Alpe du Lauzet, this tour consists of two sections, hike 57, L'Alpe du Lauzet to Le Grand Lac via the Vallon du Plan Chevalier, and hike 58, Le Grand Lac to L'Alpe du Lauzet, which can be done in one loop trip or separately. Both take you to Le Grand Lac or within sight of it, but the loop trip circles a limestone massif known as the Arêtes de la Bruyère. Hike 57 is rougher and includes a section of scrambling and a little climbing up a rock chimney that has fixed cables for assistance, whereas hike 58 is quite easy with no scrambling at all. It is possible to go to the lake via hike 57 and return via hike 58 (thus making the loop trip, or Tour des Arêtes de la Bruyère), or you can go to the lake via hike 58 and return by the same way. If you wish to make the loop trip it is best to do it clockwise, climbing up on hike 57 and descending on hike 58, rather than the reverse.

Whichever way you do it, this excursion takes you into a scenic, wild valley punctuated with limestone mountains, providing a contrast to the views of glaciers and the peaks of gneiss, schist, and granite that characterize the Ecrins massif.

Drive eastward from La Grave on N91 over the Col du Lauteret to a little place called Le Pont de l'Alpe. This is on the road, 18 kilometers from La Grave, with the village of Le Lauzet just below to your right. As you reach Le Pont de l'Alpe you will drive over a little bridge; there is a stone house to your right, and also to the right, set down a little below the road, is l'Auberge des Amis. To your left is a house with a sundial and trail signs beside it. There are two parking areas here, just before and beside the trailhead, and more parking areas past Le Pont de l'Alpe heading toward Le Monêtier-les-Bains.

56. L'Alpe du Lauzet

Rating: easy
Distance one way: 1.3 km
High point: 1,940 m

Total climb: 230 m
Time: 40 minutes

From the trailhead at signs for Le Grand Lac and Halte de Roche-Robert, start up along the left bank of the stream and in 2 minutes turn left (east); a signpost for this trail reads "Roche Robert." Switchback up a gravel road toward a waterfall that descends through a dark gray, shaly gorge. About 15 minutes later, another sign indicates Roche Robert. (For hike 57, L'Alpe du Lauzet to Le Grand Lac via the Vallon du Plan Chevalier, you will save a few minutes if you take the narrower gravel road to your left rather than the broader gravel road to the right.) The trail, which at first led east, has turned north. Arrive at L'Alpe du Lauzet in 30 to 40 minutes. Here in a green bowl with a backdrop of craggy mountains are a tiny stone chapel, a few houses, and a small restaurant named Roche Robert.

57. L'Alpe du Lauzet to Le Grand Lac via the Vallon du Plan Chevalier

Rating: strenuous
Distance one way: 2 km
High point: 2,300 m

Total climb: 360 m
Time: 1 hour 45 minutes

On approaching L'Alpe du Lauzet from Le Pont de l'Alpe (see hike 56, L'Alpe du Lauzet), you will reach a place where you can either take a narrower gravel road to your left or stay on the wider gravel road to the right. Take the narrower road that leads down to the stream. A signpost here reads "Le Grand Lac par Cheminée" and "Lac and Col de la Ponsonnière." Take this trail, which soon swings left (north) and crosses a bridge. Just beyond the bridge where the trail forks, keep to the right (east at first); then the trail bends north. It curves around to the right, then gradually climbs through a grassy area. This is the Vallon du Plan Chevalier. Big outcrops of bare rock thrust above the steep slopes. You are heading for a sort of saddle at the upper end of the Vallon du Plan Chevalier.

Arrive at the base of a boulder slide. The way up is clear at first, but a rock slide has covered much of the route and you will see only broken traces; there is also an erosion channel running down the slope. Nevertheless, you can find your way up, and rejoin the old trail somewhat to the left of the erosion channel. About an hour past L'Alpe du Lauzet reach the

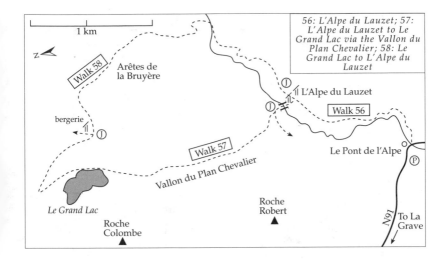

56: L'Alpe du Lauzet; 57: L'Alpe du Lauzet to Le Grand Lac via the Vallon du Plan Chevalier; 58: Le Grand Lac to L'Alpe du Lauzet

base of the rock chimney, where there is a plastic-coated steel cable. Here you must climb about 50 meters to reach the saddle in about 25 minutes. Descend about 20 meters on a dirt trail to the edge of Le Grand Lac.

58. Le Grand Lac to L'Alpe du Lauzet

Rating: easy
Distance one way: 4.5 km
High point: 2,400 m

Total climb: 100 m up, 460 m down
Time: 40 minutes up, 1 hour 30 minutes down

From the lake, which is to your left, walk along the east shore heading north. At the end of the lake turn right and climb up the slope in one big switchback, heading southeast and then south. The path seems headed toward a very narrow (as seen from this angle), multi-pointed rock peak above the lake. As you climb up from the lake there are good views of the snowy peaks across the valley. Reach a little notch, the highest point of this tour. To your left, a little higher up the slope, is a wood cabin—a *bergerie*, or shepherd's hut. Note: If you wish to and have the time, you can continue along the trail north and northwest to the Lac and Col de la Ponsonnière; it is 1.5 kilometers to the lake, and another 0.5 kilometer to the col.

From the notch, descend into a wide, high valley above which rise mountains of handsome color: ocher, rust, and dark gray. To your right (east) is the rocky tower of the Arêtes de la Bruyère (2,611 meters), and ahead (south), the rust and black Tête de la Cassille (3,069 meters). The trail is moderately steep at first, then much less so. It leads down through meadows to the stream, which you cross on stones (easy) at 2,230 meters. Walk along the left bank of the stream through a little gorge or pass it over the shoulder to the left, if there is snow in the gorge. Although you will see a bridge, do not cross the stream but keep the stream to your right as you descend. Round a corner and you will see L'Alpe du Lauzet below. From here, return to Le Pont de l'Alpe.

If you ascend to Le Grand Lac by way of this hike, do not turn left at L'Alpe du Lauzet but continue straight ahead. The grade of the climb is less steep than on hike 57. As you ascend, do not turn right (southwest) where a sign points to Le Sentier du Roy, et cetera. The trail curves gradually to the left and crosses the stream. About 1 hour 10 minutes above L'Alpe du Lauzet, cross the brook to its right bank and climb to the notch; from here you can look down upon the lake.

---

59. Les Sources de la Romanche

Rating: moderate
Distance round trip: 15 km
High point: 2,312 m

Total climb: 600 m
Time: 3 hours 30 minutes up, 2 hours 35 minutes down

Unlike the other walks in the northern Ecrins, this one (and also hike 60, The Col d'Arsine par le Sentier des Crevasses) enables hikers to view the La Meije massif from the east. This hike yields superb views of that side of the massif, and they are closer in than the views on hike 60. This is also a shorter and easier trip, although a less varied one. It follows the Romanche upstream to its sources.

From La Grave, drive east on N91 to nearby Villar-d'Arène. Just past this very small town, 4 kilometers from the La Grave post office, take D207 to the right toward the Refuge de l'Alpe and Pied du Col. Bear right for the Refuge de l'Alpe at the next junction. Pass the Gîte La Lochette, with a tennis court and a sign announcing "Refuge," "Grill," and "Bar" on your right. Immediately after the gîte drive over a bridge, turn right, and follow the unpaved road 1.5 kilometers to the parking area at its end. (Along the way, a blue arrow points to a large parking area on your left, which you should, however, pass.)

A sign at the south end of the parking area points south to the Refuge de l'Alpe and to two other huts, du Pavé and Adèle Planchard. Follow the trail along the stream that is to your right. Switchback up a moderately steep slope and in 30 minutes reach a junction separating the trails to the Refuge de l'Alpe, to your left, and to the Refuges du Pavé and Adèle Planchard, to your right. Bear right and switchback up a step, then reach a level, grassy shelf through which the Romanche flows gently to your right. Cross a sidestream on a little bridge. As you climb, the young river foams down. About 2 hours 20 minutes from the start of the hike, reach a park sign and signposted junction and turn left (southwest) for Les Sources de la Romanche and the Refuge Adèle Planchard. (The Refuge du Pavé is to the right across a bridge.)

About an hour after that junction, cross a sidestream on stones (quite easy). A grand view opens before you of the Glacier de la Plate des Agneaux. Soon, cross a bridge. The trail now bends to the right and begins to climb; the view is splendid, and although you can get closer to the glacier, the view will not be significantly better. The trail leads up the moraine on the right side of this upper valley. Pass a step where you must use your hands (easy, however). About 30 minutes beyond the bridge, the

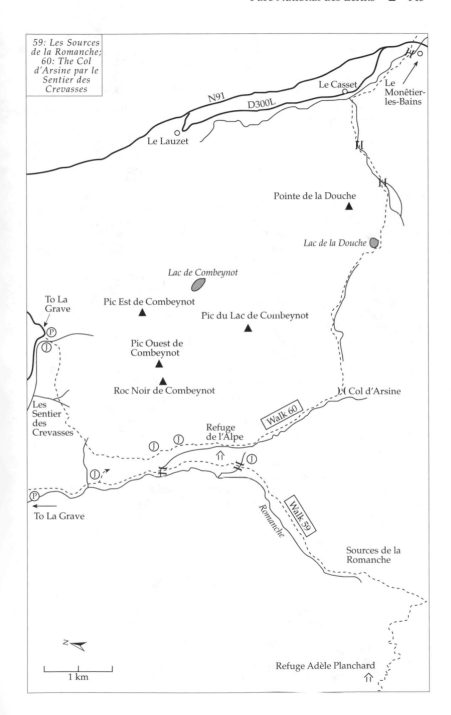

59: Les Sources de la Romanche; 60: The Col d'Arsine par le Sentier des Crevasses

N91

D300L

Le Casset

Le Monêtier-les-Bains

Le Lauzet

Pointe de la Douche ▲

Lac de la Douche

Lac de Combeynot

To La Grave

Ⓟ
Ⓙ

Pic Est de Combeynot ▲

Pic du Lac de Combeynot ▲

Pic Ouest de Combeynot ▲

Roc Noir de Combeynot ▲

)(Col d'Arsine

Les Sentier des Crevasses

Walk 60

Refuge de l'Alpe

Ⓙ   Ⓙ   ⇧   Ⓙ

Ⓙ

Ⓟ

To La Grave

Romanche

Walk 59

Sources de la Romanche

N

1 km

Refuge Adèle Planchard
⇧

trail to the Refuge Adèle Planchard begins to switchback up to the right; there is no signpost. A small side-trail continues straight ahead (south). Follow this for about 50 meters to reach a viewpoint.

60. The Col d'Arsine par le Sentier des Crevasses

Rating: strenuous
Distance one way: 19 km
High point: 2,340 m
Total climb: 380 m up, 950 m down

Time: 2 hours 50 minutes to the Col d'Arsine, 2 hours 45 minutes down to Le Casset, another 45 minutes (2.5 km) to Le Monêtier-les-Bains

This attractive trip is one of two walks (see also hike 59, Les Sources de la Romanche) providing views of the La Meije massif from the east. Despite its name, this *sentier* (trail) does not lead onto a glacier or over any crevasses—it only gives views of them. The trail begins near the Col du Lauteret, makes a halfway turn around the Pics de Combeynot, and brings you out to Le Casset. From nearby Le Monêtier-les-Bains you can get a bus at 5:35 P.M. back to the Col du Lauteret. (Check the schedule in case the timetable has changed.)

From La Grave, drive eastward on N91 to the Col du Lauteret, an easy drive with little climbing and none of the usual steep hairpin turns, as the col is only about 500 meters above La Grave. Just before the col there are two parking areas on the right. Park at the second one, positioned just before the road makes a big curve to the left to reach the col. (There are also large parking areas at the col.) It is 10.7 kilometers from the La Grave post office to this parking lot. There is a sign here for the Parc National des Ecrins and Réserve Naturelle de Combeynot. At a signposted junction a minute later, go right (west) for the Refuge de l'Alpe and the Col d'Arsine par le (by the) Sentier des Crevasses. Immediately after this, cross a small bridge and walk toward a pylon; the trail passes under a power line and for a short while runs parallel to the highway. The trail then curves left (south) around the fold of the slope and becomes le Sentier des Crevasses.

This traverse, the only delicate part of the hike, is high and exposed but generally good; however, it is occasionally very narrow—in a few spots only about 1 meter, or even 1 foot, wide. There are two short stretches with a fixed cable to help you, and one place where you must cross a stream on rocks. Getting through this section will take about 30 minutes. Emerge finally onto grassy slopes and soon find a signposted junction. Go left (southeast) for the Refuge de l'Alpe and the Col d'Arsine: here you join the GR 54 with its red and white blazes, entering here from Villard-d'Arène. You are in a superb, high valley with good views of the mountains and glaciers. Note: You can avoid le Sentier des Crevasses by taking the GR 54 to this point, described in hike 59, Les Sources de la Romanche. If you come that way you can take the bus back from Le Monêtier-les-Bains to Villard-d'Arène. However, you then will have to walk 3.5 kilometers back to the parking lot.

About 10 minutes later, a sign points right for the Refuge de l'Alpe, which is close and visible. Bear left for the Col d'Arsine and soon pass a park sign. This is an easy, lovely part of the hike through meadows, with a stream to your right; the upward grade is gentle. Almost 3 hours after the start of the hike, reach the Col d'Arsine and a good view of the Montagne des Agneaux (3,664 meters).

From the col, after 30 minutes' descent pass a pale blue pond; from here a stream cascades down the slope. Descend into a narrower, more enclosed valley. The trail switchbacks steeply down to a step. Many signs along this route beg hikers not to take shortcuts as these cause erosion, but there is one official shortcut: a sign part way down the trail points left for *raccourci* (shortcut) and right for *le sentier*. At the base of this steep section, where the grade moderates, cross a stream on rocks and reach a large pond, Lac de la Douche. The hanging Glacier du Casset appears above to your right. This is a pleasant, scenic spot, set between rock walls.

From here descend through woods (pleasantly shady on a warm afternoon), near a gurgling stream. Cross a bridge, walk along a gravel jeep road for a few minutes, then follow the blazed trail to the left into the woods again. Cross another bridge; a sign announces La Forêt Communale de Monetier-les-Bains. Beyond here, the trail becomes a dirt road. Follow this road through the woods, where cars are parked, and reach the village of Le Casset, about 2 hours 45 minutes from the Col d'Arsine.

Cross a bridge to enter this very pretty village, turn right, and go up to the church; the village is so small you can't miss it. There, cross another bridge and turn left onto the GR 54, which leads into Le Monêtier-les-Bains (thus avoiding the highway). It's 2.5 kilometers to "Monetier." As you approach the town and cross a little bridge, don't turn left (which leads to N91; you'd then have to walk along the highway for about 5 minutes) but continue straight ahead. Turn left when you reach the town, and then turn right onto the main street (which is also N91). The bus stop is on the main street on the right, just before (and across the street from) the church; look for a blue sign and a small wood shelter with a bench. If you stop for a drink or snack at Le Casset, where there's a small shop and a café, give yourself about 45 minutes to reach the bus stop at Le Monêtier-les-Bains. The ride back to the Col du Lauteret takes about 15 minutes.

EASTERN ECRINS

The Vallouise valley provides the closest approach from the east to the heart of the Ecrins massif. The trails here lead to excellent views of Mont Pelvoux, third highest mountain in the massif, and other peaks. Vallouise, a very charming small town at the opening of the valley of the same name, makes an excellent base. Its church has a fine sixteenth-century porch and there are handsome old stone houses and gardens along the town's back lanes. To reach Vallouise, drive south from Briançon on N94 to the little town of L'Argentière-la-Bessée. From there, turn northwest onto D994e, the road that extends up the Vallouise valley. As you proceed northward up the valley from Vallouise on D994e, there are hotels at the little settlements of Le Sarret, St. Antoine, and Les Claux. About 8 kilometers past Vallouise is Ailefroide, a sort of summer mountaineering center with a guides' office, a couple of hotels and a gîte d'étape, and a few grocery stores and sport shops. Another 5.5 kilometers beyond Ailefroide on the same road, now called D204T, is Pré de Mme. Carle, literally, "the meadow of Mme. Carle," where the road ends. Pré de Mme. Carle, the point of departure for many climbs and a popular hike, consists of a huge parking area, a simple chalet-hut, and an information office.

There are several colorful tales about the namesake of this intriguing place. It is said that when M. Carle returned home from war, he discovered that his wife had been unfaithful. To avenge himself, he deprived her mare of water, and then invited Mme. Carle to go out riding. The thirsty mare went mad at the sight of water in a waterfall and threw Mme. Carle, thus killing her. Another legend tells that Mme. Carle was a poor widow of this valley, with many children to feed. She possessed only one stony field, and this woman spent her life carting away the rocks and cultivating her plot of land. The inhabitants of the region gave her name to this place to honor this exemplary mother. But the real explanation is that King Louis XII gave this parcel of land to Godefroy Carle, President of the Dauphiné, and it passed to his widow (Mme. Carle) after his death.

Walks from Pré de Mme. Carle

Pré de Mme. Carle is the starting point for the trails to the Glacier Blanc and the Glacier Noir (the white glacier and the black glacier). These are the most important glaciers of the Vallouise region, each about 6 kilometers long.

The trailhead is just beside the information cabin, which is next to the chalet-hut. A broad path crosses two bridges and soon begins to switchback up along the right side of the valley. In about 30 minutes reach a signposted junction and turn either right (east) for the Glacier Blanc or left (west) for the Glacier Noir.

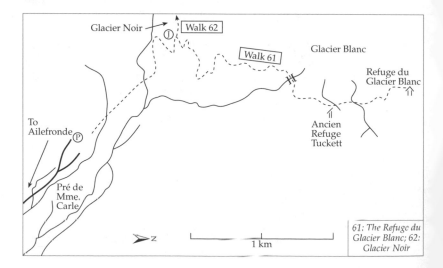

61: The Refuge du Glacier Blanc; 62: Glacier Noir

61. The Refuge du Glacier Blanc

Rating: strenuous
Distance round trip: 8 km
High point: 2,542 m
Total climb: 690 m

Time: 2 hours 30 minutes up from Pré de Mme. Carle, 2 hours 10 minutes down to Pré de Mme. Carle

This route provides the grandest views available to a hiker on this side of the Ecrins. The second part of the route is much more challenging than the first part. If you walk only as far as the snout of the glacier you will get a good view, although there are still finer views above. The second part requires a little scrambling in a few places, but the French evidently do not regard it as difficult; this is considered a *même les enfants* trail.

From the junction of the trails to the Glaciers Blanc and Noir, continue to the right (eastward). Although not inherently difficult, there are a few

Glacier Blanc

sections of trail on rocky ledges; be careful in wet weather. After another 30 minutes the trail levels out briefly to make a short traverse. Red blazes mark the way across a section of trail strewn with rocks and along a few ledges. One hour 30 minutes after starting from Pré de Mme. Carle, reach an open place with a full view of the snout of the Glacier Blanc and of the icefall, bristling with séracs, towering above. A stream issues from the glacier's tongue and runs through a bed of gravel. The more difficult part of the route is ahead, but if you turn back here you will have seen the glacier as well as Mont Pelvoux rising behind you.

To continue to the hut cross the stream on a bridge, turn right (east) and climb up a set of metal stairs attached to the rock.

A little higher you will find a choice of a few iron steps or a fixed cable to help you up a short section of rock about 10 meters high. There is a little more scrambling beyond this. At a point where you will see some blazes on the right directing you up a sort of chimney, but where a better trail seems to open up to the left, follow the blazes! They do mark the best way.

Pass a cascade to your left and about 30 minutes after crossing the stream reach a level area. The "Ancien Refuge Tuckett," an old hut that is now a small museum, is to your right. You can now see the new hut above on a promontory. Cross a very shallow stream on easy rocks. Beyond this flat area the trail switchbacks up to the hut, requiring a few minutes' scrambling just before you reach it.

The hut faces a splendid view including Mont Pelvoux, the Pic Sans Nom, and l'Ailefroide. To the right you can see the tip of the Barre des Ecrins and the Glacier Blanc; behind the hut, the Montagne des Agneaux dominates the view.

62. Glacier Noir

Rating: easy
Distance round trip: 7 km
High point: 2,445 m
Total climb: 570 m

Time: 1 hour 20 minutes up from Pré de Mme. Carle, 1 hour 10 minutes down to Pré de Mme. Carle

This glacier is called "black" because the surface of the ice is strewn with rocks that have fallen from the peaks at its back and along its sides— a blanket of gray rubble, with the ice visible here and there. The view is thickly dramatic; the glacier lies in a deep trench below the forbidding black walls of Mont Pelvoux, the Pic Sans Nom, and l'Ailefroide.

From the junction of the trails to the Glaciers Blanc and Noir, turn left (westward) and simply follow the trail for as long as you wish.

The trail is not steep; it rises very gradually, the average grade being only about 10 percent. But although not steep, the trail becomes narrow and traversing it requires concentration. It runs along the knife-edge ridge of a moraine, and although at first it is about 2 meters wide, it later narrows to 1.5 meters, then 1, and eventually is only about a foot and a half wide. You can follow the trail for 30 minutes or longer, turning back when you consider it too narrow (which for most people will probably be after about 50 minutes).

Other Walks in the Area

63. The Refuge des Bans

Rating: easy
Distance round trip: 8.5 km
High point: 2,083 m

Total climb: 600 m
Time: 2 hours up, 1 hour 30 minutes down

This is a pleasant, comparatively easy walk, culminating in a very fine view. The drive to the trailhead is more difficult than the walk to the Refuge des Bans.

The walk starts at the upper end of the Vallée de l'Onde. To reach the valley, drive on D994E across the bridge into Vallouise. When you reach the town square with its fountain, the church will be in front of you and the Syndicat d'Initiative will be to your right. Turn right at a road signed for Le Villard and Puy Aillaud. Drive 1.9 kilometers to the hamlet of Le Villard and the signposted junction of the roads for Puy Aillaud and the Vallée d'Entraigue. Bear left for the Vallée d'Entraigue and proceed up a paved road that for part of the way is narrow with only a few passing places. Reach the end of the road and a parking area 8.5 kilometers from Vallouise; there is a small *buvette* (refreshment stand) here. At the west end of the parking area is a national park sign and a sign indicating the trail to this refuge.

The trail, level for the first 10 minutes, runs alongside a gravel flood plain. It then switchbacks up to the right fairly steeply for about 10 minutes, then climbs more gradually. There is a fine view ahead of the cirque that closes off the valley: a semicircle of rugged gray teeth around a bowl with a few small glaciers clinging high on the walls. Toward the end of the walk you can see the hut above on a promontory. There is a last steep rise about 80 meters high, with a fixed cable for support on a short, rocky section about 10 meters long. At the top, turn right and reach the hut in 5 minutes, but you must purchase drinks or food in order to eat your picnic at the hut. A sign reading *"aire pique-nique"* points toward the cirque, meaning sit on any rock you like to enjoy your sandwich.

63: The Refuge des Bans

64. Lac de l'Eychauda

Rating: moderate
Distance round trip: 10.5 km
High point: 2,514 m

Total climb: 800 m
Time: 2 hours 30 minutes up, 1 hour 50 minutes down

This is a true alpine lake, nearly enclosed within walls of rock and scree slopes—a rather harsh, dry landscape.

Starting at Vallouise take D994E, the road toward Ailefroide, but turn right after about 1.7 kilometers at Le Sarret where there is a sign for l'Eychauda. Continue for 7.5 kilometers to the parking area at the end of the road at Chambran. There is a small *buvette,* a few farmhouses, and a trail sign pointing the way to the lake. The trail, initially level, heads north, passing a few sheepfolds and stone house ruins. In about 15 minutes reach a junction and take the fork to the left (north) for the lake. Follow a broad farm road up on gentle switchbacks. About 40 minutes from the start of the hike reach a national park sign and cross a small bridge. Turn right from the farm road onto the trail to cut out several loops of the road, which finally peters out anyway.

The trail switchbacks up at a moderately steep grade. Cross over an easy rock slab with a few cairns to mark the way and reach the lake in a few more minutes.

From the lake you can walk up to the Col des Grangettes; part of the trail is visible from the lake. We did not climb up to the col but were told that it is a very steep climb of about 30 minutes on slippery scree, and there is a fine view of the glaciers west of the lake.

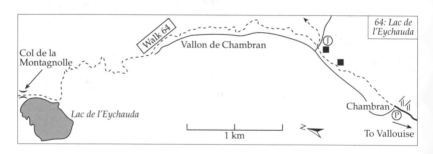

PARC NATIONAL DE LA VANOISE

This first of the French national parks was established in 1963. The ancient state known as Savoy, part of the Kingdom of Piedmont-Sardinia, once existed in the Graian Alps. Savoy was divided in the nineteenth century, the western part annexed by France in 1860, the eastern part absorbed by the new nation of Italy in 1861. The Graian Alps were thus also politically divided—between France and Italy.

The Vanoise massif is the western lobe of the Graian Alps in what is now the French Savoie. It adjoins the Parco Nazionale del Gran Paradiso just across the border in Italy. Although ancient Savoy was split asunder, the Vanoise and the Gran Paradiso are geologic brethren, and the two massifs together form Europe's largest nature reserve.

The Vanoise, a high plateau punctuated by mountains, is excellent terrain for the hiker. While the center of the Ecrins is impassable because of its cluster of glaciers, you can hike all the way across the Vanoise; its topography permits a great deal of hut-to-hut hiking. (This means that you can stay overnight at huts, which all provide blankets, and which nearly all serve dinner and breakfast, so that you do not need to carry a sleeping bag, stove, or pots; see the Introduction chapter.) Both the GR 5 and GR 55 extend across the massif. The Vanoise lies between two great valleys, the Tarentaise (bed of the river Isère) to the north and the Maurienne (whose river is the Arc) to the south. Many of the most celebrated ski resorts in France, such as Courchevel, the Val-d'Isère, and Tignes, lie on the northern edge of the Vanoise, which was the site of the 1992 winter Olympics. Those resorts are in the park's peripheral zone, however, which permits commercial development and the construction of lifts and ski runs. Such activity is rigorously excluded from the park's central zone. None of those ski resorts are prime territory for the summer hiker; they are not close enough to the best hiking trails. The villages and small resorts that do serve as hiking centers are not only closer to the rugged alpine country at the heart of the park but are also, fortunately, simpler and less artificial than the chic ski resorts. Along the northern slope of the Vanoise (the Tarentaise), unpretentious little Peisey-Nancroix with nearby tiny Rosuel and the agreeable resort village of Pralognan offer the best approaches with the greatest number of hikes. Along the southern slope (the Maurienne), Aussois and Termignon provide the best facilities and access to trails.

The Parc National de la Vanoise is the most highly organized of the French alpine parks (and much more organized than the Gran Paradiso).

Tourist offices in several towns and villages surrounding the park are set up to provide information about wildlife, hikes in the park, and accommodations and can also assist in obtaining reservations. Some offices

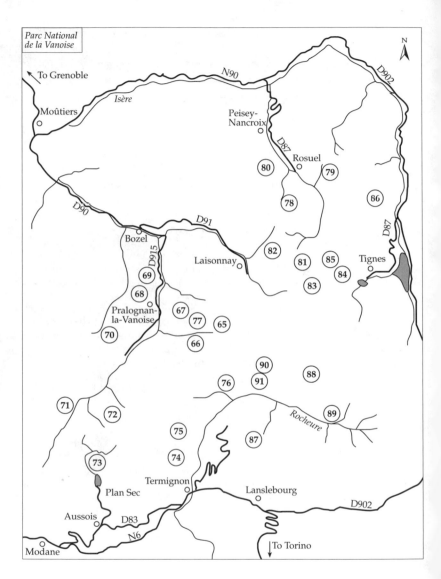

are staffed by an *hôtesse du parc* (park receptionist), also called an *hôtesse d'acceuil*—a specialist who provides very detailed information about all these matters.

There is a central reservation office at Pralognan to which prospective visitors may write or phone to make advance reservations at huts anywhere in the park. In general, though, reservations can be made a few days in advance, except for a large party. Write to Centrale de Réservation des Refuges (listed in Appendix 1). Correspondence written in English is acceptable. The telephone number is (1) 79 08 71 49. You also can write or phone La Hôtesse du Parc National at Pralognan (same address) for information (she speaks English). It is not necessary to reserve accommodations in advance for June or September. There is a per-person charge for reservations, but there is no need to send postal coupons.

Five *portes du parc*, or "gates to the park," have been established on the border of the park's central zone. The *portes du parc* are simple inns with dormitory accommodations, somewhat like alpine club huts but with indoor toilets and showers. They also provide park information, and some offer films or nature programs. Most *portes du parc* are accessible by road, and one can be reached by a park shuttle bus. They also offer a menu other than the meal of the evening. Hikers can use the *portes du parc* as a base. The five *portes* are Porte de Rosuel (near Peisey-Nancroix) and Porte du Bois (near Champagny-en-Vanoise) for the Tarentaise; and Porte d'Aussois, also known as Fort Marie-Christine (near Aussois), Porte du Plan du Lac, also known as the

Cheesemaking at the alpage at Ritord

Refuge du Plan du Lac (above Termignon); and Porte de l'Ogère (near Villarodin and Modane) for the Maurienne.

The Vanoise is also unusual in that many of its huts are either privately owned or belong to the park. These huts are exactly like alpine club huts, with one notable exception: the hut keepers will make up picnic lunches for hikers to take away.

NORTHERN VANOISE

The river Isère, flowing through the valley of the Tarentaise, forms the northern border of the Vanoise. Two pleasant, small towns lie at either end of this section of the river and serve as gateways into the region: Bourg St. Maurice to the east, and Moûtiers to the west, connected by highway N90. From the Tarentaise valley, several important tributary valleys cut deep into the mountains. The valleys offering the greatest number of hiking possibilities are the Vallée du Doron de Pralognan and the Vallée du Ponturin.

Walks from La Vallée du Doron de Pralognan: Pralognan-la-Vanoise

Pralognan-la-Vanoise (locally called Pralognan) is a small resort at the end of this valley, an upper tributary of the Vallée du Doron de Bozel (Doron means stream in the dialect of Savoie). This attractive, lively village, reached by D915, offers numerous and varied hiking itineraries. Pralognan was a traditional mountaineering center for good reason, as it is situated close to some of the most spectacular mountains in the region. It is unique in one respect: Pralognan is the only hiking center featured in this book that is a resort, and a ski resort at that, but do not be put off by that word. Pralognan bears no resemblance to custom-built French ski resorts, clots of high-rise concrete buildings that stick up like ugly, alien fungi on the slopes, which have smothered any vestiges of previous villages on the sites, if indeed there were any. Pralognan is truly an old village with a long history. In more recent times, the people of Pralognan gave refuge to several Jewish families during World War II and successfully hid them, as well as the village priest—who was active in the Resistance movement—when German troops searched the village. To retain its appearance, the inhabitants of Pralognan have chosen to ban high-rise structures. As a resort it is a very simple kind of place, with one small cablecar, a tennis court or two, and a village swimming pool. There are no elegant boutiques or glittering, grand hotels in Pralognan.

At the junction of three valleys, Pralognan offers a wide variety of hikes in several different directions. For several walks, a taxi may be convenient: you can order taxis from Intersports La Hutte, a sports shop on the main street of Pralognan (tel. 79 08 70 89), or from M. Rolland Denis (tel. 79 08 70 10).

65. The Col and the Refuge de la Vanoise

Rating: moderate
Distance one way: 6.5 km
High point: 2,530 m

Total climb: 900 m
Time: 3 hours up, 2 hours 40 minutes down

The Col de la Vanoise is one of the most popular destinations in the Pralognan area. Hikers walk there for its own sake, and it is a prime destination on a long-distance walking tour, the Tour des Glaciers de la Vanoise (see hike 76, The Refuge de l'Arpont to the Refuge de la Vanoise, and hike 77, The Refuge de la Vanoise to Pralognan), as well. The hut is located at the col.

The Télépherique du Mont Bochor operates in the summer and can be used on the way to the Col de la Vanoise. It only offers an advantage for this walk if you have no car, since the lower station is in the center of Pralognan (across from the tourist office). From the upper station, however, you must descend to join the main trail, and then climb again. If you drive, or wish to walk to the trailhead, take the road or the footpath (which cuts across the loops of the road) 2.8 kilometers northeastward to Les Fontanettes (1,650 meters), where there is a parking area and a bar/

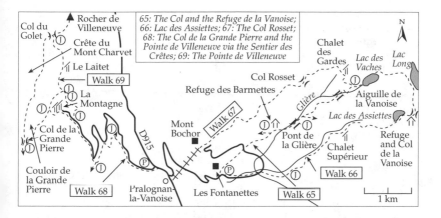

restaurant. There, a signpost points you left to the Col and the Refuge de la Vanoise.

From Les Fontanettes, start up a paved road and pass at once under a chairlift line. A moment later take the gravel trail between a second parking area to your right and a jeep road. A sign points northeast to the col. Ascend through woods, with a ski slope to your right. When you intersect the jeep road again, turn left and take it upward; it's less steep than the track you'll see up the ski slope to your right. Pass the little restaurant at Les Barmettes and cross a bridge, the Pont de la Glière. Ten minutes later, reach a signposted junction; bear right. You'll come to Lac des Vaches, a very shallow lake that you cross on a causeway of big, flat stepping stones; this takes about 5 minutes. To your right is the broad, sharp-edged slab of the Aiguille de la Vanoise, like a great adze-blade, while to your left is the impressive hanging Glacier de la Grande Casse.

Climb rather steeply and pass another lake, Lac Long, on your left. The trail nearly levels out as you reach the col, which is exceptionally broad and gently sloped. The hut on the col consists of two buildings, a large restaurant and a dormitory. It is still sometimes called by its former name, the Refuge Félix Faure, commemorating the president of the French Republic who visited this spot in 1897, accompanied by a host of generals and government ministers to inspect military preparations during a period of war fever with Italy.

You can return by the same route. Note that while the trail marked "Les Fontanettes par la Cascade" gives you a view of a waterfall, it is a longer, steeper route back than the standard one. There is a telephone at the bar at Les Fontanettes, from which you can call a taxi if you wish.

Hike 66, Lac des Assiettes, is an alternate descent route.

66. Lac des Assiettes

Rating: strenuous
Distance one way: 5 km
High point: 2,530 m

Total climb: 900 m down
Time: 3 hours to Les Fontanettes

This is a more difficult, much rougher route and offers good views of a wild, dramatic, rather hidden valley. It should not be taken in wet or threatening weather.

To return from the Col de la Vanoise via Lac des Assiettes, go behind the Refuge de la Vanoise on an unsigned trail heading southwest and soon pass a black pipe. In about 3 minutes the trail curves westward and there is a blue blaze. Soon you will see the lake below, which is dry except early in the summer. Descend along the trail with the lake to your right. Then cross the lakebed (assuming it's dry) in a straight line, heading west; if there is water, keep to this southern side of the lake to get around it. There are a few blue blazes at the end of the lake. Climb a few steps to a shallow notch with a cairn and continue westward.

You will now enter a wild valley with fine views of the Glacier de l'Arcelin to your left and of the Glacier de la Grande Casse behind you as you descend. About 30 minutes after leaving the hut, step over a rivulet; there is a ravine to your right. Descend steeply; the ground is uneven, with rocky outcrops underfoot that will be slippery in wet weather. The trail jogs to the right (north), crosses a brook, then turns left (southwest) again; the ravine is now to your left. Continue steeply down, stepping over another rivulet; there is an abandoned stone house to your left. Red blazes and a sign for Pralognan painted on a rock point left. There are fine views up to your left of a big, slab-sided rock wall. About 1 hour 30 minutes after leaving the hut, reach the river. The trail continues at first along the right bank, to which it clings; a few red blazes show the route. Twenty minutes after reaching the river, you'll see the crossing place—rocks in the river bed. The crossing is of moderate difficulty.

Once on the other side, cross a series of streams on rocks (these are not difficult). Then switchback steeply down through slippery rock outcrops. As you come to the bottom of a band of trees (1,900 meters), look to your left for a short trail that traverses to reach a main trail; here, a signpost that says "Col de la Vanoise" points back the way you came. (From this junction you can reach either the main trail to the col or a trail to the Cirque d'Arcelin and the Grand and Petit Marchet.) Turn right (northwest) and go down the main trail, passing park signs on a big rock. Descend to the river and the jeep road. Turn left (southwest) onto the jeep road; bypass a bridge but in 10 minutes, at a signposted junction, turn right and cross another bridge, then turn left onto a jeep road and soon reach Les Fontanettes.

67. The Col Rosset

Rating: strenuous
Distance loop trip: 10 km
High point: 2,545 m
Total climb: 570 m up, 740 m down
  to Pralognan

Time: 2 hours up, 3 hours 20 minutes
  down to Pralognan (ascent distance
  and time are based on starting
  from the upper cablecar station)

One of the most scenic walks in the area, this offers truly spectacular views. Although no scrambling is involved, one short section is quite narrow and exposed. Do not try this walk if there is snow on the trail, and it probably would not be safe to bring a small child here. Inquire at the park and tourist office in the village about trail conditions. For this excursion, it is advantageous to take the Mont Bochor *télépherique*, which starts from the main street—which is unnamed—of Pralognan.

From behind the upper cablecar station, take a broad path down a few steps to a signposted junction and continue straight ahead (northeast) toward the Col Rosset. On your left is a restaurant. The trail climbs through meadows, with a chairlift (inoperative in summer) to your right. The trail becomes fairly steep, then curves around to the left to avoid climbing straight up a little round hill in front of you. Soon there is a splendid view before you. The trail rises over a little bump; follow red blazes to another junction and bear left (north, then northeast) for the Col Rosset. After reaching a ski lift, a sign points you right (east) to the Col Rosset.

Approach a small notch and reach a third signposted junction: continue straight (northeast) for the col. After this point, there will be some blue blazes as well as some red and white ones. Climb more steeply and about 1 hour 40 minutes after starting the hike, reach a notch with a magnificent view of the Pointe du Vallonet, the Pointe des Volnets, and the Glacier de la Grande Casse. From here the trail continues to a higher notch overlooking a very steep drop, and then a narrow, exposed trail traverses the slope to reach the col, 2 hours from the upper cablecar station.

View from the Col Rosset

To descend, take little switchbacks eastward; the first 80 meters are steep and on scree. The trail levels out to cross a boulder-strewn ridge, still to the east; a few blue blazes can be seen. The views around are wild and wonderful. The trail rises and falls slightly, descends steeply through a cleft for 30 meters and then descends more gently to reach a bridged stream about 40 minutes below the col. Just past this is a tiny wood cabin (closed, belonging to the park) marked "Chalet des Gardes" on maps but "Cabane de Vallonet" at the cabin itself. Another 10 minutes' descent brings you to the main trail between Les Fontanettes to the Col and the Refuge de la Vanoise (see hike 65, The Col and the Refuge de la Vanoise). Turn left here for the col, or right to return to Les Fontanettes and Pralognan. Ten minutes beyond the junction reach Lac des Vaches with its causeway of stepping stones.

When returning toward Pralognan, as you reach the restaurant at Les Barmettes, you will see a sign pointing right for Plateau du Mont Bochor. This is a poor trail and not a shortcut back to the cablecar! Instead, continue down the main trail. In about 30 minutes reach a signposted junction where another trail diverges to the right for the Mont Bochor *télépherique*. This is the trail to take if you wish to return by the lift, but note that you must climb up for about 35 minutes to reach the cablecar station.

■

The Col de la Grande Pierre and the Pointe de Villeneuve

This can be divided into two walks: hike 68 is the entire loop trip, which is rather adventurous; hike 69, much easier, is just a round trip to the Pointe de Villeneuve, as it is named on trail signs; it is called "Rocher de Villeneuve" on maps.

68. The Col de la Grande Pierre and the Pointe de Villeneuve via the Sentier des Crêtes

Rating: strenuous
Distance loop trip: 14 km
High point: 2,403 m
Total climb: 1,050 m

Time: 3 hours up to the Col de la Grande Pierre, 1 hour 45 minutes for the traverse to the Pointe de Villeneuve, 2 hours down

The Sentier des Crêtes extends between the Col de la Grande Pierre and the Pointe de Villeneuve. It snakes along the top of a ridge marked the Crête du Mont Charvet on the map and is often narrow and very exposed. Do not take this trail if the weather is wet or threatening or in high winds. The landscape along this crest is bizarre, pocked with conical craters (*entonnoirs*): on each side of the trail are holes, sometimes quite deep, that taper toward the bottom. The rock, which is white or gray, eroded, cracked, and sometimes powdery, is gypsum, a calcium sulfate mineral used to make plaster. As the winter snow melts it dissolves the gypsum, which collapses to form these craters.

Walk past the tennis court of the Hôtel du Grand Bec in the direction of the Pont de la Pêche. Very soon a sign points you to the right to several destinations, including the Pointe de Villeneuve and the Col de la Grande Pierre. This is at the west edge of the village.

Follow the signs for these destinations. Walk through some woods and turn left (northwest) onto a side path that ascends. There are several junctions, all signposted. About 40 minutes from the start of the hike, cross a jeep road where a sign points up to the Grande Pierre and the Pointe de Villeneuve; this section is steep. Reach a wooden bench with white blazes nearby; turn left here and in another minute reach a signposted junction where you turn left (south) for La Montagne (an alpage) and the Col de la Grande Pierre. Note: If you go straight ahead here, you will be on the trail that heads directly for the Pointe de Villeneuve.

Climb steeply up. The trail is narrow and a little exposed. Thirty minutes past the junction, reach a dirt jeep road and turn right (north). There is now a nice view. In 5 minutes a sign points left (west), off the jeep road, for the Col de la Grande Pierre. Ascend to a meadow and bear right (north) to reach La Montagne, where there are a few small farm buildings. The path loops back (southwest) behind the alpage and then switchbacks up very steeply to the col; this final slope is marked "Couloir de la Grande Pierre" on some maps. Reach the col about 3 hours after starting the hike. La Grande Casse (3,855 meters) faces you to the east, and you can gaze down upon Courchevel to the west.

At the col turn right (north) and begin the traverse of the Crête du Mont Charvet. The trail winds along the ridge, sometimes over the crests and sometimes just a few feet below them, with gypsum craters on each side. This traverse will take about 1 hour 20 minutes, after which you'll descend to some high meadows. At a signposted junction at the Col du Golet, continue east to the Pointe de Villeneuve (or turn right—south—for Pralognan). To reach the Pointe de Villeneuve just ahead of you, climb about 100 meters; it should take 20 minutes; it offers good views. Descend from the summit to the same signposted junction near its base and follow the trail southward to Pralognan. As you descend, you'll pass several junctions for trails to the Col de la Grande Pierre. At the little saddle in the woods, by the wooden bench you passed in ascent, turn right to return to Pralognan.

69. The Pointe de Villeneuve

Rating: moderate   **Total climb:** 800 m
Distance round trip: 13 km   **Time:** 2 hours 30 minutes up, 2 hours
High point: 2,197 m   down

The Pointe de Villeneuve (as it is called on trail signs; "Rocher de Villeneuve" on maps) is a small knob at the end of a ridge, offering good views of the Vanoise massif to the east and of Courchevel to the west.

Start as for hike 68, The Col de la Grande Pierre and the Pointe de Villeneuve via the Sentier des Crêtes, but, at the signposted junction near a wooden bench, stay to the right (north) instead of turning left for the Col de la Grande Pierre. The trail climbs gradually through woods, emerging onto meadows amid which are a few old farm houses. Reach a grassy saddle, the Col du Golet, where a sign points you up to the Pointe de Villeneuve, which in any case is quite visible.

■

Walks from the Pont de la Pêche

Several popular walks begin just south of Pralognan at the Pont de la Pêche. A narrow but good paved road leads 6.5 kilometers to the Pont de la Pêche, where the road ends. There is a large parking area here. Trail signs at the southern end of the parking area direct hikers to various points. You can also walk here from Pralognan along the GR 55 or even take a taxi.

70. Le Petit Mont-Blanc

Rating: moderate
Distance round trip: 11 km
High point: 2,677 m

Total climb: 950 m
Time: 2 hours 35 minutes up, 1 hour 50 minutes down

This little mountain is quite easy to ascend—a hiker's, not a climber's, peak—and offers a good, panoramic view of the area. It was not given its name because it is particularly high (it is not), nor because it resembles Mont Blanc (it does not). Rather, it is so named because extensive areas of gypsum near its summit give it a whitish, chalky appearance. It is one of two walks near Pralognan with gypsum deposits (see hike 68, The Col de la Grande Pierre and the Pointe de Villeneuve via the Sentier des Crêtes).

From the Pont de la Pêche parking area, turn right onto the GR 55 toward the Refuge de Péclet-Polset, the Col d'Aussois, and the Col de Chavière. In a few minutes cross a bridge. Follow the trail, which at first is

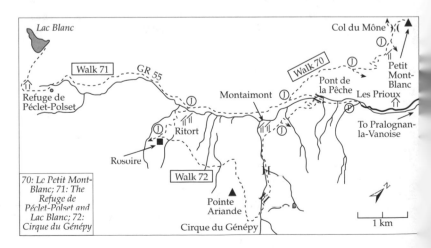

Atop Le Petit Mont-Blanc

a broad gravel jeep road, southward. In about 25 minutes you will see a sign that points right (northwest) to a path to the Col du Mône and Le Petit Mont-Blanc. Turn off the jeep road onto this path, which leads up the slope in a long, diagonal traverse. A trail merging from the right is a much steeper way that starts from the hamlet of Les Prioux, below. Pass a little stone shelter, and about 2 hours 10 minutes from the start of the hike reach a saddle—the Col du Mône—between two small peaks. Le Petit Mont-Blanc is to the right (north). Bear right and continue toward the summit. The final 100 meters are steep. The upper slopes are full of curious, cone-shaped craters, caused by erosion of the gypsum.

Close to the summit there is much exposed rock; it is white and gray and crumbles to a powdery white dust. There is an extensive view to the northeast of La Grande Casse, Le Grand Bec, and other peaks.

71. The Refuge de Péclet-Polset and Lac Blanc

Rating: moderate
Distance round trip: 15 km
High point: 2,474 m

Total climb: 760 m
Time: 2 hours 35 minutes up, 1 hour 45 minutes down

This is a straight, simple route that follows the GR 55 all the way to the hut. Lac Blanc is just behind the hut.

From the southern end of the parking area at the Pont de la Pêche, turn right onto the GR 55, signposted for the Refuge de Péclet-Polset. The trail for the first hour is almost a jeep track, with a very gentle gradient. The trail then begins to climb, although the grade is moderate. After an hour, you'll pass the signposted junction for the Col d'Aussois, but continue

161

straight ahead. After another hour and 10 minutes pass a tiny pond to your left, and reach the hut about 20 minutes later. The final hour of trail is moderately steep.

From the hut there is a fine view of the Pointe de l'Echelle just across the valley. Continue up behind the hut and in 5 minutes reach a ridge from which you can look down upon Lac Blanc, whose water is a pale, milky blue. Lovely picnic spots abound.

72. Cirque du Génépy

Rating: moderate
Distance loop trip: 14.5 km
High point: 2,449 m

Total climb: 700 m
Time: 2 hours 15 minutes up, 1 hour 30 minutes down

This is a splendid circuit with some of the best views in the region, climbing to the broad cirque carved out by the Glacier de Génépy, and then affording views of the Glacier de Péclet-Polset as you traverse the slope of the Pointe Ariande on a trail locally called the Sentier Balcon d'Ariande. This descends to the little alpage at Ritord, close to the GR 55. You can shorten the hike by just retracing your steps from the cirque.

From the parking area at the Pont de la Pêche, stay to the left; do not turn right onto the GR 55, as for hike 70, Le Petit Mont-Blanc, and hike 71, The Refuge de Péclet-Polset and Lac Blanc. After 35 minutes reach Montaimont, a small alpage with a signposted junction; both trails lead to the Cirque du Génépy, but the one to the right (south) is more direct. Continue therefore to the right, climb a little more steeply and in 15 minutes reach an open shelf from which you can see the glacier above; a stream descends noisily to your right. From another little viewpoint, you can see the torrent pouring into a little pool below; it seems to charge through its narrow, rock-walled bed. About 1 hour 30 minutes from the start of the hike, reach the shelf at the foot of the cirque. Cross a bridge and continue up along the stream's left bank, and cross a second bridge soon afterward. The sweep of the glacier above dominates the view.

To continue to the Sentier Balcon d'Ariande, follow the trail from the second bridge toward the glacier, onto the base of the moraine. The trail bends to the right (west), leaving the moraine and crossing a little brook. (A much narrower trace, which you may see to your left, leads up the knife-edge moraine and becomes very narrow, steep, and exposed.) The trail traverses to the west and then south, descending steeply to a streambed (this section can be a little tricky if there is snow) and then undulating along the slope. At Rosoire, where there is an open-air milking station, turn right (the trail to the left climbs to the Col d'Aussois). The signpost here points up to the col, but not down to Ritord (spelled this way on trail signs, but "Ritort" on regional maps). Descend a fairly steep slope to reach the alpage at Ritord, where they sell cheese made on the premises, milk, and soft drinks. You can also watch some of the cheese-making: the milk is heated in a great copper cauldron over a wood fire. (The cheese specialties here are Beaufort and Sérac Frais.) Cross the bridge just outside this *fromagerie*, reach the GR 55 in a few minutes, and turn right to return to the Pont de la Pêche.

■

Tour des Glaciers de la Vanoise

This is one of the best-known circuits in the Vanoise. A multi-day tour, it makes a loop around the cluster of glaciers known as the Glaciers de la Vanoise, just south of La Grande Casse. The tour is often done in 4 days with three overnight stops, although strong walkers can make it in 3 days. You can also walk some of its most scenic sections as day trips, either from Pralognan or from Aussois or Termignon in the Haute Maurienne (see the section Southern Vanoise, later). The classic direction is counterclockwise, starting from Pralognan, although it can be done the other way; it can also be started from Aussois or Termignon.

The major segments are as follows: Hike 73, The Col d'Aussois and the Refuge du Plan Sec; hike 74, The Refuge du Plan Sec to the Refuge de l'Arpont; hike 76, The Refuge de l'Arpont to the Refuge de la Vanoise, at the Col de la Vanoise; and hike 77, The Refuge de la Vanoise to Pralognan. Overnight reservations can be made, even just a day or two in advance, at the tourist office in Pralognan.

73. The Col d'Aussois and the Refuge du Plan Sec

Rating: very strenuous
Distance one way: 15 km
High point: 2,916 m
Total climb: 1,300 m up, 700 m down
Time: 4 hours up, 3 hours 10 minutes down

The Refuge du Plan Sec is easily accessible from Aussois. You can drive up and park near two artificial lakes, the Plan d'Amont and the Plan d'Aval, and walk to the hut in about an hour, but the longer walk described here is much more interesting.

Start as for hike 71, The Refuge de Péclet-Polset and Lac Blanc. If you drive to the Pont de la Pêche, you can leave your car for several nights in the parking area. About 1 hour after starting up the trail, turn left (southeast) at the signposted junction for the Alpage Ritord and this col. The few stone buildings of the alpage are on your left. Beyond Ritord, the trail switchbacks up to the left of a small cliff and gorge. Reach a shelf, where the trail is more gradual. You'll reach a signposted junction, where the trail that traverses the Pointe Ariande (see hike 72, Cirque du Génépy) enters from the left. Continue toward the right (southwest) to the Col d'Aussois. Two hours 30 minutes from the start of the hike, reach a stream and cross a bridge to your right. From there, climb steeply to the col over shaly outcrops, then up a slope of scree and mud. Since this is a north-facing slope, snow can linger here into July and the late melting will leave mud. A network of little paths and cairns leads up to the col about 4 hours from the start of the hike. Just to your right is a little peaklet, the rocky Pointe de l'Observatoire, that can be climbed in about 30 minutes. Hikers making this a day trip from Pralognan often climb this.

As you descend from the col its south side is less shaly, but large rocky outcrops make the descent tiring. Look for red and white and also yellow blazes. After about 1 hour 30 minutes, cross a bridge over a little brook to your left. Soon you'll be off the steep slope and onto a large grassy shelf.

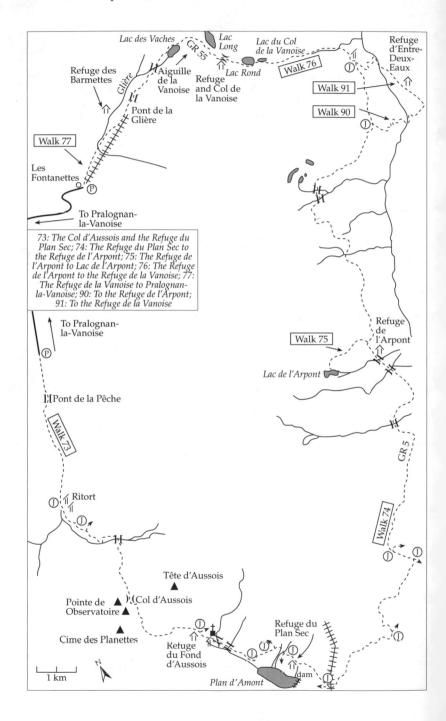

Lac des Vaches
Lac Long
Lac du Col de la Vanoise
GR 55
Walk 76
Refuge d'Entre-Deux-Eaux
Refuge des Barmettes
Aiguille de la Vanoise
Lac Rond
Refuge and Col de la Vanoise
Glière
Pont de la Glière
Walk 91
Walk 90
Walk 77
Les Fontanettes
To Pralognan-la-Vanoise

73: The Col d'Aussois and the Refuge du Plan Sec; 74: The Refuge du Plan Sec to the Refuge de l'Arpont; 75: The Refuge de l'Arpont to Lac de l'Arpont; 76: The Refuge de l'Arpont to the Refuge de la Vanoise; 77: The Refuge de la Vanoise to Pralognan-la-Vanoise; 90: To the Refuge de l'Arpont; 91: To the Refuge de la Vanoise

To Pralognan-la-Vanoise
Pont de la Pêche
Walk 73
Ritort

Refuge de l'Arpont
Walk 75
Lac de l'Arpont
GR 5
Walk 74

Tête d'Aussois
Pointe de Observatoire
Col d'Aussois
Cime des Planettes
Refuge du Plan Sec
Refuge du Fond d'Aussois
Plan d'Amont
dam

1 km
N

About 2 hours from the col, reach the little Refuge du Fond d'Aussois, a CAF hut. You can stop here, but if you push on to the Refuge du Plan Sec your next day will be easier.

Just beyond the CAF hut is a tiny stone chapel on your left, and then a few other stone buildings. Cross a small bridge and bear right at a signpost. Ahead and below you can see a reservoir of blue-green water. Pass several signposted junctions but continue toward the Refuge du Plan Sec. Cross a couple of small bridges; there will be several more signposted junctions. The last one, at La Fournache, points to the right onto a farm road. Turn left at the signpost to reach the Refuge du Plan Sec, about 1 hour 15 minutes beyond the Refuge du Fond d'Aussois.

This is a pleasant, privately owned place. The guardian's house is a restored farmhouse over 100 years old, and the present dining room was once the stable. Dormitory accommodations are in a separate building. From here, you can see two artificial lakes, the Plan d'Amont and the Plan d'Aval, quite close to each other but of different colors. This is because the upper, greenish-blue lake is fed only by run-off from glaciers and snowfields, whereas the lower, brownish lake is fed by water from hydroelectric turbines.

74. The Refuge du Plan Sec to the Refuge de l'Arpont

Rating: strenuous
Distance one way: 18 km
High point: 2,466 m

Total climb: 750 m
Time: 6 hours

As you descend from the Refuge du Plan Sec, don't take the first left but continue a little farther and turn left (east) when you reach the chairlift at a signposted junction. This joins the GR 5, which winds its way around the many folds of the slope—the type of trail the French call a *sentier balcon*.

Soon after you turn onto the GR 5, there is a short section of exposed trail with a fixed chain you can hold as you traverse the trail. Reach a gully and signposted junction and turn left (north). The trail climbs up along a gully, then switchbacks up its side. As you traverse, there will be numerous signposted junctions; follow the signs, generally pointing north or northeast, for the Refuge de l'Arpont. The views get finer and wilder. After La Turra the trail becomes a sort of narrow jeep road for a short while, then a trail once more. Nearly 2 hours from the start of the hike you'll see a section of traverse ahead that looks quite bad from a distance, but is not bad at all; it crosses a stone slide but the trail is quite broad.

About 3 hours 15 minutes after starting on the trail, cross a stream on rocks (not difficult). Some 30 minutes later the trail bridges a foaming torrent. In another 30 minutes pass an alpage offering cheese, drinks, and *couchettes* (sleeping bunks). About 40 minutes later cross a bridge with a waterfall above to your left, then cross several more small bridges to reach the Refuge de l'Arpont.

From this hut you can take a short but vigorous hike (hike 75, The Refuge de l'Arpont to Lac de l'Arpont) up to Lac de l'Arpont with magnificent views of the Glacier de l'Arpont, which can't be seen from the hut.

75. The Refuge de l'Arpont to Lac de l'Arpont

Rating: strenuous
Distance round trip: 3 km
High point: 2,666 m

Total climb: 370 m
Time: 1 hour 15 minutes up; 1 hour down

Lac de l'Arpont is a spectacular place. The broad Glacier de l'Arpont, crested with séracs, plunges right into this mountain tarn, the white ice meeting the blue water. Getting here is not a long hike from the hut but a fairly steep one, and instead of a clear trail you must do a little route finding. An advantage of staying overnight at the Refuge du Plan Sec instead of the Refuge du Fond d'Aussois is that you gain more than an hour for the next leg of the trip, and if you leave the Refuge du Plan Sec early enough (and are not too tired), you can make this an afternoon's excursion from the Refuge de l'Arpont. Or you can spend an extra night at this hut and make this trip a day's excursion.

Take the path that starts up behind the dormitory of the hut, heading west. This climbs steeply for about 180 meters, then bends to the left. The trail becomes faint, but follow a string of cairns and cross a few brooks. The terrain is rough with lots of rocks and requires a little scrambling. Climb over a final ledge to reach the lake.

Alpage on the route to the Refuge de l'Arpont

76. The Refuge de l'Arpont to the Refuge de la Vanoise

Rating: strenuous   **Total climb:** 850 m up, 650 m down
Distance one way: 14 km   **Time:** 5 hours 15 minutes
High point: 2,522 m

This is the most scenic leg of the entire tour, offering the most extensive glacier views. You can also enjoy this trail's most dramatic section as a day trip from Termignon.

A sign in front of the Refuge de l'Arpont points you left (northeast) toward the Refuge Félix Faure, now called the Refuge de la Vanoise. The trail follows the folds of the slope, and about 1 hour 30 minutes after starting on the trail, a grand panorama unfolds before you. Descend over slabs of rock to cross two streams on rocks, one about 7 meters wide and the other 10 meters wide; although there are many flat rocks, crossing in early morning is an advantage because the water level is lower then. To your left there is a view of the glaciers (at last you are able to see the Glaciers de la Vanoise) while before you is a long mountainous wall and, to your right, La Grande Casse and La Grande Motte (3,654 meters). Descend a little, cross a small brook (easy), and reach a stony area of moraine. The trail continually rises and falls a little.

Two hours 30 minutes from the start of the hike, cross a foaming torrent on a bridge and reach some meadows. Cross another stream on a plank bridge. There is a splendid view of the rock wall above you. Cross another small brook and reach first a lake and then a few small ponds. You are heading more or less east, with a tremendous view behind you of the glaciers. After 3 hours 45 minutes from the Refuge de l'Arpont, reach a signposted junction; the trail descending to the right here (east) would bring you down to the Refuge du Plan du Lac and Termignon. Continue straight ahead (north), however, along a *sentier balcon* that traverses several talus slopes. After the last of these boulder slides the trail fades out, but reach a small shelf where you pick it up again; in any case, it's clear where you must go—straight up to the notch. From there, come out into a long, high valley where the trail follows a very gentle gradient. To your right, La Grande Casse overlooks the valley. Pass a small stone house to your right. Although the trail becomes indistinct it descends to reach a broad shallow stream that you can cross on many stepping stones. On the other side of the stream, turn left on a distinct trail and go northwest through a quite level area. Pass a sign on a cross that reads "Les Barmettes." After crossing a brook on stones, come to a flooded meadow, which you cross on a long stretch of stones in the very shallow water; cairns mark the way along this. About 25 minutes beyond the Les Barmettes sign, reach a couple of aquamarine lakes and in another 15 minutes arrive at the Refuge de la Vanoise.

77. The Refuge de la Vanoise to Pralognan-la-Vanoise

Rating: moderate   **Time:** 2 hours 40 minutes (this
Distance one way: 6.5 km   distance and time is based on a
High point: 2,530 m   descent to Les Fontanettes)
Total climb: 900 m down

This retraces the descent of hike 65, The Col and the Refuge de la Vanoise. The hut is built upon the Col de la Vanoise, where a signpost points the way to Pralognan. The trail at first lies between the broad, sharp-edged slab of the Aiguille de la Vanoise to your left and Lac Long to your right, above which hangs the Glacier de la Grande Casse. Descend a short, steep section to Lac des Vaches, which you cross on a causeway of flat stones. Switchback down to a lower shelf, cross a bridge, and turn right to reach another shelf where there is a long meadow. Pass an alpage behind a long, low stone wall. Another bridge brings you to the Refuge des Barmettes, a privately owned restaurant-hut. Signposts continue to show the way down to Les Fontanettes and then Pralognan (the way to Fontanettes via La Cascade is a longer variant).

Walks from La Vallée du Doron de Champagny: The Refuge du Bois and Laisonnay

The Champagny valley provides an alternative possibility to Pralognan and Rosuel for accommodations and also hikes in the Tarentaise region. Its stream, the Doron de Champagny, joins the Doron de Pralognan at the village of Bozel, where together the two streams merge to form the Doron de Bozel, which flows into the Isère. At the upper end of the Champagny valley is Champagny-en-Vanoise, a small resort that looks prosperous and new. Beyond it, road D91b narrows to climb through a gorge and then emerges into a green and quiet upper valley where there is a very small, simple village, Champagny-le-Haut. Here you'll find the Refuge du Bois, which, like Rosuel, is one of the *portes du parc*. The Refuge du Bois is modern and pleasant and offers programs about the park and its wildlife. About 1 hour's walk (3 kilometers) farther, at the end of the road, is Laisonnay. There is a café/snack bar at Laisonnay d'en-Bas and a very charming gîte d'étape 200 meters farther at Laisonnay d'en-Haut. If you make the Champagny valley your stopping place, you can link up with some of the walks described in other sections of this chapter. Laisonnay is the trailhead for several hikes: from there you can join hike 81, Rosuel to the Col de la Grassaz and the Refuge de la Glière, and hike 82, The Refuge de la Glière to the Col du Plan Séry and Rosuel. From either hike 81 or hike 82, you can continue to the Refuge Entre-le-Lac and Rosuel, or to the Refuge du Palet. Several other walks are also accessible from the upper Champagny valley, and you can get hiking information at the Refuge du Bois.

Walks from La Vallée du Ponturin: Peisey-Nancroix and Rosuel

The upper end of this valley rises to the edge of the Vanoise high plateau and offers numerous possibilities for hikers. Many of the walks ac-

Accompagnateur and group on the route from Rosuel

cessible from here offer spacious views across the high meadows as well as dramatic views of the Vanoise mountains. One road, D87, extends up the valley, linking its villages and hamlets. Peisey-Nancroix, on the valley's eastern slope, is a quiet, unpretentious village with both modest and moderate accommodations. Higher up the slope, above Peisey-Nancroix, are two "purpose-built," artificial ski resorts, Plan Peisey and Vallandry; the buildings are all new and there is no village character. Beyond Peisey-Nancroix, there are two simple hamlets also offering accommodations: Le Moulin and Nancroix (which is separate from Peisey-Nancroix). As you continue up the valley you'll also see a gîte d'étape and a campground. At the end of the road there is a large parking lot for both day hikers and for those who are undertaking one of the longer tours that can be started from here. Just across the road from the parking lot is the Chalet-Refuge de Rosuel, one of the *portes du parc* and another possible base for hikers. At Rosuel there are simple dormitory accommodations and showers, and a restaurant where you can order the menu of the day or a la carte. You can also place an evening order for bread for your next day's picnic lunch. For more supplies, there is a grocery store just outside of Nancroix, and another in Peisey-Nancroix.

From Peisey-Nancroix it is 5.6 kilometers to Rosuel; from Nancroix it is a little over 3.3 kilometers to Rosuel.

The starting point for all walks in this section is Rosuel unless otherwise specified.

78. Lac de la Plagne

Rating: moderate
Distance round trip: 13 km
High point: 2,144 m

Total climb: 600 m
Time: 3 hours up, 2 hours down

This is the most popular walk in the area, so you will find more people on this trail than on any other hike from Rosuel.

A few steps past the Chalet-Refuge de Rosuel at the end of the road is the trailhead, with a signpost for several destinations including Lac de la Plagne. Much of the trail surface is quite rocky. Marked by a few red and white blazes, it goes southeast across a fine meadow. After an initial climb the trail levels out briefly, passes through a stand of larches, then climbs again into open meadows. Through much of this main valley there is a splendid view to your left of the wall of Mont-Pourri (3,779 meters). At its base are cliffs over which a waterfall plummets with a crashing noise; half a dozen torrents stream down the steep green meadows below. Pass a small stone cabin to your right and about 1 hour 40 minutes after starting the hike, come to a signposted junction. Stay to the right (south) for the lake.

The trail continues southward, following along the west side of the blue-green Lac de la Plagne. At the end of the lake cross a bridge and in a few minutes reach the privately owned Refuge Entre-le-Lac. Many hikers come here for lunch on its terrace, while picnickers cluster on the grassy shores around the lake.

79. The Refuge du Mont-Pourri

Rating: moderate
Distance loop trip: 12.5 km
High point: 2,370 m

Total climb: 820 m
Time: 3 hours 10 minutes up, 3 hours 20 minutes down

You'll meet far fewer hikers on this trail than on the one to the Refuge Entre-le-Lac. The trail up is quite steep but the views are striking.

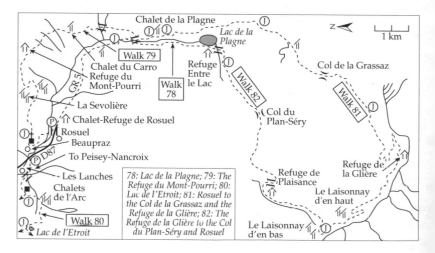

Walk along D87 toward the west end of the parking lot that faces the Chalet-Refuge de Rosuel. A minute beyond the west end of the parking lot, turn right onto a dirt road. The turn is marked by a little red and white blaze on a small rock. This dirt road bridges a stream, then turns left. At a fork stay to the left (south). Fifteen minutes after crossing the stream, a sign points to the right (north) for the Refuge du Mont-Pourri, although the legend on the sign cannot be seen as you approach it from Rosuel. Walk up into the hamlet of Beaupraz, where you'll pass a fountain. Go up a gravel road, passing below an electrical line; there is a tiny chapel to your left, and another sign points to the hut. Continue straight up toward the northeast; do not turn right when you intersect a gravel road. About 30 minutes after starting from the parking area, turn right at a signposted junction onto a narrow path through meadows, marked by occasional red and white blazes. There is a pleasing view of the meadows below.

Switchback up the slope, at first very steeply, through a stand of larches. The trail then curves to the right to begin a long traverse, less steep, to the southeast. Pass a ruined alpage. As you ascend, there is a fine view below you of the upper valley of the Ponturin. The trail passes below a rocky bluff, climbing at first gradually and then more steeply toward the east. About 2 hours 30 minutes after the start of the hike, pass an alpage with several buildings, then climb steeply to another alpage where one building, marked "Bergerie de la Sevolière," may be in use by sheep herders. Turn right here (northeast), cross a stream on stones, and reach the hut in 15 minutes.

The view to the east extends from Mont-Pourri past the Dôme des Platières to La Grande Motte; to the west are l'Aliet and the Bellecôte. Though you can return the way you came, you can also make this a loop trip by descending to the meadows that lie part way toward Lac de la Plagne, and then turning back toward Rosuel.

A sign below the hut points to Lac de la Plagne and the Refuge and the Col du Palet. Take that trail, which heads southeast. You'll pass a small stone cabin. The path cuts through a patch of monk's rhubarb and some stinging nettles. About 35 minutes after leaving the hut, cross a torrent on a bridge. An old field, also overgrown with monk's rhubarb, is enclosed within a stone wall to your left. In another 25 minutes, cross a rather swift but shallow stream on rocks, or wade across. In 15 minutes come to another unbridged stream, easier to cross. Reach the meadow floor and at a signposted junction, turn right (north) and follow a trace of path to return to Rosuel. A stream meanders to your left. About 15 minutes past the junction cross a bridge and then turn right (northwest) at a signposted junction onto the main trail between Rosuel and Lac de la Plagne.

80. Lac de l'Etroit

Rating: moderate
Distance round trip: 6 km
High point: 2,247 m

Total climb: 800 m
Time: 2 hours 25 minutes up, 1 hour
50 minutes down

This hike climbs up to a little lake from which there is a good although long-distance view of Mont Blanc. It's a popular outing for both children and adults because it passes a working alpage where there are friendly goats and you can see cheese being made.

If you start from the Chalet-Refuge de Rosuel, the trailhead is 1.5 kilometers down D87 on your left; 50 meters farther is a little grass parking area, also on your left, under the trees. If you reach a bridge and Camping les Glières, you've gone too far. If you start from Nancroix, you'll see a fork in the road and a group of little signs: Village des Larches, Chalet les Glaciers, the Refuge Rosuel, and Crêperie Félix. From this fork it is 150 meters farther to the trail junction.

A red and white blaze on a rock marks the trail, which is at first very broad—really a farm road. It takes you into woods; in 5 minutes you'll cross a stream on a bridge. The road then turns right and at once crosses another bridge. You are now on the GR 5. In a few minutes you'll see a large, two-story stone ruin on your left, site of an eighteenth-century mine. Follow the GR 5, which bends to the right here, and pass another stone house to your left. In 5 minutes (about 10 minutes from the trailhead) come to a signpost that points left to Lac de l'Etroit.

Ascend through woods and in 1 hour reach an open meadow, where the trail climbs more gradually. Soon cross a stream to your left on stones and continue up through meadows with a fine view of Mont-Pourri behind you. About 1 hour 30 minutes from the start of the hike, reach the Chalets de l'Arc, an alpage consisting of five stone buildings where cheese is made and sold. Here a sign points right (northwest) for the lake. In a few minutes cross a stream on stones, continue along a meadow, and soon cross two more little brooks. The trail curves around a shoulder, climbing southwest up to a little knoll. It bends to the right and makes a diagonal traverse up the slope to your right. About 2 hours 25 minutes from the start of the trail reach the highest point of this walk, with a panoramic view to the north and Mont-Pourri to the east. The lake is visible just below and you can descend to it in 5 minutes.

Although there is an alternative route down to the Pont Romano that would make this a loop trip, that way is extremely steep. Instead, retrace your steps. Another advantage to returning the way you came is that you face Mont-Pourri and Bellecôte, which makes for a scenic descent.

Multi-day tours starting from Rosuel. The idea of hiking in a circuit, often around a particular mountain, is very popular in France: the most famous such loop is the Tour du Mont Blanc. But there are many other circular tours such as the Tour des Glaciers de la Vanoise (hike 73, The Col d'Aussois to the Refuge du Plan Sec, through hike 77, The Refuge de la Vanoise to Pralognan). There are several tours that start from Rosuel or that pass through it, including the Tour du Sommet de Bellecôte and the Tour du Mont-Pourri.

Tour du Sommet de Bellecôte

You can do this circuit around the Bellecôte comfortably in two days, or more if you prefer. It's a very pleasant tour with some superb scenery, interesting overnight possibilities, and no difficult passages.

81. Rosuel to the Col de la Grassaz and the Refuge de la Glière

Rating: strenuous
Distance one way: 16 km
High point: 2,637 m

Total climb: 1,080 m up, 660 m down
Time: 7 hours to the Refuge de la Glière

The view from the Col de la Grassaz is one of the most splendid sights in the Vanoise.

Begin as for hike 78, Lac de la Plagne. One hour 35 minutes after leaving Rosuel, come to the first signposted junction and turn left and cross a bridge. In another 25 minutes reach the junction for the trail that descends from the Refuge du Mont-Pourri. Stay to the right and follow the track through a long, quite level meadow. Two hours 20 minutes after starting the hike, come to the signposted junction at la Plagne, an old alpage with a few cabins. Keep to the right and head south on a trail that leads to the Refuge du Palet. The trail follows a rocky crest, crossing two streams on stones; you can see Lac de la Plagne and the Refuge Entre-le-Lac below to your right, and you'll pass a couple of trails that lead down to them. You are now in a very broad, U-shaped valley with gently rounded slopes. Continue along a quite level stretch and pass the trail junction to the Col du Plan-Séry; you are heading toward the snowy dome of La Grande Motte. Three hours 30 minutes from the start of the trail, reach a signposted junction and turn right (southwest) for the Col de la Grassaz.

Pastures facing La Grande Motte

Passing a tiny stone cabin on your left, gradually ascend a wide valley through wild, empty country, with a little lake to your left amid rugged gray mountains. Reach the Col de la Grassaz about 4 hours 45 minutes from the start of the hike. The view is utterly superb: you are facing the north wall of La Grande Casse, black and very wide, pleated into sharp folds, with vertical bands of snow in the narrow furrows. Impressive as it is, La Grande Casse is only part of a huge span of mountains stretching across the landscape, glistening with over a dozen glaciers. As you approach a little closer, you'll see La Grande Motte as well. The whole scene before you is filled with mountains and glaciers.

From the pass, the trail descends through meadows, the glorious panorama all the while before you. Alpage buildings are scattered across the meadows and as you descend, curving to the right (southwest), you'll intersect a dirt farm road. You can take this down on the trail that cuts across the loops of the road. Eventually you'll turn right (southwest), rejoining the farm road. As the road starts a series of big switchbacks, you can take the trail to the left (south), which is actually part of a network of paths, some blazed with white, that cuts out most of the loops. As you look down the slope, you can see a very small stone building below, with a pitched roof of slates. This is the Refuge de la Glière, which you'll reach after a last steep descent, about 2 hours 10 minutes from the Col de la Grassaz.

Owned by the Commune de Champagny, this little hut is even simpler and plainer than other full-service huts (that is, that serve meals), but it has a special charm. With only twenty-one places it is more like a farm cottage than a hut; its keeper says it is what CAF huts used to be like before they expanded to accommodate so many hikers. Across a little lane is an old *cave à fromage*, a stone building with a barrel roof that until recently was used to age cheeses. Here you can still buy the Beaufort cheese made at the local alpages as well as butter and *sérac*, which is similar to cottage cheese. You can also purchase soft drinks and chocolate.

In fine weather, the hut keeper serves the evening meal outside at a couple of plain wooden tables. On one beautiful summer evening, we were served air-dried ham (a local specialty), a sort of *salade niçoise* with green beans and tuna, soup, rice, and *sérac* for dessert. The scene was spectacular, with the black wall of the Aiguille de l'Epéna towering above. There is also a small kitchen in the hut where you can cook your own meals.

Note: You can spend the night here or go on for about 1 hour 30 minutes more to Laisonnay d'en-Haut, where there is a small gîte d'étape of considerable charm, the Refuge du Laisonnay.

82. The Refuge de la Glière to the Col du Plan-Séry and Rosuel

Rating: strenuous
Distance one way: 11 km
High point: 2,609 m

Total climb: 1,030 m up, 1,470 m down
Time: 8 hours

From the Refuge de la Glière, walk down the farm road (southward); the Doron de Champagny river flows below to your left in a deep, V shaped bed. Just before Laisonnay, 1 hour 30 minutes from the hut, reach a signposted junction where you turn right (northeast) for the Col du Plan-Séry. A big waterfall above can also be used as a marker. The trail climbs steeply, with the waterfall to your left. Reach the top of the waterfall in about 50 minutes; the grade moderates and you are now above the trees. The trail climbs through a narrow upper valley. You'll pass a small stone house, then cross a bridge. Fifteen minutes beyond the bridge reach the small, simple Refuge de Plaisance, about 3 hours 15 minutes from the Refuge de la Glière. Restaurant service here is limited to beverages, soup, and crêpes, although overnight guests may cook their own meals. The view is very fine, extending from the Pointe de la Petite Glière to the Becca Motta.

From here a sign points northeast to the Col du Plan-Séry. The narrow upper end of this scenic valley is hemmed in by cliffs streaked with cascading streams. A moment past the hut, cross a bridge and ascend moderately steep switchbacks along the right (east) side of the valley. The trail bends to the right (east) to climb out of the valley and reaches a high meadow strewn with white rocks. Cross the Plan-Séry, a large flat area. From here, climb quite steeply to the pass, with a view to your left of yellow-gray outcrops of rock, some of which have been eroded, as is typical of limestone, into pillars and columns. Just before the col reach a little saddle, a sort of false pass, but in 5 minutes you'll be at the Col du Plan-Séry, 5 hours after starting from the Refuge de la Glière.

The descent from the col is quite steep, and the path has been eroded into gullies. In 40 minutes reach a signposted junction and turn left (northeast) for the Refuge Entre-le-Lac; the trail to the right climbs to the Col du Palet. In another 20 minutes reach the Refuge Entre-le-Lac, where you can get a meal or snack, or stay overnight. From here turn left (north), cross a bridge, and soon pass Lac de la Plagne. The trail leads northward to Rosuel, which you reach about 1 hour 20 minutes after leaving the Refuge Entre-le-Lac.

■

Tour du Mont-Pourri

This is a modified version of the classic Tour du Mont-Pourri. The standard tour makes a big loop around the mountain, with overnight possibilities on the trail or near it at the Refuge du Mont-Pourri, the Refuge Entre-le-Lac, the Refuge du Palet, the Refuge de la Martin, and the Refuge de Turia, although some other variations are possible. The standard tour is often done in 3 to 4 days.

There are several problems with the standard route, stemming from the placement of overnight facilities along it. The Refuge de la Martin and the Refuge de Turia do not serve meals or sell food (a stove, pots, and fuel are available, and hikers bring and cook their own food), and Arc 2000, a "purpose-built" ski resort, offers no accommodations for the summer hiker. For this reason, the personnel at park offices recommend that the full Tour du Mont-Pourri be started—and ended—at Arc 2000. If you were to start at Arc 2000, it would be best to leave a car there since if you conclude the circuit at Arc 2000, returning late in the day, you would need to get somewhere else for overnight accommodations. It should also be noted that there are two ways to go from the Refuge de Turia to Arc 2000; one is a shortcut that crosses Le Grand Col, a very difficult and even dangerous pass that requires climbing equipment and skills.

The modified tour proposed here begins at Rosuel, takes you to the Refuge du Palet for your first night, then to the Refuge de la Martin (where you must cook your own food) for your second. You return to Rosuel on the third day. Be sure to carry plenty of food that can easily be prepared; French grocery stores sell a variety of packaged dried soups, and some of these, with a can of tuna fish, some bread, and dried fruit, can make a good supper.

83. Rosuel to the Refuge du Palet

Rating: moderate
Distance one way: 10.5 km
High point: 2,556 m

Total climb: 1,000 m
Time: 4 hours 55 minutes

This is a section of the GR 5. Begin as for hike 81, Rosuel to the Col de la Grassaz and the Refuge de la Glière. After 3 hours 30 minutes, reach the signposted junction where the trail to the Col de la Grassaz veers off to the right; instead, keep to the left, heading south. From here, the trail climbs through a broad valley set between towers of naked rock. In another 15 minutes reach a four-way junction. Continue straight ahead, southeast,

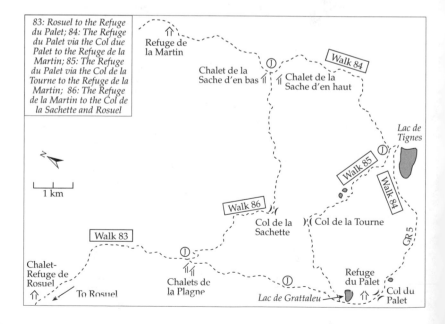

83: Rosuel to the Refuge du Palet; 84: The Refuge du Palet via the Col due Palet to the Refuge de la Martin; 85: The Refuge du Palet via the Col de la Tourne to the Refuge de la Martin; 86: The Refuge de la Martin to the Col de la Sachette and Rosuel

Dinner at the Refuge du Palet

toward the Col du Palet and soon reach Lac de Grattaleu. Cross a brook (the outlet from the lake) on a few stones and continue southward. The trail soon bends left (southeast); climb steeply for 10 minutes to reach the Refuge du Palet. The Col du Palet is 10 minutes farther up the slope, at 2,652 meters.

From the col, the view is very extensive: you can see eastward to the mountains beyond Tignes, but only the tips of La Grande Casse and La Grande Motte are visible, as they are concealed behind the peak of Pramecou. The grandeur of the view thus comes more from the sweep of the scene and the rippling lines of peaks in the distance than from a close-up view of any great mountain. If you turn to your right at the col and follow the trail to the southwest, you'll arrive in a few minutes at a sort of twin pass, the Col de la Croix des Frêtes, from which there is a good view of the north face of La Grande Casse, although La Grande Motte remains hidden. If you continued along this trail, walking southwest, you'd reach the Refuge de la Glière (see hike 81) and then Laisonnay.

There are two ways to get from the Refuge du Palet to the Refuge de la Martin. The easier route goes over the Col du Palet, the other over the Col de la Tourne; both descend near Lac de Tignes, from which you ascend to the Refuge de la Martin.

84. The Refuge du Palet via the Col du Palet to the Refuge de la Martin

Rating: strenuous
Distance one way: 14.5 km
High point: 2,652 m

Total climb: 470 m up, 870 m down
Time: 2 hours to Lac de Tignes, 3
    hours to the Refuge de la Martin

This segment of the tour descends from the Col du Palet to Lac de Tignes, a ski resort, then climbs to a hut that is watched over by a hut keeper but where there is no meal service, although stove, pots, and fuel are provided at the hut. (The hut keeper has requested that the park administration make renovations to the hut so that meal service can be offered.)

From the Refuge du Palet, climb in 10 minutes to the Col du Palet, where a signpost points down to Lac de Tignes (the name of both a lake and the resort town built on its shores). Descend eastward, gradually at first, passing a small lake to your right (south). You are on the GR 5, blazed red and white. The trail then descends more steeply. In about 15 minutes, a jeep road turns off to the right; do not take it. Continue straight ahead (eastward) on this red and white blazed trail; do not turn off onto any dirt road or ski slope. The town now comes into view; this is the least attractive section of the Tour du Mont-Pourri. The slope above the resort is strung with ski-lift cables, and the town itself is a prime example of what went wrong with French ski resorts—a cluster of high-rise buildings that has no place in an alpine landscape.

The trail eventually passes an avalanche barrier and about 1 hour 30 minutes below the col, it intersects the paved road between Lac de Tignes and the Val Claret, another ski development about 1 kilometer to the south. Continue about 300 meters into the town of Lac de Tignes. At a traffic circle, go left. Opposite the tourist office (marked "Point Information," and "I") you will find the Palafour chairlift. A signpost under it indicates the way to the Vallon de la Sache. Here the GR 5 turns right (southeast), but you must turn left (northwest) onto a dirt road which climbs the slope north of Lac de Tignes.

This dirt road follows the folds of the slope. With Lac de Tignes now out of sight, the scenery improves and you can see the larger Lac du Chevril below. Pass between two ski-lift stations, and 1 hour 10 minutes after leaving Lac de Tignes come to a signposted junction. The Col de la Sachette is to the left (west), but continue to the right (north) for the Refuge de la Martin. In another 15 minutes, at La Sache, cross a bridge over a stream; there is another signposted junction here indicating a left turn for the Col de la Sachette. Continue straight ahead as before. A rock with a red "X" painted on it blocks the upper path at a bifurcation, and a red arrow points down to a lower path. Take this path, which soon levels out. About 1 hour 15 minutes beyond the bridge, cross a series of three streams set quite close together. Large boulders help you get across the first two; you may have to walk downstream a little to find a suitable place to cross the third. Regain the trail, and reach the hut in another 15 minutes, about 3 hours after leaving Lac de Tignes.

If it is not too late and you are not too tired, it is worth taking a short sidetrip from the Refuge de la Martin. As you step out the door, take the little path to your right that climbs up toward the northwest. In 20 to 25 minutes you'll reach the toe of the Glacier de la Savinaz, cascading down in frozen motion from the Dôme de la Sache. This is a very impressive sight, a real icefall torn into séracs, and moreover you see it from a good angle.

85. The Refuge du Palet via the Col de la Tourne to the Refuge de la Martin

Rating: strenuous
Distance one way: 18 km
High point: 2,656 m

Total climb: 620 m up, 900 m down
Time: 5 hours 15 minutes

The advantage to this variant to hike 84, The Refuge du Palet via the Col du Palet to the Refuge de la Martin, is that this pass is quite wild, and you'll probably see few other hikers on the route. Also, during the ascent the slopes block the view of the network of ski-lift lines above Lac de Tignes, although they come into view on the descent. The disadvantage is that the descent is very steep, on eroded or "disappearing" trails.

From the hut, turn back (northwest) toward Rosuel and in 10 minutes reach a signposted junction; turn right (northeast) for the Col de la Tourne. Cross a rocky section where the way becomes narrow for a few steps. In another 25 minutes, at another signposted junction, turn right (northeast) for the col. The trail, marked by a few blazes and cairns, becomes steep and switchbacks up to the col, which you can reach in a little more than 1 hour from the start. The best view is just beyond the col where the slopes on either side no longer block the scene ahead. Descend very steeply. There is a small pond below to your left, and you'll pass under chairlift lines—it's impossible to escape them as soon as you approach the Lac de Tignes area. The trail for this part of the descent, as marked on the regional topographic map, no longer exists—it's been destroyed by bulldozed ski slopes and access roads—but you can see Lac de Tignes below. Descend to the edge of Lac de Tignes, where you pick up the route that climbs northward for the Refuge de la Martin, as described for hike 84, The Refuge du Palet via the Col du Palet to the Refuge de la Martin.

86. The Refuge de la Martin to the Col de la Sachette and Rosuel

Rating: very strenuous
Distance one way: 15.5 km
High point: 2,713 m
Total climb: 800 m up, 1,400 m down

Time: 3 hours 20 minutes up to the col, 3 hours 20 minutes down to Rosuel

Retrace your steps toward Lac de Tignes (hike 84, The Refuge du Palet via the Col du Palet to the Refuge de la Martin), but turn right (west) at the bridge at La Sache, which you'll reach in about 1 hour 15 minutes after leaving the hut; this is the nearest of two signposted junctions for the trail to the Col de la Sachette. This trail follows the right bank of the stream, passing a stone waterworks. A section of steep switchbacks leads to broad upper meadows where the trail levels out, and where, nearly 2 hours after leaving the hut, you pass the junction for the other branch of this trail that starts closer to Lac de Tignes. Cross a bridge to your left, and as you reach the end of this grassy shelf climb a fairly steep step to reach another, higher stretch of meadows. This is a handsome scene, with Mont-Pourri directly to your right—gray walls to which a small glacier clings, and a topping of snow above. Ahead are the eroded forms of naked grayish-tan rock peaks, while around you in the meadows much edelweiss may be found among the wild purple asters.

The final steep climb to the col will take about 1 hour. The trail, up the right side of the valley, is rather exposed and one section is quite stony; care is required. Reach the col about 3 hours 20 minutes after starting the hike from the Refuge de la Martin. The best view is mainly the scene behind you of the peaks to the east. Looking west from the col, you'll see limestone pinnacles to your right.

The first 20 minutes of the descent are on boulders, although the way is quite clear and marked by cairns, along the right side of the valley. Reach a stretch of smaller stones and eventually a dirt trail; none of it is exposed, like the final stretch of trail on the other side of the col. Descend to meadows and cross a little brook on stones (easy) and pass a small stone house to your left. There is a good view of the snowy dome of La Grande Motte and the black wall of La Grande Casse across the meadows, and of Mont-Pourri behind you. The trail makes broad switchbacks down the east side of the valley. About 2 hours below the col, reach the stone houses at La Plagne; at the signposted junction here, turn right (north) for Rosuel, as in hike 79, The Refuge du Mont-Pourri. Reach Rosuel about 3 hours 20 minutes from the col.

■

SOUTHERN VANOISE

The river Arc, flowing through the valley of the Maurienne, marks the southern border of the Vanoise massif. The slope rises abruptly, so there are no long valleys pushing into the massif as there are from its northern side; instead, you must hike in. And there are no fancy ski resorts along this southern slope, but much simpler villages. The most convenient bases for hikers are Aussois or Termignon, or one of the hamlets between these two. The N6 road extends along the valley of the Haute Maurienne and connects Modane and Termignon. Aussois, however, is located above the national road, on the valley's northern slope. From Modane, cross the river to its northern bank and take D215 up to Aussois. Aussois is a very old community that has turned itself into a sort of sleepy, minor resort with a small village center that retains its traditional character. Termignon, a little farther to the east, is slightly less attractive; since N6 runs through this little town it is also a little noisier than Aussois, which is built higher on the slope, away from the highway and set among fields. Termignon, however, is more conveniently located for some of the walks described here. In addition, there are a couple of tiny, pleasant hamlets between Aussois and Termignon: Sardières and Sollières-Sardières, also set among fields and off the main road, offer accommodations. They are on D83, a road that connects Aussois and

Termignon. Modane, a large town to the west, is a busy, commercial town.

One other very unusual overnight possibility should be mentioned. Just south of Aussois is the Fort Marie-Christine, one of the *portes du parc* but unlike any of the others. It is actually an old fort, double-walled and surrounded by a moat, with a cobblestone courtyard. Even if you are not planning to stay the night it is worth a visit, as one of its halls is now used as an exposition room, and the upper story retains embrasures for cannons. One of the barrel-vaulted chambers has been converted into a very attractive restaurant. To get there, follow the signs in Aussois to "Gite Marie Christine" or to "Porte du Parc de la Vanoise." Take the D26 road about 1 kilometer south, then turn right at a signpost onto a gravel road.

Fort Marie-Christine is one of the Forts de l'Esseillon, built early in the eighteenth century when this region was part of the kingdom of Piedmont Sardinia in order to protect its border against the French. You can visit all five of these forts on foot by an easy trail, or by car.

You can hike or drive north from Aussois on D108e to two artificial lakes, Plan d'Amont and Plan d'Aval, with parking areas for each. From the parking area at Plan d'Amont, you can walk eastward for about 1 hour to the Refuge du Plan Sec, or northwest for 1 hour 30 minutes to the Refuge du Fond d'Aussois. Both huts are along the Tour des Glaciers de la Vanoise, hike 73, The Col d'Aussois and the Refuge du Plan Sec, and hike 74, The Refuge du Plan Sec to the Refuge de l'Arpont.

Bellecombe. Many of the classic hikes in this area start from a spot called Bellecombe, near the top of the steep southern slope at the edge of the Vanoise high plateau. To drive to Bellecombe, go east (and then briefly north) on N6 past Termignon for 0.5 kilometer, then go straight across the road onto a narrow, paved road with a sign for "Parc National Bellecombe." (At this point, the N6 curves to the right, but you must cut across it.) This narrow road winds up for 14 kilometers and ends at Bellecombe, which is a large parking area; driving up takes about 20 minutes.

The *navette* (shuttle van). A shuttle plies daily in the summer season between Termignon and Bellecombe and also makes a few other stops at signs that say "Arret Navette" and show a small picture of a bus. To find the *navette* stop in Termignon, walk out of the town square on the main street (which is the N6) to the west end of town; it's just a few hundred yards to the *navette* stop, on your left, near a *boucherie* (butcher shop). At Bellecombe the stop is at the north end of the parking area. Beyond Bellecombe, the *navette* uses farm roads to make a small circuit; there are stops named Entre-Deux-Eaux, Femma, and Plan du Lac. The latter is near the Refuge du Plan du Lac, one of the *portes du parc*, and easily accessible because of the *navette*. You can pick up a current *navette* schedule at the tourist office in the town square at Termignon.

87. Tour de la Pointe de Lanserlia

Rating: moderate   **Total climb:** 470 m
Distance loop trip: 11.5 km   **Time:** 4 hours 30 minutes
High point: 2,774 m

This walk makes a circuit around a small mountain just east of the Refuge du Plan du Lac. Much of it is off trail so you must do a little route

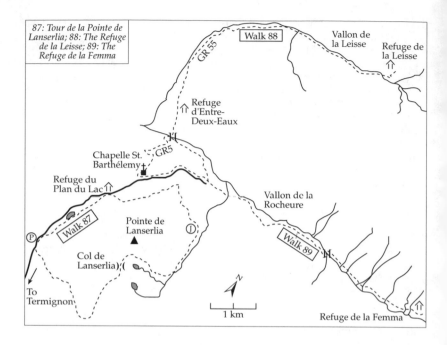

87: Tour de la Pointe de Lanserlia; 88: The Refuge de la Leisse; 89: The Refuge de la Femma

finding. This is not difficult, as the direction you must go in to make the loop is very clear; nevertheless, this should not be done on a day with poor visibility. There are no other dangers, although the final descent is quite steep.

From the north end of the Bellecombe parking area, follow the signposted trail northward to the Refuge du Plan du Lac, which you'll reach in about 20 minutes. This hut is set in a meadow with a splendid view, and there is an orientation table near the hut to help you identify the peaks and glaciers before you. Continue past the hut and at a signposted junction, keep right (northeast) toward the Refuge de la Femma. The trail bends around a shoulder; about 1 hour 20 minutes later reach a stream, with a trace of trail. You'll see a hump of rock with cliff-like sides in front of you and a moraine. Turn right (south) here from the stream and make your own switchbacks up the slope. There are a few traces of trail. Ascend up a small gully and reach a little lake with another lake just beyond it. In 15 minutes reach a third lake, with another trace of trail. In another 10 minutes a fourth small lake can be seen to your right, if you walk off the trail a few paces toward the right. About 2 hours 35 minutes from the hut reach the Col de Lanserlia; from this notch there are superb views of the Glaciers de la Vanoise and the mountains to the west.

Descend on a trail to the southwest. The first 50 meters are steep, then it becomes a little less so. Orientation is not difficult as you can see the Bellecombe parking area below. Continue mainly southward down the slope, with only traces of trail, until you intersect a farm road about an hour below the col. Turn right here and pass an alpage with its name,

"Piou," on a small wood sign that announces the sale here of butter and cheese. The farm road winds downward gradually and you reach Bellecombe about 1 hour 30 minutes below the col.

88. The Refuge de la Leisse

Rating: easy
Distance round trip: 16.5 km
High point: 2,487 m
Total climb: 580 m

Time: 1 hour 45 minutes up from the *navette* stop of Entre-Deux-Eaux, 1 hour 25 minutes down to the *navette* stop, and 1 more hour to the Refuge du Plan du Lac.

This walk starts at the Entre-Deux-Eaux *navette* stop and returns to the Bellecombe *navette* stop. Otherwise, start at Bellecombe and walk to the Refuge du Plan du Lac, as in hike 87, Tour de la Pointe de Lanserlia, and continue from there to Entre-Deux-Eaux, thus adding 5 kilometers to the hike. (You can further shorten the walk by taking the *navette* for your return from Entre-Deux-Eaux.) A well-worn trail heads north over the meadow, descending 300 meters to a bridged stream and a signposted junction; just beside this is the *navette* stop for Entre-Deux-Eaux. (Between Bellecombe and this point you are on the GR 5.)

Cross the bridge (you are now on the GR 55) and continue up the slope heading northward, reaching the Refuge d'Entre-Deux-Eaux in 15 to 20 minutes; if you walk here from the Refuge du Plan du Lac instead of taking the *navette* to the Entre-Deux-Eaux stop, it will take about 1 hour 15 minutes. Privately owned, the Refuge d'Entre-Deux-Eaux is a smaller, more intimate place than the Refuge du Plan du Lac. Follow the trail northward; the Vallon de la Leisse opens to your right, curving to the northeast. As you head up this rather narrow, wild valley, the rubble-strewn lower slopes of La Grande Casse and La Grande Motte are to your left. The gradient is moderate; reach the Refuge de la Leisse about 2 hours 30 minutes beyond the Refuge d'Entre-Deux-Eaux. (The GR 55 continues over the Col de la Leisse to the Lac de Tignes area, where you can pick up hike 84, The Refuge du Palet via the Col du Palet to the Refuge de la Martin.)

89. The Refuge de la Femma

Rating: easy
Distance round trip: 12 km
High point: 2,364 m

Total climb: 220 m
Time: 2 hours up

The Vallon de la Rocheure is a broader, greener, gentler valley than the Vallon de la Leisse, with several alpages, whereas the Vallon de la Leisse is quite wild and uninhabited. If you take the *navette* to the Femma stop, you will be at the entrance of the Vallon de la Rocheure. From here, the signposted trail rounds the shoulder of the slope, following the farm road, then descends to the stream. Cross on the bridge; the farm road ends soon afterward. The gradient of the trail is quite moderate until a final short ascent to the hut.

If you start at Bellecombe, walk northward to Plan du Lac (as for hike 87, Tour de la Pointe de Lanserlia) and continue on the trail to the signposted junction for Entre-Deux-Eaux. Turn right, following the farm road. The round trip distance from Bellecombe is about 21 kilometers.

■

Tour des Glaciers de la Vanoise, from Termignon

This multi-day circular tour is described earlier as hike 73, The Col d'Aussois and the Refuge du Plan Sec, through hike 77, The Refuge de la Vanoise to Pralognan, starting and ending at Pralognan. You can also start the Tour des Glaciers de la Vanoise from Termignon, or you can walk part of the tour as a day hike from Termigon. Part of one of the most scenic segments of the tour, described in hike 76, The Refuge de l'Arpont to the Refuge de la Vanoise, can be done as a day trip from Termignon (or from either the Refuge du Plan du Lac or the Refuge d'Entre-Deux-Eaux).

90. To the Refuge de l'Arpont

Rating: moderate
Distance round trip: 16 km from the Entre-Deux-Eaux *navette* stop
High point: 2,561 m
Total climb: 700 m from the *navette*
Time: 2 hours 30 minutes from the *navette* stop, 2 hours down

From Bellecombe take the *navette* to the Entre-Deux-Eaux stop (or walk past the Refuge du Plan du Lac down to the bridged stream, as in hike 88, The Refuge de la Leisse). Instead of crossing the bridge at the *navette* stop, turn left (west) at the signposted junction. You'll soon come to a second bridge over the Torrent de la Rocheure; cross this, and then cross one more bridge over the Torrent de la Leisse. The trail bends left at first, then right, passing a few farmhouses. Switchback steeply up the slope to reach a junction with the main trail (described as hike 76, The Refuge de l'Arpont to the Refuge de la Vanoise, on the Tour des Glaciers de la Vanoise). If you turn left (southwest) at this junction you'll be headed toward the Refuge de l'Arpont; if you turn right (north) you'll be headed toward the Refuge de la Vanoise (also see hike 76). If you take the turn toward the Refuge de l'Arpont and walk part way there, you'll see the most spectacular segment of the whole 3-day tour, with a grand view of the glaciers.

91. To the Refuge de la Vanoise

Rating: moderate
Distance round trip: 12 km
High point: 2,522 m
Total climb: 600 m
Time: 3 hours 30 minutes up, 2 hours 30 minutes down

From Bellecombe take the *navette* and then walk to the Refuge d'Entre-Deux-Eaux (as in hike 88, The Refuge de la Leisse), or walk past the Refuge du Plan du Lac to Entre-Deux-Eaux. From Entre-Deux-Eaux, continue northward for 30 minutes. You'll then see a stone bridge, the Pont de la Croé-Vie, to your left; there is a signposted junction. Turn left here and cross the bridge. Switchback rather steeply up the slope, mainly westward. Pass two concrete bunkers; the trail curves to the left (again, westward) to enter the upper valley that leads to the Col de la Vanoise.

Opposite: *On the way to the Rifugio Benevolo*

THE ALPINE PARKS OF NORTHWEST ITALY

PARCO NAZIONALE DEL GRAN PARADISO

In northwestern Italy the snowclad peak called Gran Paradiso rises amid an expanse of mountains and glaciers at the center of the great park that bears its name—a landmark site in the annals of preservation. The Parco Nazionale del Gran Paradiso deserves its name not only for its physical beauty, but also as a sanctuary for wildlife, especially the ibex, the largest alpine wild animal. The park logo is the head of this noble creature, which Italian conservationists were instrumental in saving after it had been hunted to extinction in most of alpine Europe.

The events that led to the park's creation began in 1821, when even the Gran Paradiso area had only a hundred or so ibex left. Joseph Delapierre, a forestry warden and also an alpinist (he is better known to mountaineers under the name of Zumstein, for whom one of the summits of Monte Rosa was named), appealed to local officials on behalf of the endangered animal. One of the king's officers, Thaon de Revel—a man remarkably ahead of his time—forbade hunting the ibex in this territory. In a decree dated September 21, 1821, de Revel proclaimed that the people are required to exert the utmost diligence to conserve animal species in danger of extinction. He not only forbade all hunting of the ibex but also the sale and purchase of its flesh, fur, and horns, upon pain of a fine. His powers were limited, however, and hunting the ibex remained the right of the royal family of Savoy. In the long run this undemocratic arrangement played its part in the story. A subsequent king, King Victor-Emmanuel II, was a passionate hunter; in 1856 he declared the Gran Paradiso area a royal hunting reservation and installed a corps of vigilant gamekeepers whose presence made poaching very difficult and thus kept the ibex from total extinction. The motive of Victor-Emmanuel II was to preserve this noble game for his own rifle rather than to save the species, yet paradoxically that was the result he achieved. But he was no naturalist; he offered a bounty to his gamekeepers for killing such predators of the time as the lynx, wildcat, bearded vulture, and eagle, resulting in the extinction of the former three species in the area.

During World War I poaching increased and the ibex population again dwindled. Finally, in 1919, Victor-Emmanuel III ceded the royal prerogative in the area and offered up the lands he personally possessed toward the creation of a national park. A government report at the time spoke of the importance of conserving alpine flora and fauna and especially of the need for a reserve to prevent the extinction of "the beautiful species of the ibex, of whom the last surviving examples in Europe are found in these mountains." A few years later, in 1922, the Parco Nazionale del Gran

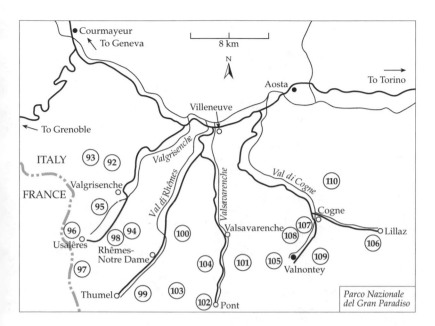

Paradiso was created—the first national park established in Italy and the cradle for the regeneration of the ibex throughout the Alps. From the surviving stock in the Gran Paradiso, colonies of ibex have been reintroduced into France and the other European alpine countries. Today, large numbers of these handsome animals roam the Gran Paradiso—the greatest ibex population in the Alps. Other forms of wildlife are also bountiful here; eagles soar over the park, and the bearded vulture is being reintroduced.

As in France, there is a degree of local resentment over the intrusion of the national government and the regulations imposed upon the territory of the park. Graffiti near the entrance of the Val di Rhêmes reads "P.N.G.P = S.P.Q.R." The first set of initials refers to Parco Nazionale del Gran Paradiso; the second set stands for ancient Rome.

Rising to a height of 4,061 meters, the peak called the Gran Paradiso is the only mountain above 4,000 meters entirely upon Italian territory. It does not stand alone but is the crowning point of a great massif filled with a host of other snowclad mountains and glaciers. The park that bears its name is situated in the eastern Graian Alps. Just across the western edge of the park in the western Graian Alps is the French Parc National de la Vanoise, making the two parks part of the same geologic unit. The border between them, a political one, is an arbitrary line. Both regions were once a single unit called Savoy, part of the kingdom of Piedmont–Sardinia. Western Savoy was annexed by France in 1860 and eastern Savoy by Italy in 1861, when that country was unified. Savoy was culturally and linguistically French, and French is still the first (and apparently the preferred) language of native-born inhabitants on what is now the Italian side, although they are bilingual. This simplifies matters for travelers to the western Alps, since with a little French one can get along in the Alps of both France and northwestern Italy. The local people also speak a dialect (*patois*) that has minor variations from one valley to the next. (In one version of *patois*, *bonjour* is *bondzo*; *toujours* is *todzor*; *champs* is *zan*; *vache* is *vatz*; and *chapelle* is *tzapelle*.) This region is autonomous within Italy, allowing it a certain measure of self-government; many local people, however, had hoped for greater autonomy and even for independence, fearing that their *patois* and their culture will eventually disappear. The names of many villages and geographic features are French but have been Italianized, and many trail signs are in French, although the same place names appear on maps in Italian. A trail sign may read "Col Fenêtre," but on the map it's "Colle della Finestra." When you actually reach the Rifugio Savoia, the sign for it reads "Refuge de Savoie."

The major valley of northwestern Italy is the Val d'Aosta, which divides the Pennine Alps to the north from the Graian Alps to the south. It is also called the Valle d'Aosta, and the Val or Vallée d'Aoste in French; in *patois* this is the Val d'Otain, and the people of the region are Valdotains. Rising southward from the Val d'Aosta, four major valleys penetrate the massif of the Gran Paradiso: from west to east, these are the Valgrisenche, the Val di Rhêmes, Valsavarenche, and the Val di Cogne. The Gran Paradiso park limit runs along the mountainous ridge dividing the Valgrisenche and the Val di Rhêmes so that the Valgrisenche is not within the park proper, but it is so obviously part of this geographic and cultural unit and is, moreover, so appealing that it is included in this book.

Named for Caesar Augustus, Aosta is the chief town of the region. You can reach it in 1 or 2 hours from any of the villages mentioned in this chapter, and it provides a good alternative on a rainy day—or if you just want a break from hiking. Its Roman ruins include town walls, a triumphal arch, a Praetorian gate, and a theater. The medieval church of Sant'Orso with its very graceful twelfth-century cloister is also worth a visit. There is quite a handsome town square and attractive shops along a traffic-free street. A number of castles (notably Fenis, Issogne, and Verres) are scattered along the Val d'Aosta and may prove an attraction for travelers with children, and even for those without them.

Alte vie are high routes, like the Swiss *Höhenweg*. Two such *alte vie* extend across the mountains on both sides of the Aosta Valley (the Pennine Alps to the north of the valley, and the Gran Paradiso massif to the south). They are numbered "1" and "2," with 2 being the southern route. The part of *alta via* 2 that traverses the Gran Paradiso area enters the Valgrisenche at the Col di Planaval, crosses over the Col Fenêtre to the Val di Rhêmes, crosses the Col d'Entrelor to the Valsavarenche, and crosses the Col Lauson to Valnontey. It is often blazed with the number "2" inside a triangle.

To walk the *alte vie* from end to end and return to your car, you need to use local buses. Check with the information office for bus schedules and parking information.

There is an excellent information office at Villeneuve. The office is situated right on the Aosta valley highway and is close to the entrances to all the valleys described here. Some of the personnel speak good English (you can also write to them in French). They can assist you with informa-

Planaval

tion about hotels, transportation, trails, and general conditions. (They publish an annual booklet listing all hotels in the region, the *Annuario Alberghi* or *Liste des Hotels,* and they publish a booklet listing the mountain huts (*Elenco Rifugi* or *Liste des Refuges*). There is another office in the Place E. Chanoux, the main square of Aosta, offering information about the town and the entire region. The Villeneuve office, on the other hand, specializes in the Gran Paradiso national park region (including the Valgrisenche). See Appendix 1 for addresses.

There are several conditions unique to this region of which you should be aware.

Driving. If you are driving in Aosta, a white disc surrounded by a red ring means the road is not open to motor traffic, a blue disc with a diagonal red stripe means "no parking," and a blue disc with a white "P" means that parking is allowed.

Trail blazes and markers. Unlike other alpine countries, in which red and white paint marks are generally used to blaze trails, in the Gran Paradiso park and the Valgrisenche yellow blazes are the trail markers. Many hiking trails are numbered on the maps sold in this region (see

Maps, later), and the trails are sometimes blazed with a yellow triangle, in the center of which their number is painted in black, and sometimes only blazed with a yellow stripe. In this region, red and white blazes are markers for property boundaries, so do not be led astray!

Trails are often a little rougher and less groomed than alpine trails in Switzerland and Austria.

Stream crossings. In the Gran Paradiso area many brooks and streams are left unbridged, and a pair of trekking poles is very useful for crossing on rocks.

Maps. Maps of the Gran Paradiso are not perfectly accurate and sometimes contain errors. Although routes are numbered and keyed to the maps, the numbers you see on the trail do not always correspond to the numbers on the maps.

VALGRISENCHE

The Valgrisenche, a quiet, unspoiled valley, is an undiscovered delight. Although the highest mountains of the Gran Paradiso massif are to the east, the Valgrisenche has abundant charm. Besides lovely scenery and good walks, it is less touched by tourism than any other valley in the region and, thus, a good place to pick up some of the flavor of the old Val d'Otain. Scattered along the valley are several old villages that seem unaware of how appealing they are in their utter simplicity. These villages offer mostly modest accommodations but some very good food. The valley is as peaceful a place as you can find outside a real wilderness—an ideal retreat for anyone with jangled nerves. (In one hotel we stayed at, the cook told us they had once before had two American guests, some years ago.)

The village of Arvier, in the Aosta valley, is the entry point for the Valgrisenche. Accommodations are available along the valley at Planaval, Valgrisenche (which bears the same name as the valley), and Bonne, each of which is a modest, unassuming hamlet. There is also a food market and a post office at Valgrisenche. Bonne is perched above a reservoir, Lago di Beauregard, the creation of which was (and is still) much resented by the local people. It is said that you can sometimes faintly see the village of Fornet, which was covered with water to create this reservoir that is not even used to capacity.

In the nineteenth century the curé of Fornet kept a journal that has now been locally published. In it, two old ladies explain in *patois* (translated into French) their recipe for cooking marmot. (1) Bury the marmot in the ground for 24 hours, to get rid of the gamy taste. (2) Boil it. Thus the simple life of the Valgrisenche! (Note: No one today admits to eating marmot, and you won't find it on any menu.)

The walks listed here begin from several points in the valley.

92. Plan Petet

Rating: easy
Distance round trip: 8 km
High point: 2,284 m

Total climb: 800 m
Time: 2 hours 30 minutes up, 1 hour 45 minutes down

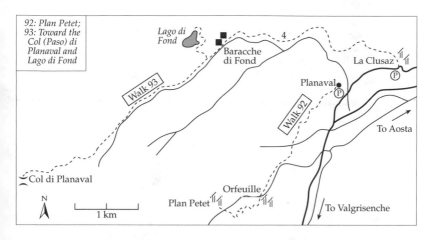

92: Plan Petet;
93: Toward the
Col (Paso) di
Planaval and
Lago di Fond

Lago di Fond

Baracche di Fond

4

La Clusaz

Planaval

Walk 93

Walk 92

To Aosta

Col di Planaval

Orfeuille

Plan Petet

To Valgrisenche

N

1 km

An easy, short excursion to the small alpage of Plan Petet, this is a good walk to get your legs into condition for longer, higher walks. It gives a nice view of the Ghiacciaio di Château Blanc, a glacier known locally as "le Glacier Blanc."

You can drive up to the edge of the hamlet of Planaval (there is only one road to Planaval, and it is unnamed); there is a parking area to your right, just before the hotel. Walk back down the road to your right, and turn right at a big rock with yellow arrows painted on it. Walk up this paved road for 5 minutes and come to a three-way intersection. Here the paved road turns right, and there is a dirt road to the left; however, continue straight ahead on a dirt and gravel road that ascends slightly. (The ways to the left and right do not ascend.) This dirt and gravel road is marked with a sign, a white disk within a red circle, indicating that you may not drive up it unless you have a special permit. On your left are some beehives—square boxes with metal roofs, like little houses. About 200 meters up from the three-way intersection is a yellow blaze, a triangle with the number "4" painted in it, on a rock on your left. Start up this dirt and gravel road, which ascends on long switchbacks.

Stay on this; do not go off on an old section of road, but take the switchback to the right. Pass a concrete sluicegate to your left. In about 1 hour 30 minutes, you'll reach Orfeuille, which was a rather muddy construction area when I was there; a large new communal stable of reinforced concrete, partly underground, was being built to hold eighty cows. Nearby are a few very low stone huts, also partly underground, some of which have rounded concrete roofs. These are not military bunkers but stables built to protect cows against avalanches. Look for a square, one-story building of stone and concrete with a few tiny windows. The trail goes up to the right of this, starting at the right (southwest) corner of this structure. There are no blazes, but you'll see traces of old paths that switchback up the grassy slope. Follow almost any of these tracks up to the southwest. The trail gets more distinct as you ascend and leads around a few rocky ledges. Reach a tiny alpage called Plan Petet about 2 hours 30 minutes above Planaval. There are more small stone huts, partly underground, that have rounded concrete roofs. This is in a small valley with a stream. Above is a rock wall topped with a small glacier—the Glacier du Château Blanc—whose rounded top echoes the shape of roofs on the shepherds' huts and barns. Two peaks, the Testa del Rutor and Mont Château Blanc, are just visible behind the glacier. As you descend, retracing your steps, there is a nice view down onto the clustered stone roofs of Planaval, set picturesquely among its fields.

93. Toward the Col (Paso) di Planaval and Lago di Fond

Rating: moderate
Distance round trip: 16 km
High point: 2,600 m
Total climb: 1,100 m

Time: 4 hours up, 40 minutes down to Lago di Fond, 1 hour 45 minutes down from Lago di Fond

This outing takes you to splendid upper meadows with very scenic views. A nice feature of the walk is that the scenery is rewarding almost as soon as you reach the upper meadows, so if you go no farther you need not feel cheated. Or you can wander up the valley to the edge of the glacier.

You can walk to the trailhead from Planaval, or drive through Planaval and continue for 1.5 kilometers on a narrow paved road past La Clusaz, which is a cluster of stone farmhouses. There, the road takes a bend to the left; follow this. Soon after, there is a sign for Lac du Fond (French for Lago di Fond) and the Glacier du Château Blanc (French for the Ghiacciaio di Château Blanc) on the right side of the road. Park just below the sign, on the grass beside the road. The path is on your left, across the road from the sign; there are yellow arrows and triangles marked "2" and "4." (As you climb, the trail will sometimes be blazed with a "2," sometimes "4.")

Ascend westward on a narrow but distinct trail that traverses up along the west slope of the Valgrisenche, rising rapidly but not too steeply on small switchbacks. There are good views down upon the village and the valley. An hour from the trailhead, reach a ruined stone cabin and a small concrete building, which are part of the local hydroelectric project. Climb more steeply above the last trees and pass concrete waterworks on your left; stay to the right of the cascading stream. In another 45 minutes reach a shelf of grassy meadows; if you go no farther, you'll still have lovely views from here of "le Glacier Blanc." About 15 minutes later cross the stream on some wooden boards to its right bank and follow the yellow blazes up the rocky slope. In 20 minutes cross the stream again on boards, then head northwest. You'll reach a group of about eight stone huts, the remains of a hamlet called "Baraques du Fond" on a signpost ("Baracche di Fond" on the map).

Continue past this hamlet, following yellow blazes beside the stream and bearing left at a bifurcation. Watch for a yellow blaze on the other side of the stream, then hop across to the right bank; it's shallow and you could wade. The trail climbs diagonally along a ridge on the left (east) side of this upper valley but later dips toward the valley's center. Reaching the col requires stepping onto the glacier, which untrained and unequipped persons should avoid. Instead, you can remain up on the ridge to the left, where the view is more extensive than in the center of the valley. Follow traces of trail and a few cairns (no blazes) as far as you wish until stopped by the moraine or the glacier, about 1 hour 45 minutes beyond Baraques du Fond.

Here is the best way to find the trail up to Lago di Fond. Return to the outskirts of the ruined hamlet on its southwest side (closer to the glacier). Then, start up again toward the col, as before, but near the bifurcation watch very sharply for a faint third trail to the right, about 5 minutes past the hamlet. Take this and climb toward the northwest; within 5 minutes you'll see a few stone steps. Pass the steps, hike up the right (east) side of the upper valley, and in about 15 minutes reach small, dark blue-green Lago di Fond, with a view from its bank of the glacier. Retrace your steps for the descent.

Toward the Paso di Planaval

94. Toward the Colle della Finestra

Rating: moderate
Distance round trip: 15 km
High point: 2,840 m

Total climb: 1,100 m
Time: 3 hours 45 minutes up, 2 hours
10 minutes down

This excursion takes you up to a wild, high alpine meadow enfolded between steep, rocky ridges. The trail becomes strenuous when snow is present, but the scenery from the meadow is good enough so you won't mind not going all the way to the col if there is lingering snow on it.

On approaching Lago di Beauregard from the northern end of the valley, the road forks at the hamlet of Valgrisenche. You can drive completely around the lake; most people take the road along the east side of the lake, a narrow, one-lane road with scarcely any pull-offs. The road on the west side is much better; although partly unpaved, most of it is wider, with better visibility. The public road ends at Usalêres; only those with special permits may drive farther south. Many trailheads are located around the southern end of this reservoir, at or near Usalêres, which consists only of a parking area and a small restaurant. At nearby Surier, there are a few farm buildings.

From the Usalêres parking area, walk southward on the road. After 10 minutes, at a sign for the Refuge de l'Epée, turn sharply left up the slope onto a jeep road. In about 35 minutes you have a choice: continue up the jeep road, or turn right onto the *Sentiero Panoramico*, as it is called on the signpost here. (The jeep road is longer and more gradual, with big switchbacks—a duller route, although the views are still good.) The *sentiero*, a steeper footpath, switchbacks up through the woods. About 55 minutes after starting up the *sentiero panoramico*, a broken sign points to the Refuge de l'Epée. Cross a boggy section with a few farm buildings to the left on the other side of a stream; a few more ruined stone huts can be seen above to your right. Heading northeast, cross this stream on a bridge. Walk past the front of a new concrete building and come out onto the jeep road. Follow this road for about 2 minutes, past the last of the farm buildings. Then

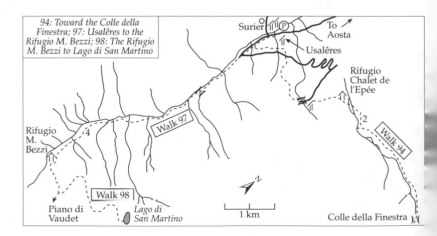

94: *Toward the Colle della Finestra; 97: Usalêres to the Rifugio M. Bezzi; 98: The Rifugio M. Bezzi to Lago di San Martino*

a rusty brown signpost on the slope above to your right indicates the continuation of the *sentiero;* the trail climbs northeastward up the slope, while the jeep road continues northward to reach another alpage.

Ascend very steeply on small switchbacks; the trail here is narrow but distinct. Go left at a fork (the way to the right is part of an old switchback). The trail eventually curves to the right, rounding a rocky shoulder. Although boulders and ledges are strewn about, the way remains distinct. At a big cairn the trail joins the jeep road; turn right onto the road, pass another small alpage, cross a bridge, and reach the hut, 2 hours 30 minutes from Usalêres. The hut, privately owned, is new and attractive.

At the hut, a signpost indicates the Col Fenêtre (French for Colle della Finestra) to the southeast. Start up a short section of jeep road (blazes and the number "2" mark a shortcut off this to the left); a stream is to your right. When you reach a meadow, head east, then southeast, on traces of trail marked by some yellow blazes. This is a wild, lonely, splendid place. The trail to the col rises in switchbacks, leaving the meadow to traverse up through talus along the left (north) slope of the valley. A final, very steep section switchbacks up to the col.

95. Toward the Rifugio Scavarda

Rating: strenuous
Distance round trip: 13 km
High point: 2,920 m

Total climb: 1,130 m
Time: 4 hours 30 minutes up, 3 hours down

The Refugio Scavarda is located below a craggy ridge that forms part of the wall of the Testa del Rutor, which, at 3,468 meters, is one of the highest mountains in the Valgrisenche. The hut is closed, partly destroyed by fire several years ago. The scenery around it is rugged, and there is a sweeping view of the peaks that close off the valley to the south.

You can start this walk from the southern end of the hamlet of Bonne. Walk southward along the road (there is only one) for 15 minutes and then take the jeep road that ascends to the right; there are signs here for the Rifugio Scavarda and other destinations. In 10 minutes go left (northwest) at a fork, continuing up a jeep road; this is blazed "3," "4," and "5." In about 1 hour, a rock blazed "3" indicates a way to the right (northwest) off the road. A network of little trails all lead to the same place. Pass two ruined stone cabins on your left, and in another 2 minutes you'll reach the several stone buildings of Alpe Vieille (marked Arp Vieille on the regional map; Arp is Alpe in *patois*).

A sign above this alpage points right to the Rifugio Scavarda, and is numbered "3." The trail starts on the south side of the sign; go past the sign to a concrete trough. There is a blaze on the side of a ruined stone house, but you don't see it because it's on the opposite side. If you don't spot the trail, start up the rough, steep tractor road that ascends from Alpe Vieille; in a few minutes you'll see the trail to your left, marked by a yellow blaze. Climb up on small switchbacks and cross a narrow brook on stepping stones. About 1 hour 50 minutes after starting the hike, reach a rather level area, the floor of a basin; you'll see a sluicegate, a little dam, and a ruined stone cabin. Looking straight ahead (west), the rounded notch you see is the Forcla du Bré; the path to the Rifugio Scavarda is to

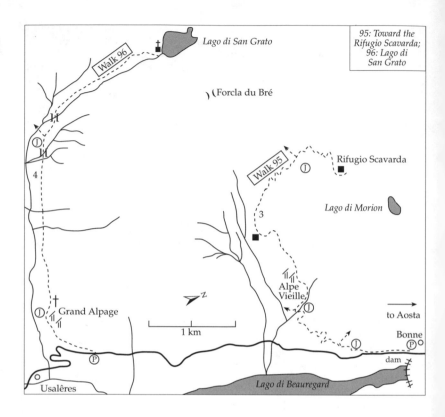

your right, leading over a rocky wall. The trail now goes northwest, taking you up the right side of the basin. Ascend for 1 hour, and turn right (northeast) at a junction blazed "4." This passes to the right of a rocky wall. In another 40 minutes the trail turns slightly to the right (east) and switchbacks up the slope. Twenty-five more minutes bring you up to the ridge, from which you look down upon the ruined hut and a small lake. In clear weather, it is said that you can see the Matterhorn and Monte Rosa from here.

96. Lago di San Grato

Rating: moderate
Distance round trip: 10 km
High point: 2,462 m

Total climb: 540 m
Time: 3 hours 10 minutes up, 1 hour 50 minutes down

This excursion climbs to an alpine lake at the base of a cirque below the Testa del Rutor. When we were there the only tricky part was that a bridge had been destroyed by an avalanche, and we had to make a detour to get around and over the stream. This may still be the case, since no one was sure when the bridge would be repaired. (I heard much grumbling about centralized authority, even in this autonomous region, and about decisions getting bottled up in Rome.)

See hike 94, Toward the Colle della Finestra, for initial driving directions. If you park at Usalêres, cross the bridge at the southern end of the road and start up along the west side of the lake. A footpath cuts across the loops of the road, but the path is rather faint. After about 1 hour turn left onto a jeep road that goes up to the Grand Alpage; a sign indicates both the lake and the Col du Mont. You can cut out this part of the walk by driving up to the junction of the jeep road; there are a few places where you can park along the road west of the lake. The time, distance, and total climb figures given here are based on starting at this junction. Continue up by footpath or jeep road to the Grand Alpage, a cluster of stone buildings. Just beyond this cluster, past a long stable, turn right (northwest) at a fork. Ascend gradually, traversing above the stream. (A stone monument above testifies to a disaster that occurred here during World War II. German officers were forcing captive workers to carry supplies up to the Col

Lago di San Grato

du Mont, although the local people warned the Germans that conditions were dangerous, as it was getting warmer. An ensuing avalanche killed workers and Germans alike.)

If you learn that the bridge has been repaired, turn right off this jeep road at a blaze marked with a "4," 45 minutes past the Grand Alpage. This will lead you to the bridge; cross that, follow the trail over the big hump before you, and continue to the lake.

If the bridge is still not in use, do not turn right at the blaze marked "4." Continue to the left toward the Col du Mont. Cross a small wooden bridge and then another, and turn right (north); the trail to the Col du Mont climbs to the left. Where you turn right, there is no trail. Walk upstream until a point where two small tributary brooks join to form the stream. Cross these on stones, then climb the big green hump between two cascading streams (you should see the ruined bridge below to your right). Rejoin the trail, which leads along an upper valley with a very gentle gradient; a stream is to your right. A steep step that takes 10 to 15 minutes to climb leads up past a small stone chapel to Lac de St.-Grat, as the lake is known in French. The lake is framed by a rugged cirque with a strip of glacier on top.

97. Usalêres to the Rifugio M. Bezzi

Rating: easy; moderate beyond the Rifugio M. Bezzi
Distance one way: 5 km
High point: 2,284 m
Total climb: 500 m
Time: 2 hours 10 minutes up, 1 hour 30 minutes down

It's a relatively short walk to the Rifugio M. Bezzi, beyond which several excursions are possible. If you are staying at a hotel in the valley, you can come up here and spend a night, hike a little farther the next morning, and get back to your hotel by evening.

See hike 94, Toward the Colla della Finestra, for initial driving directions. From Usalêres, walk southward up the jeep road; the stream is to your right. Pass a few ruined stone cabins. After 1 hour 15 minutes the jeep road ends, and in another 20 minutes the trail begins to climb. By now you will have crossed a few sidestreams on bridges. An old path, with "Rif. Bezzi" painted on a rock, leads to the left, but instead stay to the right, closer to the stream but farther from the valley wall (and any falling stones). You'll pass the cable line used to supply the hut, which is just above a tiny pond.

From the hut you can continue along the left side of the valley; a signpost near the hut points to the Col Bassac Derè, signed "4" and "11," and to the Rifugio Benevolo. The trail climbs toward the big glacier at the southern end of the valley (you are not hiking down the center of the valley, but along the slope above it). Cross a couple of brooks on stepping stones; you'll see occasional yellow blazes marked with "4" and "11" and a few cairns. Go as far as you can or wish, stopping short of the glacier and the Col Bassac Derè. You'll probably stop at about 2,960 meters, if not before, after a walk of 2 hours (an ascent of about 700 meters) from the hut; the distance from the hut to the edge of the glacier is about 3 kilometers. Allow about 1 hour to return to the Rifugio M. Bezzi. The upper end of this valley is very scenic, with a big, exposed icefall and a rim of mountains above. The Grande Sassière (3,751 meters), the highest peak of the Valgrisenche, dominates the view.

98. The Rifugio M. Bezzi to Lago di San Martino

Rating: moderate
Distance round trip: 7 km
High point: 2,800 m

Total climb: 700 m
Time: 3 hours 45 minutes up, 2 hours 30 minutes down

This cross-country ramble offers the challenge of route-finding and a grand view at the end. Your objective is a small lake east and slightly north of the Rifugio M. Bezzi. There are only traces of trail but because the terrain is open above treeline, you can scout your way in clear weather. Don't try this route, however, in clouds or mist. There are almost no blazes and the track peters out; you must be competent with compass and map to complete this route safely.

Start from the east side of the Rifugio M. Bezzi, the side away from the stream (see hike 97, Usalêres to the Rifugio M. Bezzi), and look for yellow blazes that are on two different rocks. Switchback directly up the slope (the east side of the valley) on a network of little trails; this is steep going for 1 hour, generally southeast. Reach a crest, then descend a little through a trough, and cross a shallow stream on stepping stones. Follow traces of trail that switchback up the other side of the trough; the faint trace then turns left (north) and soon comes to an end. Go due east over meadows called "Piano di Vaudet" on the map. Continue up and down across the folds and ripples of the land, turning a little northward at 2,750 meters, until you see the lake. There is a large cairn at its north end, and it has a few tiny islands. Immediately southeast of the lake is a ridge about 50 meters higher, offering a splendid view of La Grande Traversière and Punta (Pointe) Bassac. This is spectacular, open terrain, consisting of meadows and rolling alpine tundra, with great views of snowy mountains—a rim of peaks surrounding you in virtually all directions.

When returning to the Rifugio M. Bezzi, be careful not to overshoot the trail leading down the slope of the valley to the hut, as there are cliffs if you go too far to the north. If in doubt, follow a compass heading of 260 degrees instead of 270 degrees upon returning.

THE VAL DI RHÊMES

The Val di Rhêmes is a broader valley than its neighbor to the west, the Valgrisenche. The entrance to it is at Villeneuve in the Val d'Aosta. At Introd, a village just above Villeneuve, the road forks; stay to the right for the Val di Rhêmes (the road to the left leads to the Valsavarenche). The chief villages in the Val di Rhêmes are Rhêmes–St. Georges and Rhêmes–Notre Dame; accommodations are available at both, as well as at several other points, and you can buy provisions at Rhêmes–Notre Dame. (If you are seeking them, you can also find fancier hotels here than in the Valgrisenche, although there are simple places as well. There are also more people here than in the Valgrisenche.) At Rhêmes–Notre Dame a national park information center provides literature and displays. The public road ends at Thumel, where there is a large parking area.

99. Thumel to the Rifugio Benevolo and Truc Santa Elena

Rating: moderate
Distance round trip: 16 km
High point: 2,470 m
Total climb: 600 m

Time: 2 hours up to the hut, 1 hour 30 minutes down; 1 hour 15 minutes from the hut to the Truc Santa Elena, 1 hour back to the hut

If you walk as far as the Rifugio Benevolo, you'll get an excellent view of the Granta Parei (sometimes referred to as Granta Parey), the big, sheer-walled mountain that dominates this valley, and of the Ghiacciaio di Golettaz (Golettaz Glacier in French). You can also continue beyond the hut to the Truc Santa Elena for an even closer view, but this requires route-finding skills because there is no clear trail.

From the parking area at Thumel, walk down the paved road, southwest, and soon turn left at a fork onto a dirt trail with yellow blazes, heading south. (The road continues upward to the right; although the public may not drive up it, some hikers take it as a less steep route to the hut.) Cross a sidestream on a bridge and climb to an attractive valley, with broad meadows sloping up to jagged peaks. Watch for a bent blaze shaped like an arrowhead and turn sharply left (southeast), crossing a narrow sidestream on stones (easy). Be careful here; the thunderous roar to your left is the foaming waterfall you saw just below. Cross several boggy sections and then a small bridge. About 1 hour 20 minutes after starting the hike, reach a dirt jeep road (the one mentioned earlier on which the public may not drive) and cross a good bridge just below two spectacular waterfalls. Turn left and continue along the jeep road, crossing another good bridge in 2 to 3 minutes. Then immediately turn right off the road onto a trail that climbs steeply and is marked with blazes. When you reach a small alpage, you'll again meet the jeep road. Continue now along the road instead of taking the blazed trail in order to avoid a steep section on what appears to be marble, very slick and treacherous despite a fixed cable. Reach the hut in 2 hours or a few minutes less.

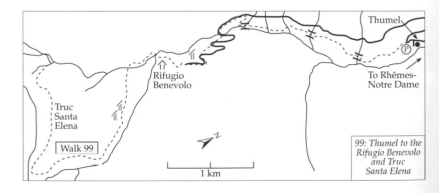

Thumel

Rifugio
Benevolo

To Rhêmes-
Notre Dame

Truc
Santa
Elena

Walk 99

1 km

99: Thumel to the Rifugio Benevolo and Truc Santa Elena

The Rifugio Benevolo is at the edge of a broad, sloping meadow; to your right there is a fine view of the Granta Parei's huge wall (Granta Parei means grand wall in *patois*), stark and vertical, and a broad glacier is before you.

The Truc Santa Elena (its name in *patois* is Tsanteleyna; in French it is the Truc Ste. Hélène) is a big hill, closer to the mountains and glaciers. Behind the hut and toward the glaciers is a boulder blazed "4" facing the picnic tables. Start down this path. Cross a bridge and almost immediately afterward at a rather faint fork, turn left onto a trace of narrow trail and follow this, generally southeast. Traces of path lead to the Alpage du Fond; here you "join" Route 13c as marked on the local map, although there is no real trail. At the alpage, keeping the stable to your right, walk along the base of the cliff to a notch, keeping the cliff to your right. Pass through this narrow notch. You may see traces of trail and a few blazes. Eventually curve to the right around the base of the Truc Santa Elena and stop wherever you like. Count on about 1 hour 15 minutes to reach the meadows above the moraine, a fine viewpoint and the farthest you'll probably want to go. Give yourself 1 hour to return to the hut.

100. Rhêmes–Notre Dame to the Col di Entrelor

Rating: strenuous   **Total climb:** 1,350 m
Distance round trip: 12 km   **Time:** 5 hours up, 3 hours down
High point: 3,007 m

This trip takes you through several zones: woods, meadows, and then the wild, empty country above. The hike up to this col will give you a good workout as well as a view of the Gran Paradiso and Grivola peaks.

At Rhêmes–Notre Dame cross the bridge; as you do so, reaching the river's right bank, the park information center is just to the left. Take a steep path up the slope, and in a minute or two intersect a jeep road. Turn left; in another minute you'll see a sign pointing left to Entrelor Sort. Pass by this, but turn sharply left (southeast) almost immediately after onto a path that ascends. About 35 minutes after starting the hike, reach a signposted junction and turn right (southeast) for the Col di Entrelor (in French, Col d'Entrelor). Climb steeply through woods and in another 45 minutes reach a grassy shelf. There is a small alpage—the Alpages d'Entrelor—in a hollow in the center of this shelf.

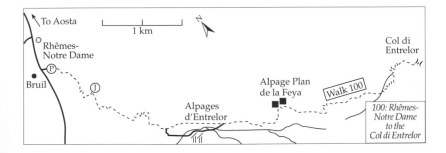

Ruined alpage

Continue up the north side of the valley. Cross a shallow brook on stones (easy); switchback up another slope, and 1 hour 20 minutes from the start of the trail reach a small ruined alpage at Feya (Feye in French) where some of the stone cabins have rounded roofs for avalanche protection. Continue up around a shoulder, bearing left. You'll reach a higher shelf with a circular, level meadow. In front of you will be a broad wall of moraine, looking like gravel; the trail to the col goes to the left of this. There is a big wall of rock to the left of the moraine wall, and the trail leads to the left of that too. As you ascend, there is also a steep rock wall close by to your left as you head toward a talus slope. At 2,930 meters, the trail, blazed, turns right (southeast). Traverse across the talus slope at the base, then turn left (east); you'll find a dirt track that climbs up to the col, with the talus slope to your left.

VALSAVARENCHE

The lovely valley of Valsavarenche offers numerous walks and some of the most splendid views in the Gran Paradiso. It is the historical heart of the park; when Victor-Emmanuel II first came to the Val d'Aosta to hunt, he was so delighted with the Valsavarenche that he established a royal hunting reserve here. His descendant, Victor-Emmanuel III, eventually ceded the reserve to the state, leading to the creation of this first Italian national park.

The point of entry is Villeneuve, on the highway along the Val d'Aosta. Shortly above, at the village of Introd, the road forks; bear left for Valsavarenche. Also called Dégioz, Valsavarenche is the name of a small village here as well as the name of the valley; there are also hamlets at Eaux-Rousses and at Pont, where the road ends. Accommodations are available at all these settlements, and there is a large campground at Pont, with a small general store; there is another grocery store and bakery at Dégioz.

101. The Rifugio F. Chabod and the Rifugio Vittorio Emanuele

Rating: strenuous; moderate if you only go to one hut
Distance loop trip: 15 km (4.5 km to the Rifugio F. Chabod)
High point: 2,750 m
Total climb: 1,300 m up, 1,150 m

Time: 2 hours 35 minutes to the Rifugio F. Chabod, 3 hours 5 minutes for the traverse to the Rifugio Vittorio Emanuele, 2 hours down from the Rifugio Vittorio Emanuele to Pont

The Rifugio F. Chabod and the Rifugio Vittorio Emanuele, above the east slope of the Valsavarenche, are popular destinations. They can be visited separately, as two different excursions, but it's also possible to combine them by traversing between the two. Although the walk is described here starting with the Rifugio F. Chabod and finishing with the Rifugio "V. Emanuele," it can of course be done in reverse. If you do the full excursion in the direction given here, you must start at the parking area for the Rifugio F. Chabod, and you will end up in Pont. Of the two huts, Chabod is newer, more attractive, and less crowded.

The ascent of the Gran Paradiso is easier from this valley than from the Valnontey on its eastern side, and it is most often climbed from the Rifugio V. Emanuele. Among those who have climbed to its summit from the Valsavarenche is Achille Rati, who later became Pope Pius XI. The Rifugio F. Chabod was named for a native Valdotain, a climber and scholar: Professor Frédéric Chabod, considered one of Italy's greatest historians, also became the first president of the Val d'Aosta after it was granted autonomy.

There is a parking area for the Rifugio F. Chabod about 2 kilometers north of Pont. From it, cross a bridge to the right bank of the Savara River, where there is a signpost. Pass to the left (east) of a little white house; the trail is just ahead. Cross under a power line and you'll see a yellow "5" blazed on a rock. The broad trail switchbacks up through woods. Keep to the right (south) at a junction. Continue up on switchbacks; turn right at another junction, cross a bridge, and stay to the left for the Rifugio F. Chabod, following blazes marked with "4" and "5." The way is always clear. Reach the hut in 2 hours 35 minutes. It's an attractive place, with a good view not only of the north face of the Gran Paradiso but also of the long ridge of mountains of which that peak is the highest, as well as of several glaciers.

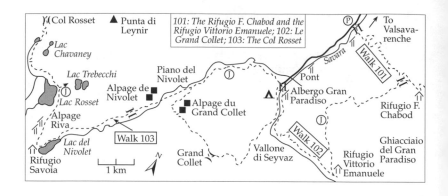

To traverse to the Rifugio V. Emanuele, start back down the trail up which you ascended. In 10 minutes turn left to cross a bridge. You'll see a few blazes marked with "1a" and some cairns. Descend a bit, cross a stream on stones (easy), then ascend again. Reach some broad rock slabs. Here the route descends somewhat to the right toward the valley; there are many yellow blazes and some cairns. Cross a bridged stream, beyond which the trail is cut into a rocky slope. The way continues up and down across a series of little ridges and troughs as it contours around the folds of the slope. You'll be heading more or less southwest or south. Cross a boulder slide, descending slightly—there are many blazes—then ascend again, and cross another boulder field. At last you can see the glacier at the upper end of the Valsavarenche, and you can also look down upon Pont. About 2 hours 20 minutes after leaving the Rifugio F. Chabod, intersect a trail up to the Rifugio V. Emanuele, and turn left (south). The hut is soon visible. You must cross a number of rivulets and an area with flat slabs of rock, but blazes and cairns mark the way. Reach the Rifugio V. Emanuele about 3 hours after leaving the Rifugio F. Chabod.

Although most climbers use this hut as a base from which to climb the Gran Paradiso, you can't actually see its peak from the hut. You get a good view, however, of the mountains south of it: the Tresenta, Ciarforon, and others.

The trail from the Rifugio V. Emanuele back to Pont is a well-beaten one, and you cannot get lost on it. At one place it divides, but the two branches reconnect. After 50 minutes, pass two ruined stone cabins on your left; soon afterward there is a good view of a cascade to your right. Switchback down below treeline, and about 1 hour 30 minutes after leaving the hut, cross a bridge to your right over a stream, then cross a shallow brook on stones (easy). The trail turns right (north) as it reaches the Savara, the river in the center of the valley. Follow the level trail northward along the right bank of the Savara and pass the long stone cabin of a private youth camp. Then turn left to cross a wooden bridge and reach the Pont campground, 2 hours after leaving the hut.

102. Le Grand Collet

Rating: strenuous
Distance loop trip: 11 km
High point: 2,832 m

Total climb: 900 m
Time: 3 hours 45 minutes up, 4 hours
down

This is a rugged, scenically splendid walk that requires some route-finding. The Grand Collet, although a small pass, deserves its title because of the magnificent view—one of the grandest in the park—it affords of the Gran Paradiso. You are almost certain to see ibex and probably chamois as you descend from the pass, and maybe some on the way up as well. You may even see an ibex "nursery": a herd of young animals, who sometimes engage in playful combat. It's hard to give a precise time for this walk because it's impossible to say how long one might want to spend watching the wildlife (as well as admiring the view). Anywhere from 30 minutes to 1 hour should be factored in for watching animals, looking at the scenery, and finding the route. The most challenging part of the hike is the descent, where you need to find your way from cairn to cairn, although none is beyond the visible range. You must find the best way to go between the cairns while descending, sometimes over talus slopes. The descent is steep, and occasionally you may want to use your hands while descending over boulders—a little easy rock scrambling. This route should never be attempted in mist or rain because it would be difficult to spot the cairns and the wet rocks would be slippery. It's a good idea to have a compass and a map with you.

At Pont there are two bridges between the Hotel Genzianella and the campground. The trailhead is just past the second bridge to your right as you walk from the hotel toward the campground. There, a sign points toward the Col del Nivolet, which you must head for at first. In 5 minutes, at a little fork, turn right onto a wider trail. There are occasional yellow blazes. Switchback up rather steeply, with a stream to your right; you'll also see a power line. After 1 hour 10 minutes the trail levels out, heading eastward across a grassy basin. Then it climbs a little more to reach a slightly higher shelf with a few boggy areas. About 1 hour 30 minutes after starting up the trail, go left (southwest) at a junction; to your right you can see a small wooden bridge. Ascend a few more small steps and reach a broad, level meadow—the Piano del Nivolet. Hike along this for about 40 minutes until you see three or four ruined stone huts to your left: this is the Alpage du Grand Collet. Leave the main trail and walk to these houses; one is blazed "12A."

This old alpage is built at the base of the eastern slope of the Piano del Nivolet. Look for a narrow but distinct track, and begin switchbacking up the very steep slope. To your right a stream descends the steep pitch of a narrow side valley, and there is a talus slope to your left. There are no blazes at first, but eventually a very few yellow blazes and a number of cairns may be seen. Above to your left is a big hump of broken rock, its top rounded, and to your right, a more pointed rock peak. Head for the notch between the hump and the point. The trail is now indistinct and sometimes nonexistent, but cairns mark the route. A final steep climb brings you up to this notch—the Grand Collet—and a scenic feast of mountains and glaciers.

The return to Pont is more difficult than the ascent from the Nivolet valley, because the route negotiates a way down various intermediate steps, swinging about to bypass several bands of cliffs. When you reach the notch of the Grand Collet, go to your left (to its east corner) for the descent, steeply down on a visible track. If there is snow at the notch, don't step to the edge: there may be a cornice or overhanging lip of snow, which can be dangerous. Reach a little shelf about 50 meters below the notch. Keeping to the right (south), cross the shelf, and look for little cairns. Don't go to the left, which would require you to descend a talus slope. There are traces of trail here. Reach a lower shelf (1,750 meters) and bear left, crossing a brook. Near a cairn, swing left (northeast). Watch for a trace of path that descends first to the left and then bears right over some talus. Cross several rivulets, then descend over more boulders, and at 2,680 meters bear left again (northeast). Watch for cairns all the way.

Ruined stone cabins

Cross another brook, heading first right and then left. At 2,620 meters you'll see "2A" blazed on the southeast face of a huge rock; there are more blazes to be seen as you descend below this. This may be about 1 hour below the Grand Collet. A view of the glacier opens up to your right. At 2,500 meters turn left (north), and soon you can see Pont below to your left. At 2,450 meters, there is a rock with "PONT" painted on it and a white arrow pointing north. You'll pass another white arrow on your left, pointing to "G. Collet, 2A." In another 10 minutes (at 2,400 meters), the trail descends to the right, a brief section heading straight for the valley floor. You may see several white blazes near here. Soon it turns left (north) again, passing two ruined stone cabins at 2,350 meters. Descend on switchbacks below the cliffs and reach a level dirt trail about 3 hours 20 minutes below the Grand Collet; this descent estimate includes several stops to look at animals. Continue to the campground.

If you ascend this way, you must walk past the campground at Pont until you see a long, one-story stone house across the river. To your right a yellow blaze marked with "2A" indicates the way up.

103. The Col Rosset

Rating: very strenuous
Distance round trip: 8 km one way to the Rifugio Savoia, 5 more km to the col, 26 km round trip

High point: 3,023 m
Total climb: 1,100 m
Time: 5 hours 30 minutes up, 4 hours down

This is a long, strenuous hike offering magnificent views that can, however, be made easier by making it a 2-day excursion. Moreover, you don't have to go all the way up to the col to enjoy superb views; go only as far as you wish. You can stop overnight at either the privately owned Rifugio Savoia or a hut belonging to CAI, the Rifugio Città di Chivasso. Beyond the huts the route is not signposted or well marked.

Begin as for hike 102, Le Grand Collet. At the Alpage du Grand Collet, where that route turns left for the Grand Collet, continue straight ahead. You'll pass another ruined alpage to your right. Cross a bridge and continue up the broad valley (the Piano del Nivolet), heading southwest. The trail leads under a power line; just above, to your right, is a paved road. Pass a lake to your left, and 3 hours after starting you'll find the Refuge Savoie (Italian name on the map, but French name at the hut). Turn right just before reaching the first of its several buildings; there is a sign for Leynir.

Switchback up the slope, and in 20 minutes reach an alpage. Here the trail turns to the right. Pass in front of the alpage (that is, keep the alpage to your left as you ascend) and climb up a broad dirt trail. Blazed "9a" here, the trail heads northward, then swings to the left. A lake is below to your left, and there is a glorious panoramic view of the impressive Levanna range to the south—snowy, folded mountains. As you climb to Lago Rosset there is a grand view of the Gran Paradiso and Ciarforon, so even if you go no farther the excursion is rewarding. Lago Rosset is the largest of several lakes strewn across the slopes below the Col Rosset.

The trail passes around Lago Rosset to the east and north. A very clear trail veers right (northeast), but do not take that—it goes to the Col di

Leynir. Instead, follow traces of trail along (and about 30 meters above) the north side of the lake. Walk along this north side until you pass a waterfall on your right (northeast): this waterfall is the key landmark. It is roughly where you'll see a second lake. At a junction a path heads left (south), blazed "4," between the two lakes; do not take that. The path to the Col Rosset begins to ascend, generally northwest, on broad switchbacks. Head to the left at first (northwest), then generally west as you ascend up to a little shoulder. The waterfall will be on your right as you start these switchbacks up the shoulder. Note: On descent do not take the very clear trail, blazed "4," that goes between the two lakes; it leads ultimately to an unbridged, cascading torrent.

As you reach the top of the shoulder, you'll see a big rocky wall to your left (west), with a little lake below it. Head north; the col is straight ahead, visible as a slight dip or very small saddle. The top of the shoulder is a level area, with cairns and blazes. Climb another step to another level area, with small rocks strewn about. Cross this and ascend a very steep wall of small rocks and scree to reach the col; the way up is clear although a few steps are "delicate." The view from the top is superb.

104. Lago Djouan, the Colle della Manteau, and the Valle delle Meyes

Rating: moderate for reaching Lago Djouan; strenuous for the entire trip
Distance one way: 17 km
High point: 2,795 m

Total climb: 1,350 m up, 950 m down
Time: 3 hours 30 minutes to Lago Djouan; 3 hours 10 minutes down to Pont

This can either be done in its entirety, as described here, or be divided into two separate round trips. The views are first-rate for much of the trail. The only problem with the entire excursion is that the distance between its starting and end points is about 7.5 kilometers, but a friendly hotel keeper might be willing to drive you to one end of the walk or pick you up at the other end. We struck up a friendship with some Italian hikers who drove us one way. (They had a car at each end.) The description here begins at Dégioz and ends at Pont. You may also be able to take a bus one way, depending on the schedules.

It is better to start at Dégioz than at Eaux-Rousses, although the way up from Eaux-Rousses to Lago Djouan appears more direct and shorter. It gets off, however, to a rough start, steep and eroded.

At Dégioz, drive across the bridge at the northern end of the hamlet to the left bank, and ascend a little to the smaller hamlet of Vers le Bois. There is a parking place and a sign to your left, but you can drive higher into Vers le Bois and to the end of the road. Cross the road and start walking up to the right through the woods on a very broad, gradual, excellent trail blazed "8." This "trail" is, in fact, the old carriage road used by King Victor-Emmanuel II to reach the hunting lodge he built on the slope above, which was later destroyed by an avalanche. You may spot a plaque on a rock to the right, indicating that this is the "Sentiero Marialuisa." In about 2 hours you should be above treeline on a nearly level trail that

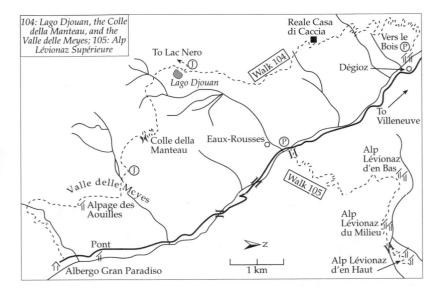

104: Lago Djouan, the Colle della Manteau, and the Valle delle Meyes; 105: Alp Lévionaz Supérieure

heads across a wide meadow with a splendid panorama to your left, across the valley, extending from the Grivola past the Gran Paradiso to the Becca di Montchair.

At Orvieille, 2 hours 10 minutes after starting the hike, pass a fenced-in white house belonging to the park and closed to the public. At the corner of the fenced area, to the right, a signpost points left to Lago Djouan and other destinations. Pass the white house (it's to your left) and a water tap with a sign reading *"eau potable"* (potable water). In another 15 minutes reach an alpage (there are some ruins below to your left). Climb up behind the alp building, pass by it, and continue straight ahead (do not turn right on a little narrow path that ascends steeply up the slope). Follow the trail south and southwest across sloping meadows, with the beautiful panorama of the Gran Paradiso chain always in sight. Ascend a moderate grade and reach Lago Djouan about 3 hours 20 minutes after starting the hike.

Optional: A trail leads from Lago Djouan up to Lago Nero and then to the Col di Entrelor, a pass leading to the Val di Rhêmes (see hike 100, Rhêmes–Notre Dame to the Col di Entrelor).

To continue to the Colle della Manteau, take the path around the northwest and west side of Lago Djouan. The trail climbs diagonally across a rocky ridge—there is a short stretch over boulders—and then switchbacks up to the pass. Although the slope is rocky, the trail is wide, distinct, and good, except for a short section across the boulder slide, which is well blazed. Reach the col about 1 hour 10 minutes beyond Lago Djouan.

From the col descend southward into an empty valley, wilder than the one from which you just climbed: this is the Valle delle Meyes (pronounced "my-ess"). A tiny turquoise lake lies below. Do not turn left at a small junction but continue southeastward to a stream, which you cross on rocks. Follow the trail along the right bank and then as it veers off to the right. Ascend a little and walk around the corner of the next ridge, thus leaving the Valle delle Meyes. When you get around this corner, there are fantastic views of the upper Valsavarenche, with all the mountains and glaciers that close off the southern end of the valley. You should reach the edge of this ridge about 2 hours after leaving Lago Djouan.

After rounding the corner pass a small pond to your left and cross a stream on a little causeway of stepping stones. You'll soon reach another tiny pond. Several curious mounds of rocks, about 4 feet high, lie about the meadows. At a signposted junction, descend to the left on a trail blazed "3," "3a," and "4." Arrive at a jeep road, where another sign points down (south) to Pont, and descend, passing the abandoned Alpage des Aouilles. The path turns left, passes under a power line, and crosses a bridge, turning left. You will then reach the trail that extends between Pont and the Col del Nivolet (the northern end of this trail is used for hike 102, Le Grand Collet, and hike 103, The Col Rosset). Turn left and descend to Pont. It may take 3 hours 10 minutes to descend from the Colle della Manteau to Pont.

105. Alp Lévionaz Supérieure

Rating: strenuous   **Total climb:** 1,100 m
Distance round trip: 17 km   **Time:** 4 hours up, 3 hours down
High point: 2,730 m

This hike takes you up toward the Col Lauson (which some hikers, following an *alta via*, use for passage to the Valnontey), although this route diverges just below the col. It climbs past three alpages: lower, middle, and upper Lévionaz. The place names on signposts reflect the local *patois*, and although quite recognizable they're not identical to the names on the map. Although the finest view is above, you could stop at the lower of the three alpages and just picnic in the pleasant meadow there.

Begin at Eaux-Rousses; there is a parking area along the road. Cross the bridge to the right bank of the river. The trailhead is signposted; take an immediate right and walk under a power line. For a minute you head up the valley toward Pont, but then turn left. The trail is blazed "2." It climbs between stone walls and you pass beneath a second power line. Continue up beside a low stone wall, heading east. Switchback on a good, graded trail through woods and reach Alp Lévionaz Inférieure ("Lévionaz d'en Bas" on the map; both mean "lower Alp Lévionaz") about 2 hours from the start of the hike.

As you turn a corner toward the southeast, a view opens up of the mountains ahead. Here you enter a broad, inviting meadow. The trail descends a bit to a lovely stream on your left. Reach the streambed, but do not cross the bridge here to your left. Instead, cross a second bridge over a rivulet; the trail is blazed "2." It soon starts to switchback up along the right side of the valley. Two stone huts visible across the meadow are Alp Lévionaz du Milieu—the middle Alp.

The trail switchbacks upward, and a rock wall is to your right; the grade is moderate and the trail surface quite good. Climb generally eastward. About 45 minutes beyond the lower Alp Lévionaz, turn left to cross a good bridge over the upper Lévionaz stream, here a swift torrent. Continue on switchbacks up the other side (above the right bank now). In another 10 minutes pass a small stone ruin to your right, and 5 minutes beyond that turn left (north) at a fork where a rock is blazed "2," with a painted sign indicating a left turn for the Col Lauson, a right turn for l'Herbetet. In another 25 minutes reach a signposted junction. Turn right here, departing from the trail to the Col Lauson, and in 10 more minutes reach Alp Lévionaz d'en haut (Lévionaz supérieure)—the upper alp. You can continue a little farther to the right (southwest), crossing two brooks on stones; follow traces of trail and in about 15 minutes (beyond the ascent time given for this walk) you can reach the top of a ridge, with an excellent and close view of mountains and glaciers. On a clear day you can see Mont Blanc in the distance.

THE VAL DI COGNE, VALNONTEY, AND THE VALLONE DI VALEILLE

The Val di Cogne attracts more visitors than any other valley in the Parco Nazionale del Gran Paradiso. The entrance to this big valley is between St. Pierre and Sarre, just west of Aosta. Unlike the other major valleys of the Gran Paradiso region, which cut directly south into the massif, the Val di Cogne swings southeastward. However, its two tributary valleys, Valnontey and the Vallone di Valeille, veer off directly south, rising into the high mountains; Valnontey points almost straight toward the Gran Paradiso. Valnontey and the neighboring Valsavarenche therefore offer the closest access to the park's highest mountains.

The little town of Cogne, in the Val di Cogne, is the only resort in the park, although it is a modest place compared to any major alpine resort. Despite its shops and hotels, Cogne is a true (not an artificial) town, and an old one, with a maze of little streets. Near the entrance to Valnontey is a small hamlet of the same name. It has several hotels, a small grocery store, a campground, and a large parking lot, to accommodate the many visitors staying in Cogne who come here for the hikes. Lillaz, 6 kilometers east of Cogne at the head of the Vallone di Valeille, is similar to Cogne but smaller.

Valnontey

The upper end of this tributary valley is closed off by a magnificent cirque of glaciers and mountains. Splendid views of the cirque can be had from either of two vantage points high on the valley slopes: L'Herbetet on the western side and Alpe Money on the eastern side of Valnontey.

106. Valnontey to Alpe Money

Rating: strenuous
Distance round trip: 12 km
High point: 2,325 m

Total climb: 660 m
Time: 3 hours up, 2 hours 30 minutes down

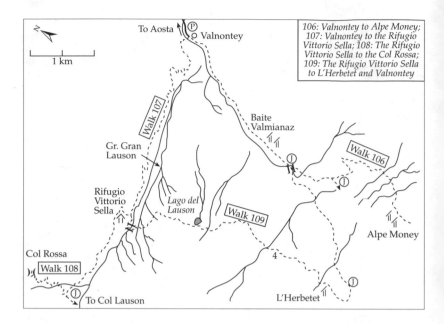

106: Valnontey to Alpe Money;
107: Valnontey to the Rifugio
Vittorio Sella; 108: The Rifugio
Vittorio Sella to the Col Rossa;
109: The Rifugio Vittorio Sella
to L'Herbetet and Valnontey

This is a steep climb, somewhat exposed in a few places, to an old alpage on a high meadow overlooking the great cirque at the end of the valley. This route is slow going because there are many rocks underfoot, but the trail is sufficiently wide and is essentially good.

From the hamlet of Valnontey, take the broad dirt road heading south toward the mountains. After 40 minutes pass a cluster of old stone and log cabins called "Baite Valmianaz." About 10 minutes past here, just before the trail reaches the riverbank, there is a rock to your left blazed "4," on which the names "Herbetet" and "Money" (pronounced "monay") are also painted. Ignore this; it's for a section of trail destroyed by a boulder slide. Continue on the main trail for a few minutes more to the edge of the river. There, where the trail jogs left to rise above the riverbank, turn left onto a path marked with "104." This is about 15 minutes past the cluster of cabins. (The path to L'Herbetet continues straight ahead.) Until here the trail has been almost level.

Ascend a slope on steep switchbacks; the trail surface is rather rocky. About 50 minutes after starting up this slope, the trail turns left to make a long traverse along a ledge and then loops upward to another series of switchbacks. In another 30 minutes it levels out, traversing around a shoulder. Cross a boulder slide and a stream on rocks (moderate), and a few minutes later turn right at a fork (although both are blazed "20," the trail to the left goes to Bivouac Money, a small shelter for climbers that is much higher up the slope). Cross an area of rocky ledges, some of which have shallow water running over them, and descend to Alpe Money—a

On the way to Alpe Money

few ruined stone buildings on a grassy shelf. (One of the huts has been re-paired and is owned by the Don Bosco society, a Catholic youth organization.) From these meadows there is a superb view of the great amphitheater of mountains at the end of the valley, with glaciers tumbling below them.

■

Valnontey to the Rifugio Vittorio Sella and L'Herbetet

This 2-day tour is a very popular excursion. The hike up from Valnontey to the Rifugio Vittorio Sella is fairly short; if you arrive early enough and are not too tired, you can add an optional afternoon excursion to the Col Rossa. The next day, make the high-level traverse to L'Herbetet, from which you descend to Valnontey. You can of course break this up into separate excursions by, for example, hiking from Valnontey along the lower trail to L'Herbetet and back by the same trail, in the same day.

107. Valnontey to the Rifugio Vittorio Sella

Rating: moderate
Distance one way: 5.5 km
High point: 2,590 m

Total climb: 900 m
Time: 2 hours 40 minutes up

Vittorio Sella, for whom this hut is named, was an Italian banker and a photographer, who ventured out to such places as the Himalayas, the Caucasus, Alaska, and Africa at the end of the nineteenth century and again very early in the twentieth century—long before it was either fashionable or easy to do so. His photographs, some of them panoramic views, are remarkable. The hut keeper has a book of Sella's photographs and seems willing to show it. The hut itself originated as one of King Victor-Emmanuel II's hunting lodges.

At the hamlet of Valnontey, find the bridge; you really can't miss it. Cross the bridge to the left bank of the river and at once bear left (south). You'll soon see a signpost for the hut and other points and a blaze marked with "2." Follow the broad trail that switchbacks up the slope on the west side of the valley. As you climb you'll see a cascading torrent to your left. After you rise above treeline, you'll see a stone building across the torrent; this is an alpage, not the hut. Follow the blazes marked with "2" up along more switchbacks. You'll see an ocher-colored stone building; again, that's not the hut but a park house. Descend a few steps beyond the park house; the hut is just behind it.

108. The Rifugio Vittorio Sella to the Col Rossa

Rating: strenuous
Distance round trip: 8 km
High point: 3,195 m

Total climb: 610 m
Time: 2 hours 10 minutes up, 1 hour
15 minutes down

The largest colony of ibex—about 300 of them—in the Parco Nazionale del Gran Paradiso, and surely in all the Alps, frequents the high meadows behind the Rifugio Vittorio Sella. For any walk behind the hut, allow a lot of extra time for wildlife-watching. From the hut a trail crosses these meadows and then forks, with one branch climbing to the Col Lauson and the other to the Col Rossa (which you may also hear called the "Col de la Rousse"). The Col Lauson trail is much more frequented because it's on an *alta via* and is the pass to the Valsavarenche. The Col Rossa, however, has grander, more open views. Beyond the meadows the route to the Col Rossa is rough and the terrain is wild. You can, of course, just spend a few hours wandering through the meadows, where you are as sure as you can be anywhere in the Alps of seeing ibex, perhaps large numbers of them, especially in the late afternoon when they come down to graze. The scenery is another attraction; the upper valley in which the meadows lie is surrounded on three sides by mountains, as if by a horseshoe, and also offers good views across Valnontey.

The trail starts behind the hut (see hike 107, Valnontey to the Rifugio Vittorio Sella) on its west side and heads westward. A lovely stream to your left bisects the meadow. Look for a rock blazed with a yellow arrow, followed by another rock blazed with a "4"—these are about 50 meters from the northwest corner of the hut. Proceed to a trail that leads up to the higher meadows, partly enclosed within the U-shaped loop of mountains; there is a fine view of the snowy peaks across the Valnontey. About 30 minutes above the hut, at 2,790 meters, there is a picnic table and bench.

Follow a narrow track to the right (north), and in a few minutes cross a bridge over a brook. About 10 minutes past the bridge, there is a bifurcation; a sign painted on a rock indicates that the "Colle della Rossa" and the "Colle della Nera" (the red col and the black col) are to the right; another rock, on the other side of the brook, is painted "Colle Loson." Cross another brook on boulders (a little difficult). After this the trail switchbacks to and fro, making two easier crossings across a brook. The more difficult crossing on boulders can be avoided by taking a shortcut, not blazed but very distinct. It takes you along the left (northeast) bank of the stream.

Switchback steeply up a rocky wall between two cascading torrents. Turn to the right to cross the torrent on your right on stones: it's pretty shallow here, although there is a lot of water streaming over the stones. Climb steeply up to the top of this wall, after which the grade eases off. There are occasional yellow blazes marking the way. Another steep section of switchbacks, on muddy scree, leads up to the Col Rossa, from which there are sweeping views. It is said that on a clear day you can see the Matterhorn, which appears as a black shape, and the Monte Rosa, as a white one.

109. The Rifugio Vittorio Sella to L'Herbetet and Valnontey

Rating: very strenuous
Distance one way: 15 km
High point: 2,656 m

Total climb: 150 m up, 1,100 m down
Time: 2 hours 45 minutes up, 4 hours 10 minutes down

The view from L'Herbetet is the finest in Valnontey and some say the best in the entire park. It's a panorama of the great cirque of the Gran Paradiso and its satellite peaks, all hung with glaciers, similar to the view you see from Alpe Money (see hike 106, Valnontey to Alpe Money) but from a closer, better angle, and encompassing a greater sweep. There is a slight catch: between L'Herbetet and Valnontey you must cross a rather wide, unbridged mountain stream. The trail between the Rifugio Vittorio Sella and L'Herbetet has a short but very difficult spot as well, so there is no easy way to reach this wonderful viewpoint. Nevertheless, large numbers of Italians of all ages venture up here, braving the torrent and the tricky trail, to enjoy the magnificent view. Note: This route should never be taken in wet or threatening weather, or by persons who have vertigo or who would be frightened by a very exposed traverse on very small footholds.

From the Rifugio Vittorio Sella (see hike 107, Valnontey to the Rifugio Vittorio Sella), walk up toward the Col Lauson and the Col Rossa for a minute, then cross a bridge to your left. The trail turns left and then bends to the right and is blazed "4." At first the trail is very good and distinct, crossing an area of flat stones marked with blazes and cairns. It winds around the folds of the slope, passing an area where there was a great rock slide, but you don't have to hop over boulders: there is a good route through the rubble. About 50 minutes after leaving the hut, reach the difficult part of the route, a section of traverse where the trail becomes quite narrow and exposed. It may take about 15 minutes to pass the worst sec-

Unbridged torrent on L'Herbetet route

tion of trail; it's not a long stretch, but there are a few very "delicate" steps where one must proceed with extreme caution. At one point you must hold onto a fixed cable and swing out over the ledge. Once past that, the trail, although narrow and often exposed, is relatively good: a high balcony walk. There is a superb scene ahead and another to the east.

Continue into a deep fold, and cross a torrent on stones (or ford it). The trail continues through two areas of boulder slides. About 2 hours 40 minutes after starting the hike, reach a small meadow where the trail is no longer exposed and the view is stunning. As you climb a little higher the view becomes even grander—an amphitheater of rugged black peaks and glaciers with multiple torrents cascading down cliffs and ledges toward the valley far below.

Descend from these meadows to a stone house belonging to the park— the spot is marked as "L'Herbetet" on the map. Immediately below it at a junction, turn left (southeast) for Valnontey. A good trail switchbacks down; you'll pass a plaque honoring a park warden, with a tribute that translates as follows: "The balance of nature is a patrimony that belongs to me; to protect it is a question of civic decency and wisdom." Nearly an hour below the park house, cross a bridge, and then cross a gentle brook on stones (easy). The trail descends by a series of broad, gradual switchbacks. About 20 minutes after crossing the bridge, reach the main trail along the valley floor and turn left at a signposted junction. In another 20 minutes, reach the unbridged torrent mentioned earlier, which you must cross on rocks. Somehow or other—usually with the help of bolder, steady friends—people do it. Early in the season or after heavy rains, the torrent will be even more difficult. One should not attempt it alone. Beyond this torrent descend a rocky section of trail, turning right where there is a blaze to avoid a section of boulder slide. You'll then reach the riverbank. Turn right to cross a bridge, then turn left on the other side. Follow the trail along the right bank, crossing a sidestream on logs or stepping stones. In another 15 minutes pass the place where the trail begins climbing to Alpe Money, and continue northward along the broad, nearly level trail to Valnontey, which you will reach about 3 hours 30 minutes beyond L'Herbetet.

■

110. The Vallone di Valeille and Lago di Loie

Rating: strenuous
Distance loop trip: 14 km
High point: 2,380 m

Total climb: 800 m
Time: 2 hours 30 minutes up, 3 hours down

This is one of the standard walks of the region, often done as a loop trip up from Lillaz to this small lake, then down into the Vallone di Bardoney where you round a little mountain called Testa Goilles, and then return to Lillaz. A description of the complete route is given here, with some reservation. The direct way up from Lillaz to the lake is popular not only be-

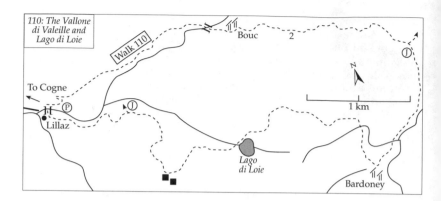

cause it's shorter but also because you can see Mont Blanc as you climb (that is, if you look behind you). This part of the trail, however, is not only steep but very rough, full of rocks and ledges; the route for the descent through the Vallone di Bardoney, although longer, is gentler and a far more pleasant trail—only the last 140 meters of descent is on a poor, eroded trail. You may well wish to climb up to the lake via the Vallone di Bardoney and descend the same way; I would not recommend a descent by the direct route—nor an ascent by it in wet weather.

Reach Lillaz 6 kilometers east of Cogne. There is a large parking lot at the entrance to Lillaz, with a trail sign at the northeast corner where a bridge leads into the village. After crossing the bridge you'll soon see a sign pointing left (east) to Lago di "Loye" and Cascate; go left here. In 5 minutes come to a picnic area along the left bank of the stream; a minute or two beyond this, you'll see a waterfall to your left. Follow a trail marked with "12" that branches off to the right (south) and begins climbing. In 5 minutes the trail forks; a sign points right (upward) to the lake, and in another 5 minutes, the trail bends left, crossing a brook on good rocks that are close together.

The way becomes steep and rocky, blazed by red bands painted around trees. At a park sign bear left (east). After an hour of clambering up and over rocks, reach a level meadow with some stone ruins. Bear left here following blazes, cross a short and fairly level stretch of boulders, then ascend another slope that is less steep. After reaching treeline, round a shoulder, cross a tiny rivulet, and reach the lake, which is enclosed in a bowl and so offers no view. It will take about 2 hours 30 minutes to get here.

To descend, climb around the shoulder just east of the lake, curving to the right. The trail descends steeply to a boggy meadow and into a beautiful, wild valley—this is the Vallone di Bardoney. Climb over another little hump and descend to a lower meadow, heading left (east) on a trail blazed "102"; you can see Alp Bardoney to your right (southwest). Continue straight ahead; soon, a sign points right to the alpage, where milk and cheese are sold. There is also a stream to your right. The trail goes left (northeast). Continue along the stream's left bank; you'll see a small waterfall to your right, then a gorge, and then another waterfall. Descend now through woods and reach a field, where you turn left at a junction blazed with "2." Soon you'll reach a bridge next to a spillway. Cross the bridge, turn left, and take the path along the right bank of the stream. A signpost at Gollie points you straight on (westward) to Lillaz. At a point where the trail separates into two variants, the lower one is better (there is a road above). The trail back to Lillaz is blazed with many numbers—"6," "10a," "10," "101," and others—and sometimes the word *sentiero*, which means trail. You'll also see red blazes as well as the usual yellow ones. Turn left at a fire hydrant and descend about 140 meters to the parking lot. You should be down about 3 hours after leaving the lake.

APPENDICES

1. Useful Addresses

FRANCE

The following central administrative offices for each park will provide general information, including the addresses for information offices that are near the parks.

Parc National du Mercantour
23, rue d'Italie, BP 316
06000 Nice cedex 1, France
tel. (1) 93 87 86 10

Parc National des Ecrins
Domaine de Charance, BP 142
05004 Gap cedex, France
tel. (1) 92 51 40 71

Parc National de la Vanoise
135, rue du Docteur Julliand, BP
705
73007 Chambéry cedex, France
tel. (1) 79 62 30 54

Centrale de Réservation
Maison du Parc et du Tourisme
73710 Pralognan-la-Vanoise,
France
tel. (1) 79 08 71 49

Parc Naturel Régional du Queyras
avénue de la Gare, BP 3
05600 Guillestre, France
tel. (1) 92 45 06 23

Accommodations

For information on gîtes d'étape or chambres d'hôte, write to the Gîtes de France, either at the general office in Paris or at one of the regional offices. Also listed here are addresses for the various accommodations guides noted in the Introduction.

Maison des Gîtes de France
35, rue Godot-de-Mauroy
75439 Paris cedex 09, France
tel. (1) 49 70 75 75

Mercantour

Gîtes de France
55, promenade des Anglais, BP 602
06011 Nice cedex 1, France
tel. (1) 93 44 39 39; fax (1) 93 86 01 06

Queyras

Gîtes de France
5 ter, rue Capitaine-de-Bresson,
BP 55
05002 Gap cedex, France
tel. (1) 92 51 35 45; fax (1) 92 53
96 68

Ecrins

Gîtes de France
Maison des Agriculteurs
40, avénue Marcelin-Berthelot
38100 Grenoble, France
tel. (1) 76 40 79 40; fax (1) 76 40 79 99

Vanoise

Maison du Tourisme
24, bd de la Colonne
73000 Chambéry, France
tel. (1) 79 33 22 56; fax (1) 79 85 71 32

Michelin
Services de Tourisme Du Pneu Michelin
46 avénue de Breteuil
F-75324 Paris Cedex 07, France
tel: 33(1) 45 66 1234

Hotel Guidebooks

Michelin
P.O. Box 19001
Greenville, SC 29602-0987

Fédération nationale des Logis de France
83 avénue d'Italie
75013 Paris, France
tel. (1) 45 84 70 00; telex: LOGIAUB 202 030 F; fax (1) 45 83 59 66

General Information

Club Alpin Français
24 avénue de la Laumière
75019 Paris, France
tel. (1) 42 02 68 64

French Government Tourist Office
610 Fifth Avenue
New York, NY 10020-2452
tel. (212) 757-1125; fax (212) 247-6468

Bureau des Guides et Accompagnateurs de la Vallée des Merveilles
BP 12
06430 Tende, France
tel. (1) 93 04 62 64

ITALY

For infromation on the Parco Nazionale del Gran Paradiso, contact:

Parco Nazionale del Gran Paradiso
Via Rocca, 47
10123 Torino, Italy
tel. (011) 817 11 87

Accommodations and General Information

For information and to receive booklets listing all the hotels and mountain huts in the region, write (in Italian, French, or English) to one of the following addresses.

Office du Tourisme
Loc. Champagne, 18
11018 Villeneuve (AO)
Vallée d'Aoste, Italy
tel. (0165) 9 50 55; fax (0165) 9 59 75

Azienda Autonoma di Soggiorno é
   Turismo di Aosta
Ufficio Informazioni Turistiche
   (Syndicat d'Initiative)
Piazza E. Chanoux 8
11100 Aosta, Italy
tel. (0165) 356 55 or 236 627; fax
   (0165) 34 657

Club Alpino Italiano
Via Fons. Pimentel 7
20100 Milano, Italy
tel. 022614 1378; fax 022614 1395

Club Alpine Italiano
Piazza Chanoux 8
11100 Aosta, Italy
tel. (0165) 40 194; fax (0615)
   3634244

Italian Government Travel Office
Rockefeller Center, Suite 1565
630 Fifth Avenue
New York, NY 10111
tel. (212) 245-4822; fax (212) 586
   9249

2. Correspondence

Following are some sample letters of inquiry, in French and Italian, asking to reserve a room. In both countries, calendar dates are written with the day first, followed by the month, so December 5 is written as 5/12 (5 décembre or dicembre), not as 12/5. The following months, days of the week, and numbers are given in French and Italian, respectively.

January: janvier or gennaio; February: février or febbraio; March: mars or marzo; April: avril or aprile; May: mai or maggio; June: juin or giugno; July: juillet or luglio; August: août or agosto; September: septembre or settembre; October: octobre or ottobre; November: novembre or novembre; December: décembre or dicembre.

Sunday: Dimanche or domenica; Monday: lundi or lunedi; Tuesday: mardi or martedi; Wednesday: mercredi or mercoledi; Thursday: jeudi or giovedi; Friday: vendredi or venerdi; Saturday: samedi or sabato.

one: un or une, or un, uno or una; two: deux or due; three: trois or tre; four: quatre or quattro.

FRENCH

Hotel xxx

France

Cher Madame/Monsieur:

Nous souhaitons (Je souhaite) réserver pour deux personnes (une personne) une chambre double [note: means a double room] [for several nights] pour les nuits du 20–23 août inclu. Nous comptons (je compte) arriver l'après-midi du 20 et repartir le matin du 24.

[for one night] pour la nuit du 20 août (arrivée l'après-midi du 20 et départ le matin du 21).

Nous souhaitons (Je souhaite) être en demi-pension.

[You may add *Nous voudrons prendre demi-pension*—"we would like to have half-pension".]

Je vous serais reconnaissant [reconnaissante if the writer is a woman] de bien vouloir répondre par courrier avion, et vous trouverez ci-joint deux coupons-réponse internationaux. Si vous désirez des arrhes, le numéro de ma carte de VISA est *xxx xxx xxx xxx*. La date d'expiration est le *xx/xx/xx*. En attendant votre réponse, veuillez agréer, Madame, Monsieur, l'expression de mes sentiments distingués,

Jane Brown

Translation

Dear Sir/Madam:

We (I) would like to reserve a room at your hotel for two people (one person) for

the nights of August 20–23. We (I) will arrive on the afternoon of the 20th and will leave on the morning of the 24th.

the night of August 20. We will arrive on the afternoon of the 20th and will leave on the morning of the 21st.

We (I) would like to have half pension. [You can wait until you arrive to say that. Note that if you're staying in a small village in either France or Italy, it's generally understood and assumed that you'll eat dinner and breakfast at your hotel or gîte.]

Please reply by airmail. Enclosed are two international postal coupons. If you would like a deposit, the number of our (my) VISA card is *xxx xxx xxx xxx*; the expiration date is *xx/xx/xx*. I look forward to your reply.

Sincerely yours,

ITALIAN

Hotel *xxx*

Italy

Egregio Signore o Egregia Signora:

Vorremmo (vorrei) prenotare una camera doppia (singola)—preferiremmo (preferisco) un letto matrimoniale—per le notti (la notte) dal 20 agosto fino al 23 agosto, con inclusa la mezza pensione.

Includo due vaglia postali internazionali per la Sua risposta. Per favore, rispondere per Via Aerea. Se è necessario un deposito, il nostro (mio) numero VISA é *xxx xxx xxx;* la data di scadenza è *xx/xx/xx.* Speriamo (spero) in una risposta favorevole.

Distinti saluti

Jane Brown

Translation

[The only difference between this letter and the French one is that this requests a double bed (*un letto matrimoniale*), as sometimes Italian hotels have twin beds (*due letti*) in double rooms. A single person can simply leave out the phrase *preferisco un letto matrimoniale.*]

For gîtes d'étapes, chalet-refuges, *portes du parc,* and refuges (*rifugi*), which generally have dormitories:
Nous souhaitons réserver deux places (une place), pour la nuit du ... (We wish to reserve two spaces (one space), for the night of ...). Some gîtes have a few private rooms; if you want to request one private room, write the following: *Nous souhaitons réserver deux places où si possible une chambre pour deux personnes si c'est possible* (... or a room for two if that's possible).
To reserve two places in Italian: *due posti (un posto) per la notte di ... .*

3. Metric Conversions

CELSIUS	FAHRENHEIT		KILOMETERS	MILES
0	32		0.5	0.3
10	50		1.0	0.6
20	68		1.6	1.0
30	84		2.0	1.3
			5.0	3.1
METERS	FEET		8.0	5.0
100	328			
300	984		HECTARES	ACRES
500	1,640		1	2.47
1,000	3,280			
1,500	4,920			
2,000	6,560			
2,500	8,200			
3,000	9,840			
3,500	11,480			
4,000	13,120			

4. Interchangeable Italian and French Place Names in the Gran Paradiso Region

HIKE	ITALIAN	FRENCH
	Val d'Aosta, Valle d'Aosta	Val d'Aoste, Vallée d'Aoste
92	Ghiacciaio di Château Blanc	Glacier du Château Blanc
93	Col (or Paso) di Planaval	Col de Planaval
	Lago di Fond	Lac du Fond
	Barrache di Fond	Barraques du Fond
94	Colle della Finestra	Col Fenêtre
	Rifugio Chalet de l'Epée	Refuge de l'Epée
96	Lago di San Grat	Lac de St.-Grat
98	Punta Bassac	Pointe Bassac
99	Truc Santa Elena	Truc Ste. Hélène
100	Col di Entrelor	Col d'Entrelor
	Alpage Plan de la Feya	Feye
102	Col del Nivolet	Col de Nivolet

5. Topographic Maps

FRANCE

The French maps are produced by and can be ordered from the Institut Géographique National, 107 rue de la Boétie, 75008 Paris, France, tel. (1) 43591083

Mercantour

Hikes 1 through 10 and 12—Série Bleue 37410, Alpes-Maritimes, Vallée de la Vésubie, 1:25,000

Hike 11—Massif et Parc National du Mercantour, 1:50,000, or Série Bleue, Tende, 1:25,000

Queyras

Hikes 13 through 15—Top 25 3537 ET Guillestre, Vars-Risoul

Hike 16—Top 28 25 3637 OT Mont Viso, St.-Véran–Aiguilles

Hike 17—Top 25 3537 ET Guillestre, Vars-Risoul, and Top 25 3637 OT Mont Viso, St.-Véran–Aiguilles

Hike 18—Top 25 3537 ET Guillestre, Vars-Risoul

Hikes 19 through 23—Top 25 3637 OT Mont Viso, St.-Véran–Aiguilles

Hike 24—Top 25 3537 ET Guillestre, Vars-Risoul, and Top 25 3637 OT Mont Viso, St.-Véran–Aiguilles

Hike 25—Top 25 3537 ET Guillestre, Vars-Risoul, and Top 25 3637 OT Mont Viso, St.-Véran–Aiguilles

Hike 26—Top 25 3637 OT Mont Viso, St.-Véran–Aiguilles

Hikes 27 through 32—Top 25 3637 OT Mont Viso, St.-Véran–Aiguilles

Hikes 33 through 35—Top 25 3537 ET Guillestre, Vars-Risoul

Hikes 36 through 38—Top 25 3538 ET Aiguille de Chambeyron

Hikes 39 and 40—Top 25 3637 OT Mont Viso, St.-Véran–Aiguilles

Ecrins

Hike 41—Massif et Parc National des Ecrins, 1:50,000 Massif and Parc National des Ecrins, or Top 25 3336 ET Les Deux Alpes Olan Muzelle

Hike 42—Top 25 3437 OT Champsaur–Vieux Chaillol

Hikes 43 and 44—Top 25 3436 ET Meije Pelvoux, and Top 25 3437 ET Orciéres-Merlette

Hikes 45 through 51—Topo 25 3436 ET Meije Pelvoux

Hike 52—Massif et Parc National des Ecrins, 1:50,000, or Top 25 3336 ET

Hikes 53 and 54—Top 25 3436 ET Meije Pelvoux

Hike 55—Top 25 3436 ET Meije Pelvoux, and Top 25 3336 ET Les Deux Alpes–Olan Muzelle

Hikes 56 through 64—Top 25 3436 ET Meije Pelvoux

Vanoise

Hikes 65 through 73—Top 25 3534 OT Les Trois Vallées–Modane

Hikes 74 through 76—Top 25 3633 ET Haute Maurienne-Grande Casse

Hike 77—Top 25 3534 OT Les Trois Vallées–Modane

Hikes 78 through 80—Top 25 3532 ET Les Arcs-La Plagne

Hikes 81 through 86—Top 25 3532 ET Les Arcs-La Plagne, and Top 25 3633 ET Tignes–Val-d'Isère

Hikes 87 through 89—Top 25 3633 ET Tignes–Val-d'Isère

Hikes 90 and 91—Top 25 3633 ET Haute Maurienne-Grande Casse

ITALY

GRAN PARADISO

The Italian maps are produced by and, in theory, can be ordered from the Instituto Geografico Centrale, Via Prati 2, 10121 Torino, Italy. In practice, it will prove difficult and expensive.

Hikes 92 and 93—Il Parco Nazionale del Gran Paradiso, 1:50,000

Hikes 94 through 104—Map 102 Valsavaranche, Val di Rhêmes, Valgrisenche, 1:25,000

Hikes 105 through 110—Map 101 Gran Paradiso, La Grivola, Cogne, 1:25,000

GLOSSARY

ENGLISH	FRENCH	ITALIAN

Accommodations and Services

bank	banque	banca
bath	bain	bagno
B&B-type lodging	gîte chambre d'hôte	
campground	le camping	campeggio
closed	fermé	chiuso
cubicle	box	scompartmento separato
dormitory	dortoir	dormitorio
exchange (currency)	échange	cambio
free	libre	libero
full (hotel)	complet	completo
furnished rental apartment	locations de vacances	
hiker's inn	gîte d'étape	tappa
hotel	hôtel, auberge	albergo
hotel list	liste des hôtels	annuario alberghi
hut keeper	gardien	custode
mountain hut	refuge	rifugio
mountain inn	chalet-refuge	chalet-rifugio
occupied (toilet)	occupé	occupato
open	ouvert	aperto
overnight cost	la nuitée	
parking	le parking	parcheggio
pay phone cards	télécartes	
pay phone tokens		gettone
room	chambre	camera
sheet or mattress cover	drap housse/couchette	coprimaterasso
sheet sack	sac à viande	zaino
	sac de couchage	copripiumino
shower	douche	doccia
sleeping bag		saco a pelo
sleeping bunks	couchettes	
toilet	W.C., toilette	toilette, gabinetto
tourist office	office du tourisme	azienda di soggiorno é turismo
tourist office	syndicat d'initiative	ufficio informazioni turistiche

Food

bakery	boulangerie	panificio, panetteria
bread	pain	pane
breakfast	petit déjeuner	prima colazione
butcher shop	boucherie	macelleria
dinner	diner	pranzo, cena
full pension, full board	pension complète	pensione completa
grocery store	alimentation, épicerie	alimentari, drogheria
half pension, half board	demi-pension	mezza pensione
herb tea	tisane	tisana
herb tea (mint)	infusion de (menthe)	infuso di (menta)
huge supermarket	hypermarché	ipermercato
lunch	déjeuner	pranzo
peanuts	cacahuètes	arachide
picnic	pique-nique (picnic)	picnic
picnic area	aire pique-nique	
shops (prepared foods)	charcuterie	rosticceria
raisins	raisins secs	uva secca
shop	magasin	mercato, negozio
shop where bread is sold	dépôt de pain	
snack	casse-croûte	spuntino
snack bar, refreshment stand	buvette	buvette
supermarket	supermarché	supermercato
whole-grain bread	pain complet	pane integrale

Geographic Features

bridge	pont	ponte
crest, ridge	crête	cresta
dam	barrage	diga
field of old snow	névé	nevaio
flat place	plan	piano
footbridge	passerelle	passerella
glacier	glacier	ghiacciaio
hill	colline	collina, colle
lake	lac	lago
mountain	mont, montagne, pic	montagna, picco
mountain stream	torrent	torrente
pass, notch, saddle	col	passo
peak, summit	sommet, cime	cima
reservoir	réservoir	serbatoio
ridge	arête	cresta, crinale
river	rivière, fleuve	fiume
scree, talus	éboulis	frana, smottamento

stream, brook	ruisseau, courant	corrente, ruscello
valley	val, vallée	valle
woods, forest	forêt, bois	bosco, foresta

Hazards

attention warning	attention	fare attenzione
dangerous	dangereux	pericoloso
forbidden	defense de	vietato
help	secours	soccorso
rabies	la rage, hydrophobie	rabbia
stonefall, falling rock	chute de pierres	caduta massi, caduta di sassi

Hiking

backpack	sac à dos	sacco da montagna
balcony trail, high trail	sentier balcon	sentiero panoramico
boots	chaussures de montagne	scarpone da montagna
cablecar	télépherique	funivia
cairn	cairn	mucchio di pietre
chairlift	télésiège	seggovia
east	est	est
first ascent	premiére montée or ascension	prima salita
hike, ramble	randonnée	escursione a piedi
hiking guide	accompagnateur	
hour, minute	heure, minute	ora, minuto
last departure	dernière descente	ultima discesa
left	gauche	sinistra
loop	boucle	cappio
map	carte	cartina
north	nord	nord
one way	aller (descente) simple	sola andata
right	droit	destra
round trip	aller-retour	andata e ritorno
section	tronçon	scompartimento, parte, sezione
shepherd's hut	bergerie	ovile
shortcut	raccourci	scorciatoia
south	sud	sud
stroll, ramble	balade	passeggiata
tow-lift	téléski	sciovia
trail	sentier, chemin pédestre	sentiero
trail blaze	balisage	segnaletica

(trekking) poles	batons	bastone
west	ouest	ovest

Travel

bus	autobus, autocar	autobus, autoservizi, pullman
bus station	gare routière	stazione degli autobus
bus stop	arrêt autocar	fermata
highway	autoroute	autostrada
information	information, renseignements	informazione
jeep road	une route pour voiture	
jeep, four-wheel-drive vehicle	quatre-quatre	jeep, fuoristrada
railway	chemin de fer	ferrovia
railway station	gare	stazione
road	route	strada
shuttle	navette	navetta
timetable	horaire	orario
trail bike	vélo tout terrain, VTT	
train	train	treno
way, road (incl.trail)	chemin, route	strada, camino

Weather

cloudy	nuageux	nuvoloso
cool, cold	frais, froid	fresco, freddo
fine weather	beau temps	bel tempo
fog, mist	brouillard, brume	nebbia
ice	glace	ghiaccio
lightning	éclair, foudre	lampo, fulmine
rain	pluie	pioggia
snow	neige	neve
storm	tempête	tempesta, burrasca
sunny	ensoleillé, du soleil	soleggiato
thunder	tonnerre	tuono
thunderstorm	orage	temporale
warm	chaud	caldo
weather forecast	météo, prévision de temps	previsione del tempo
wind	vent	vento

Wildlife

chamois	chamois	camoscio
eagle	aigle	aquila
ibex	bouquetin	stambecco
marmot	marmotte	marmotta

INDEX

About the Author

Marcia R. Lieberman is a freelance writer whose work has focused on mountains and mountain people. She is the author of *Walking Switzerland: The Swiss Way* (The Mountaineers: Seattle, 1987), and *The Outdoor Traveler's Guide: The Alps,* (Stewart, Tabori, & Chang: New York , 1991). She has published over a dozen travel articles in the *New York Times*, mainly about the Alps and the Himalaya, and has also published articles in *Trilogy, Himal,* and *The Rhode Islander* magazines. She holds several English degrees: a B. A. from Barnard College, an M. A. from Columbia University, and a Ph. D. from Brandeis University; and she also holds an M. A. from the Graduate Writing Program at Brown University.

About the Photographer

The work of photographer Philip Lieberman has been shown at the Bertha Urdang Gallery in New York and in galleries in Providence, Boston, and Bern, Switzerland. His work was included in Contemporary Art in Rhode Island, a 1994 show at the Museum of the Rhode Island School of Design, and is part of the permanent collection of the Museum and also of the Brooklyn Museum in New York. He holds B. S., M. S., and Ph. D. degrees from the Massachusetts Institute of Technology, and is the George Hazard Crooker University Professor and Professor of Cognitive and Linguistic Sciences at Brown University. He has published seven books and over 100 articles on speech, language, and the evolution of human beings and the human brain.

Their love of the mountains has led the Liebermans to hike in the Alps for some 10 years, to trek in the Himalaya five times, and to hike in Colorado, the Canadian Rockies, California, and the White mountains.

THE MOUNTAINEERS, founded in 1906, is a nonprofit outdoor activity and conservation club, whose mission is "to explore, study, preserve, and enjoy the natural beauty of the outdoors...." Based in Seattle, Washington, the club is now the third-largest such organization in the United States, with 14,000 members and four branches throughout Washington State.

The Mountaineers sponsors both classes and year-round outdoor activities in the Pacific Northwest, which include hiking, mountain climbing, ski-touring, snowshoeing, bicycling, camping, kayaking and canoeing, nature study, sailing, and adventure travel. The club's conservation division supports environmental causes through educational activities, sponsoring legislation, and presenting informational programs. All club activities are led by skilled, experienced volunteers, who are dedicated to promoting safe and responsible enjoyment and preservation of the outdoors.

The Mountaineers Books, an active, nonprofit publishing program of the club, produces guidebooks, instructional texts, historical works, natural history guides, and works on environmental conservation. All books produced by The Mountaineers are aimed at fulfilling the club's mission.

If you would like to participate in these organized outdoor activities or the club's programs, consider a membership in The Mountaineers. For information and an application, write or call The Mountaineers, Club Headquarters, 300 Third Avenue West, Seattle, Washington 98119; (206) 284-6310.

Send or call for our catalog of more than 300 outdoor titles:
The Mountaineers Books
1011 SW Klickitat Way, Suite 107
Seattle, WA 98134
1-800-553-4453